The Warrior's Path

The Warrior's Path

Reflections
along an
Ancient Route

Casey Clabough

The University of Tennessee Press • Knoxville

All photographs by Gene Adair. *Frontispiece:* Shenandoah Valley farmland, Virginia, with view of Bue Ridge Mountains. *Page xii:* Monocacy River near Frederick, Maryland. *Page 10:* Potomac River, looking toward Harpers Ferry, West Virginia, and Maryland Heights. *Page 26:* Field and subdivision near Charles Town, West Virginia. *Page 42:* Natural Bridge, Rockbridge County, Virginia. *Page 94:* Farm near Radford, Virginia. *Page 134:* Cherokee Lake near Bean Station, Tennessee. *Page 152:* Gatlinburg, Tennessee. *Page 176:* Country road, East Tennessee.

Map (page xi) by Julie Krick.

This book is printed on acid-free paper.

Clabough, Casey Howard, 1974–
    The warrior's path : reflections along an ancient route / Casey Clabough.
        p. cm.
Includes bibliographical references.

ISBN-13: 978-1-57233-602-5 (pbk.: alk. paper)
ISBN-10: 1-57233-602-1 (pbk.: alk. paper)

1. Appalachian Region—Description and travel. 2. Clabough, Casey Howard, 1974—Travel—Appalachian Region. 3. Trails—Appalachian Region. 4. Valleys—Appalachian Region. 5. Maryland—Description and travel. 6. Virginia—Description and travel. 7. Tennessee, East—Description and travel. 8. Frontier and pioneer life—Appalachian Region. 9. Appalachian Region—History. 10. Natural history—Appalachian Region. I. Title.

F106.C545 2007
917.4—dc22   2007009520

For my kin, dead and living, distant and near,
especially the children of Pinkney Clabough and Viola Huskey Clabough

Alle die grossen
Bilder ib mir, im Fernen erfahrene Landschaft,
Städte und Türme und Brücken und un-
vermutete Wendung der Wege
und das Gewaltige jener von Göttern
einst durchwachsenen Länder:
steigt zur Bedeutung in mir
deiner, Entgehende, an.

> —Rilke, "Du im Voraus"

Sic Juvat Transcendere Montes.

> —Alexander Spotswood

It is like an echo
Of something I have always known.

> —R. H. W. Dillard, "The Greeting"

Contents

Preface

This narrative seeks at once to begin to reflect the experience of the eighteenth-century mid-Atlantic North American frontier (what is identified by some as eastern Appalachia—the areas along the Blue Ridge chain of mountains), recount certain aspects of the natural and cultural development of that region, and connect these historical variables to the cultural and environmental realities that exist in the area now through the visceral account of one person's journey. The book's title is drawn from the Iroquoian word *Athowominee*, which translates variously as "the path of the armed ones" or "the warrior's path." Formed centuries ago by migrating animals and the native North American people who followed them, the route spanned from the Iroquois country of what is today New York State down the Appalachian valley system into the Cherokee country of Tennessee and North Georgia. Generally following the courses of rivers and creeks, it ran through the Cumberland Valley of Pennsylvania, the Shenandoah Valley and southern valley network of Virginia, and the Holston Valley of Tennessee. Native Americans used the route for hunting, trade, and war. When the first European explorers ventured west, they discovered the path, and in time it was enlarged and used as the dominant avenue for settlers moving into the interior of the continent (as it grew and changed its course it would come to be known by several names, among them the "Great Wagon Road"), with one of its major offshoots (the "Wilderness Road") passing westward through the Cumberland Gap into what is now Kentucky.

Among those to follow *Athowominee* were my own Germanic ancestors, who had immigrated to the Pennsylvania interior from a region of eastern Bavaria in the 1730s. At the end of the eighteenth century they followed the path from western Maryland to the Smoky Mountains of Tennessee. Having read a number of seventeenth- and eighteenth-century accounts that pertained to the route and the areas along it, I resolved to repeat the journey of my ancestors, noting and comparing what I observed against the narratives of earlier travelers and explorers.

I should emphasize here that this book is not solely a personal memoir, nor is it the story of one family. On the contrary, I use information about my ancestors and facts and events drawn from my contemporary journey as spring-boards for underscoring the route's and the region's centrality in our country's history. Historians have estimated that between two and three hundred thousand hopeful settlers would follow the same portion of the path between 1775 and 1810—an extraordinary number given North America's sparse population at the time. Perhaps as many as three out of every four contemporary Americans has an ancestor who followed the route at some point. This then is not merely the story of my trip, nor of a single family's journey, but rather the representative tale of many—a fundamentally American story that attempts to imagine how European settlers first traveled west along and beyond the eastern mountains and valleys of middle North America.

In terms of the book's design, I follow what is, on the surface, a linear chronological structure based on the unfolding of my journey. Although the text is chiefly concerned with history, its sections or chapters are organized around the areas through which I passed and the events that occured along them while following portions of the modern highways that once constituted *Athowominee* (there were, in fact, a number of significant stretches where the location of the original trail remained uncertain or altogether unknown to me). Although the unfolding of the book is linear and chronological, it is interspersed with frequent flashbacks to the central historical events that pertain to the specific areas I encountered during my journey, as well as intellectual musings and information on changes in the cultures and environments of these places. Errors and misinterpretations are inevitable in a book of this nature, and I take full responsibility for them, along with whatever moments of true insight or tenuous value may have been achieved along the way.

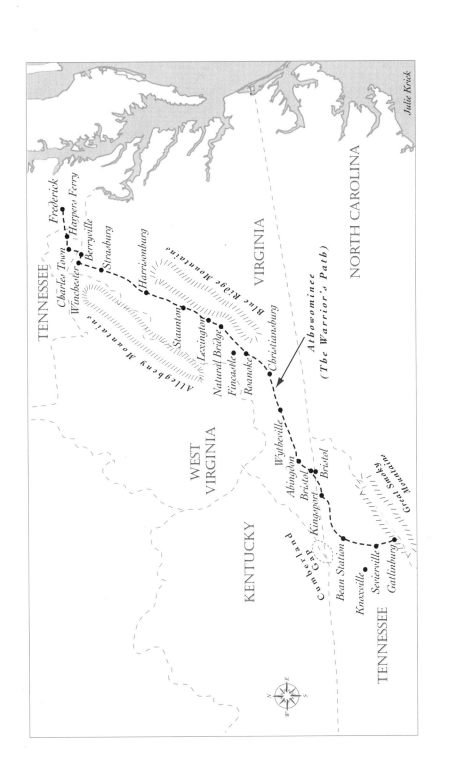

Julie Krick

MARYLAND

Here: Monocacy River Valley

I shall have to . . . trace my story from its small beginnings up to these recent times when its ramifications
are so vast that any adequate treatment is hardly possible.
— Livy, *The Early History of Rome*

When the virus of restlessness begins to take possession
of a wayward man, and the road away from Here seems
broad and straight and sweet, the victim must first find
in himself a good and sufficient reason for going.
—John Steinbeck, *Travels with Charley*

I am standing, only just arrived but already sweating, beneath a late-morning
end-of-July sun, in a newish-looking housing development at the circular
dead end of Grossnickle Court, off Biggs Ford Road in Frederick County, Maryland, gazing westward, toward the river valley of the Monocacy and, beyond
it, long Catoctin Mountain, hazy in summer. Like you, I might be anywhere
but I happen to be here, now, in this eastern part of southern North America,
standing where pavement turns to grass and then, beyond, a field of hay, thick
but carrying in its near spent green the inevitable hints of late summer's harvest
brown. "Here" is usually something we take for granted, but its simplicity of
connotation ever blurs in our minds its inherent insinuations of both position
and time. The traveler asks himself, "How do I get there from here?" or, mea-
suring the position of the sun against his fatigue, suggests to his companions,
"Let us stop here for the night and resume our journey at dawn." It may also
refer to a minute topic or specific subject, as in "Here, I must disagree with you";
yet, more dynamically, it may too demand action: "Come here!" Beyond, in all

these things, the word embodies an affirmation of life, of being, now. To the one who, uncertain of our presence, calls our name, we reply, "Here."

"Here" is the bashful and more shadowy companion of "place." As with here, the idea of place, any place, remains one of our most basic yet slippery concepts: it is a space with boundaries but its limits may be definite or indefinite; it might be construed as an abstract mental or spiritual location, "There is a place for you in my heart," or as a literal blank domain, "This is the place where you write your name"; it may also refer to a small particular occupied spot, as when your finger touches the place where your head hurts, or to a point someone has achieved or come to only to then lose it, as in this book: "I've lost my place." Place is irrevocably wedded to context, for the space your body occupies is a place, but so is the earth and what scientists call the solar system. And, at once more abstract and more central, it is also a proximity of yearning, of desire; as the writer Wendell Berry says, "The mind still hungers for its earth, its bounded and open space."

Most humans of the twenty-first century seem to be attempting to get somewhere: a better place to live, a specific place in their lives, or perhaps just a place to call their own—a place to come to. Americans, at this particular place in time, exist in a civilization that goes to great lengths to try and tell them where they are, where they should be trying to get, and when—the answer to which always seems to take the form of an emphatic "Now!" Most humans of the twenty-first century live amid numerous manufactured signs and mark-ers—bright, loud, subtle, and subliminal—to tell them where they are, or where they are supposed to think they are: road names, county lines, city limits, prop-erty boundaries, and the like. These are the markers of our own time, seeking to position us in relation to other acknowledged and collectively believed-in places of the present. Yet, their very attachment to this particular era ensures their gen-eral irrelevance in determining or directing us to the places of times long since bygone, the signs of which have passed, faded, or never were. Dwelling upon and surveying the here of long ago invites other, at once more fundamental and abstract, determinants of place and direction to coalesce and lend themselves, drawn back reluctantly across time, like ghosts revisiting the places they once haunted.

As I walk some distance into the field of tall alfalfa and orchard grass, there comes into view before me, toward the river called Monocacy, a rough line of woods. That the field, having stretched away from grass, asphalt, and houses, should, in its turn, dissolve into trees is essential—as basic and obvious as it must seem—to understanding this place in the present, as well as the more recent past. Land-scape is a story that fields and trees help tell, though the form and content here in eastern, southern North America and most of the world over have long been influenced if not dictated by humans, most notably the people of the past four hundred years, though the comparatively sparse earlier populations had their own distinct narrative styles as well. Before the arrival of Europeans nearly all of this particular area would have been covered in forest, except for the few open places that had been burned over, the result of flames set loose upon dead wood or dry grasses by lightning, or of native hunters and gatherers easing their tasks with sporadic soil-enriching burnings, usually along rivers and creeks. Though the people we call Indians and their forebears had frequently passed through this place, it is believed for now that they never lived here for any significant length of time, camping for a while perhaps as they journeyed through, onward or homeward, in the midst of seasonal expeditions bent on game and forage. For better or for worse, most often for the worse, to know the land for what it is is to know the people who have trodden upon it, broken it open, and rearranged it to their ostensible advantage, ordering it into some semblance of a system believed to help facilitate survival or, more recently, the gross acquisition of the material goods of others.

Since the greatest man-made changes to the landscape are the more recent, to understand what I am looking at is to trace the more proximate human cata-lysts of change. The transition of this area from a forest to what is before my eyes now began with the arrival of colonists from the Germanic states of northern Europe in the early eighteenth century. To realize, in turn, the manner and assumptions of these people in their relation to this place is to know something of their reasons for coming to it. Groups of Germans began journeying to North America in earnest in 1683, arriving to the north in the colony of Pennsylvania, lured by embroidered British propaganda of great opportunity in the "New World" and the very real religious tolerance of the utopian thinker and colonial proprietor William Penn. By 1709 there were nearly fourteen thousand of them peopling mostly what would come to be the more western central counties of Pennsylvania, and they would be followed by Scottish Presbyterian families and other English-speaking folk generally dissatisfied with life and conditions in the British Isles. Although German men brought with them numerous trade skills—among them were blacksmiths, mechanics, shoemakers, watchmakers, gunmiths, butchers, and cabinetmakers—that helped build and support village and county economies, they and their families were often viewed with suspicion by their English-speaking neighbors—convenient objects of the old archetypal human fear and hatred of that which is different. Writing in 1725, James Logan, provincial secretary of Pennsylvania, reported that the Germans "come in crowds, and as bold, indigent strangers from Germany, where many of them have been soldiers. All these go on the best vacant tracts and seize upon them as places of common spoil. . . . Many of them are Papists—the men well armed, and as a body a warlike, morose race." Foremost in the minds of Logan and others were the dangerous cultural differences of the Germans, which, coupled with their large and able numbers, presented a perceived threat to the otherwise dominant English element of the American colonies. Years after Logan's warning, distrust of German settlers lingered. As Benjamin Franklin fearfully theorized, "Why should Pennsylvania, founded by the English, become a colony of aliens, who will shortly be so numerous as to Germanize us, instead of our Anglicifying them, and will never adopt our language or customs any more than they can acquire our complexion?" Taking Logan's uncongenial caricature a step further, Franklin emphasized the distinct possibility of a hostile cultural takeover—a "Germanization" —by "aliens" of a divergent "complexion." Inherent in Franklin's disconcerting rhetoric is his portrayal of the Germans as an implacable separate race, resistant to change and probably engaged in the conscious undermining of their rightful English masters.

The upshot of such cultural hostility, the search for greater social freedom, and the lure of cheaper land led Germans southward from the Pennsylvania counties along the Cumberland Valley, generally following the courses of mountains and rivers and the old trails of Indians that strayed along their ridges and banks. In March of 1732, Charles Calvert, the fifth Lord Baltimore, seeking to create a kind of strategic buffer for the English colonists of eastern Maryland against the Indians on the frontier, had offered two-hundred-acre tracts between the Potomac and Susquehanna rivers to willing families with the assurance that they would not have to make payments on the land for three years. Pennsylvania Germans were quick to inhabit the territory, and it was along the Monocacy River or Frederick Valley (between the only two villages existing in western Maryland at the time: Monocacy, the site of which remains uncertain, and Fredericktown), where I am standing now, that my own ancestors recorded their first extant land deed in 1742 on a portion of riverfront property that was part of a nine-thousand-acre tract called Monocacy Manor, a landscape that would appear strange to our eyes now, where old growth brooded amid a shadowy canopy and the lush grass of the rare open areas had never felt blade nor plow. A place all but lost to family memory, a distant legend even in the time of my great grandfathers, who carried with them to their graves a story that cannot be retold.

Having abandoned the field for the shade of the woods, I discover, under a swell in the ground, beneath a thin layer of dried leaves and dark humus, a buried pile of large, roughly rectangular river rocks. They could have been carried from the field, heaped along the edge so as not to hinder plow or hoe again; or, more likely, since they are uncommonly flat and uniform on all sides, they might have been used as part of a rock foundation, the piled building blocks of a barn, a home, of lives. The hewn beams that rested on these rocks have long since passed beneath the forest floor, as have the feet that once walked upon them. But I am here and you are here. Here, we are. Enter with me these buried legends, brushing away the damp clinging leaves and soil. The rocks piled here were not moved by one man. Lift with me these stones from the earth. Let us raise them into sunlight.

Though the isolated life of the German settlers existing in this bucolic area would have been difficult, it was not completely unknown to their experience and history. Many had been farmers in the Old Country, and in antiquity the Roman historian Tacitus had described the people of the Germanic tribes as living "scattered and apart, just as a spring, a meadow, or a wood has attracted them." But of exactly how they existed here, how they came to shape this place, more must be said. As Tacitus's fellow Roman historian Livy, once wrote, "I invite the reader to the much more serious consideration of the kind of lives our ancestors lived." Upon arriving at the place where they planned to raise a house, the ground to become "here," or *"hier"* as they more properly called it, trees were cut and logs were squared and fit into one another to form a rectangular shape over a foundation of flat-shaped rock, precisely of the sort I discovered, carried from the best potential field site or a nearby stream. The logs were then chinked, usually with wet, clay soil. Roofs and floors consisted mostly of wooden planks hewn by a whipsaw. Often a family would live in a primitive lean-to while the cabin's preliminary construction sped along, perhaps aided by neighbors if they were fortunate to have any near enough. Refining the structure, openings were cut for doors and windows, which were then attached with driven wooden pins. A chimney of flat rock and clay was raised through a hole cut in the roof. All this work conspired to create what William Eddis, an English official who traveled to the Frederick County area in autumn 1772, called "a rude construction."

For settlers, the archaic or visually wanting manner of their homes was of little moment. Necessity and survival were their primary concerns. Accordingly, the *Küche,* or kitchen, was the first room completed, after which attention would turn to the barn, essential for the livelihoods of crop storage and livestock, and, later, when leisure allowed, adorned with hexes, *Distelfinken,* and other symbols of south German custom. Sometimes the barn was even connected to the kitchen, the primary subsistence structures joined by an umbilical cord of wood. The other rooms, and perhaps an ice or spring house and smoke house, were built in due course, along with strong beds, benches, and tables, held together by driven wooden pins, smoothed with an adz, and painted by firelight with bright depictions of tulips, birds, and other traditional Bavarian designs. China plates and eating utensils were rare; the food container of choice usually was a carved wooden bowl, the drinking vessel a conveniently shaped gourd, the utensils carved of wood if they were used at all. The brief time between dinner and sleep generally was spent reading in the heavy family Bible, hinged with brass or iron clasps, consulting the almanac for the forecasts of sun and moon so crucial to planting, and educating the children. During the day, boys who did not work in the fields usually followed the Germanic tradition of learning a trade, the inherited knowledge passed on, the young acquiring the ways and wisdom of a land foreign to them that remained their point of cultural origin—a place hardly any of them would ever see.

Settlers would try to build close to a natural spring, but if the land did not permit it, a good branch of dogwood, peach, or witch hazel could be employed for the purpose of dowsing for underground water, after which a primitive well would be dug. Shortly after arriving, even while the house was being built, settlers would go about the business of clearing land and planting crops. Corn, wheat, and other vegetables were sown around the stumps of cleared land, which usually were left to rot rather than be toilsomely uprooted. The rest of the tree provided firewood, and the rocks that inhibited plowing were carried out of the field and used to build fences and foundations. If a family enjoyed the unlikely good fortune of having a mill somewhere within a twenty-mile radius of their home, corn and wheat would be ground following the harvest, the miller taking a share in payment. But this was a rare luxury early on. Pork and corn were the most common foods at the table, the pigs running wild in the woods, feeding on nuts, roots, and an assortment of other organic matter. Those that were large enough usually were slaughtered during winter's first cold spell, over a two-day period, which, if one had neighbors, might take the form of a community event, the killing and cleaning occurring on the first day and the following morning devoted to the cutting of the various parts. As with building, the harvest, and various other tasks, working together made the killing, cleaning, and dividing of the pig all the more swift, efficient, and enjoyable.

The pig was a fundamental part of several dishes, including *Leberwurst, Pfann-hase* (boiled pig juice mixed with cornmeal), and ham, which was buried in ash to preserve it. Prepared in suspended pots over the fireplace or even down among the flames, traditional German meals like *Schnitz und Knöpf* and *Sauer-kraut und Speck* retained their popularity among the settlers. Women struggled to bring variety to the table, and families constantly looked for ways to diversify their menu. If they had the seed, settlers were quick to plant fruit trees. Germans were particularly fond of making cider or brandy from apples, and they used other specialized agricultural techniques they had brought with them from Europe, employing crop rotation and fertilizing their land with the droppings of livestock. In late summer they watched closely for the time of harvest, studying the weather as they walked their furrows at dawn, grasping the wheat to weigh its teeming, testing golden kernels with their lips. Families generally helped one another at harvest, and once a local mill was established, each family would have their appointed day for the purpose of grinding their corn and wheat, the coarse or leftover parts of which could be retained to feed livestock through the bare-pastured winter months.

Men and women alike worked hard and occasionally their tasks overlapped. Among their more common responsibilities women daily swept the dirt yard around the house with hickory brooms, their short gowns allowing the dirt to collect about their ankles without soiling their clothes. Women also generally were responsible for sewing, making lye soap from animal lard, and composing many a family's beautiful *fraktur* drawings, which, framed by colorful borders, recorded genealogical information and significant dates. With the family's constant toil, clothes wore out quickly, and women were constantly working wool, flax, or yarn—or some combination of the three—into garments, blankets, and other useful items. Much of this kind of work was performed in the evenings by the fire since other artificial light remained a luxury. Animal grease could provide an inexpensive source of light though it carried with it a strong, usually unpleasant, odor. Candles were very expensive and the majority of folks usually went to bed at nightfall amid the utter dark, save perhaps the distant pale glow of the evening star or a gleaming moon, and the soft sounds of a nocturnal landscape peopled but little, the nearest neighbor perhaps miles away, falling asleep quickly after a full day of labors upon which their lives depended.

All this unfolded, just as things are unfolding now, more than two and a half centuries ago in a portion of western Maryland, of eastern North America, called the Piedmont, an Italian word that means "foot of the mountains." Although there are several new suburban developments in this area, there lingers enough farmland, planted mostly in corn and potatoes, to imagine it a sparsely populated, rural landscape. The fecundity of the ground ensured the area's relatively rapid clearing and settlement during the eighteenth century. As William Eddis explained in his letters, "The richness of the soil, and the salubriety of the air, operated very powerfully to promote population." By the time of the American Revolution, most of the flatter or rolling areas had been transformed from great forests into finely cultivated fields. J. F. D. Smith, a Scotsman loyal to England who was imprisoned at Frederick—or Fredericktown, as it was known then—during the war, described the land as "heavy, strong, and rich, well calculated for wheat, with which it abounds, this being as plentiful a country as any in the world."

The enduring richness of the area does not stem from the soil itself but rather from the ground's close proximity to the river, the primal shaper and architect of the valley, rising and falling over the course of centuries, carrying things away and bearing them here, ever rearranging what is. Although their crops grew well here, few of the original German settlers who came to the region in the 1700s stayed indefinitely. Moving for various reasons at different times, they swept on like the waters, southward or farther west, to distant lands as wild as these had been before the first man brandished his axe in the crisp morning air. My own ancestors left this place for the Smoky Mountains at the end of the eighteenth century, and like the disappearing current flowing in the Monocacy on the morning of their departure, no token remains of the manner of their passing, nor its reason. Like the water here, now, they passed on, the mystery of their leaving having given way to the silence of their absence—the air's sudden quiet in the faded wake of a creaking wagon wheel, the last rustle of a leaf.

I descend deeper into older woods and then below the humid trees, down to the moist coolness of the river, the scattered stones of its sandy shore. The Monocacy is murky, brown, and sluggish despite the wet summer. Many of the trees along it here look to reach back a century in age, left in peace to grow for what in our time is considered a long time, a venerable age. Whether it passes in the sudden contracting span of a wink or with a slow, deep exhalation, short or long, truncated or enduring, the here of the present remains determined by our being in it, which in turn derives from a long series of others' existences, of which we are the present remainders. And if we cannot know entirely the manner of their being, we can at least attempt to trace their journey to us, to walk in their footsteps toward ourselves. And so this place—what at one time was to become here, what then became *hier* for my ancestors—will soon be left by me, as it was by my fathers of two centuries ago, to itself and others who will know it by different names; the stories of who I am, who we are, ever bearing us away on the journeys whose final destination is the domain where existence fades, which is also that misty country that serves as the embarking point of others. Time wanes even as we linger, the undisclosed interval collapsing amid the hesitation that is our nature. Though I have only just arrived, my departure is at hand. Walk with me then for a while, in the footsteps of others toward myself, ever leaving even as we arrive. Let us pass together as others have, neither going nor coming, but here for a moment and gone, the spent instant our invisible wake, the nothing of space now empty. . . .

MARYLAND

Departures: Catoctin Mountain and Potomac River Valley

Then I journeyed forth and became a stranger. . . .
—Stefan George

We leave the port, and lands and towns retreat.
—Virgil, *The Aeneid*

Take a look down your highway,
Tell me what you see.
Well if you're down my way,
It could well be me.
—Roy Harper, "Highway Blues"

The Monocacy River of western Maryland runs slow, creeps, a small green maple leaf on the surface taking what seems like an eternity to pass where I am standing, the small stone I cast after it bringing hardly a splash or a ripple, as if muffled by the river, swallowed in a placid murky silence that gives no sign of what has passed. These waters afford neither view nor reflection; they hold close their secrets, obscuring them with a dark cloudiness, bearing them away slowly, elsewhere. . . .

Why my ancestors left this area of western Maryland for the foothills of the Smoky Mountains at the end of the eighteenth century remains a mystery that I may never understand, the clouds that veil the stars pressed close, unwilling to abate. Perhaps it was something akin to the dominant reason for their journey from Pennsylvania to Maryland, namely affordable land and greater cultural tolerance or isolation. Or it could have been something completely unlooked for, something averse to historical circumstance, a reason altogether unlikely. Dwelling on this question I realize that my travel-based supposition, my vague feeling that following their route today might potentially provide answers or insight into their reasons for going, is perhaps the most ridiculous aspect of the entire undertaking, for it hinges altogether on the indistinct and evasive phenomenon of human experience. Whereas history may hold close her secrets from scholars and scribes, experience gladly doles out his brutal knowledge, however grudgingly, to those who, however foolishly, seek him out. History and experience are estranged lovers, the latter the event and the former the teller. Both are mysterious and perhaps ultimately unknowable, but that is precisely what makes them so seductive, both to each other and to us. The Spartan general lies dying on a field of battle twenty-four hundred years ago, perhaps wondering who will tell his story and recall his glory or dishonor, while the fragmentary data left in his wake fascinates the young historian, centuries later, hunched at a desk, in search of lost time, trying to make sense of, or even imagine, a place and worldview so far removed from hers that it might be considered alien. Therein lies the challenging and all too often hopeless quality of the discipline. As the French poet Paul Valéry warned, "History is the most dangerous concoction the chemistry of the mind has produced. Its properties are well known. It sets people dreaming, intoxicates them, engenders false memories, exaggerates their reflexes, keeps old wounds open, torments their leisure, inspires them with megalomania or persecution complex, and makes nations bitter, proud, insufferable, and vain. History can justify anything you like. It teaches nothing, for it contains and gives examples of everything." Hardly an endorsement of the field. Yet, for all this, for all history's faulty detours and dead ends, agendas and distortions, illusions and compulsions, historians have ever echoed the Roman historian Livy in ultimately deeming "antiquity a rewarding study."

History is twined and fraught with tales of departures, of migrations—vanishings from certain places recounted across epochs: sudden flights by single tribes or outcasts and great movements of entire populations over centuries. In the eighteenth century, in this particular area of southeastern North America, travel generally was a small sporadic affair involving usually a single family or perhaps a handful of them. Yet most of the routes they followed were already there, beaten down over the centuries by migrating animals and the humans who followed them. Wandering early settlers traveled mostly by foot or packhorse along these narrow Indian paths, marked occasionally by blazed tree boughs in places where they became dense with foliage or were otherwise indistinct. Later, on broadened paths, families who could afford them began using Conestoga wagons, an innovation of Pennsylvania German carpenters and ironsmiths. The finest were built of hickory planks and deftly balanced on iron wheels with black gum hubcaps. A series of bent iron rods provided an elongated arched frame over which could be stretched a canopy—a roof to keep travelers and their goods dry. The fact that American steering systems are on the left side of the automobiles of our own time stems from the location of the wagon's driver seat, which was just to the inside of the left front wheel. From that position the driver vigilantly held the jerk line, which was attached to the bit of the left front or "wheel" horse. Tethered behind the wagon there might have been a cow or a pig or a dog, and it was not unusual to find a chicken coop attached to the end of the bed, while beneath the better wagons there hung a tar bucket from the rear axle, the slick lubricant easing the wagon's labored turning over roads that often resembled little more than muddy bogs or rutted elongated clearings.

No matter the mode of travel, settlers left in the hopes of arriving ready to work, with dried food, seeds for planting, and tools for building. Yet many things conspired to slow or even foil entirely the progress of their journeys: foul muddy weather, unfamiliarity with the route, the uncertainty of Indian encounters. All these things presented themselves to the traveler with a variable degree of uncertainty that might carry with it dire consequences. However, as the old saying goes, "No amount of careful planning will ever replace dumb luck," and so the prepared and knowledgeable occasionally perished even as the more foolhardy travelers, hungry and cold, undersupplied and barely outfitted, lucked their way onto good building sites and fine ground, missing, by pure chance, the marauding Shawnee war party, late spring flood, or early autumn snow storm. Such is the pitiless and ironic hue history may sometimes take—an impressionistic montage of chance disasters and near misses randomly visited upon sage and fool alike. I can only hope my own ignorance and many other deficiencies will serve me as well, countered by the vagaries of history's favorable chaos, of unlooked-for good fortune.

I cross the Monocacy River by way of the bridge on Biggs Ford Road, the water's shallowness here indicating that in the time before the first bridge spanned the river it had once been a natural crossing place for wagons, horses, and the people who walked among them. Reaching Catoctin Mountain Highway, a busy four-lane road, I turn south along it, clinging to the outer portion of the shoulder, as far from the racing traffic as possible. Catoctin itself, the long-risen geological feature off to my right, constitutes a kind of small easterly hiccup of the Blue Ridge, the range of which lies beyond my view to the west. I had once lived on a similar manner of mountain in the central country of Virginia, just south of the James River, the highest point from where it looms southeast of the Blue

Ridge to the Atlantic Ocean, some two hundred miles distant. Because there were hardly any mountains to the east, this one afforded—despite its humble summit of sixteen hundred feet—a stunning view of the horizon that stretched unimpeded, concealing, far beyond my gaze, morning or evening, an invisible landscape.

Here, on the road, below the interminable vistas of such easterly North American ridges, the horizon presses much closer, peppered by trees, homes, and automobiles—the latter both at rest and in the process of furious motion: reving, honking, passing each other in rapid vehement pursuit of unknown sundry errands. Though occasionally they inadvertently jump a guard rail or, shifting down into four-wheel drive, stray into fields or forests, automobiles for the most part are thankfully confined by the roads that have been built, often thrown together haphazardly, for them. Over the long duration of his many travels, John Steinbeck noted that "roads change, increase, are widened or abandoned so often in our country that one must buy road maps like daily newspapers," the various routes—appearing, growing, vanishing—coming to resemble strange overlapping conjectures rather than authentic or definite avenues of transit. As the poet Laura Riding observed, "The map of places passes. The reality of paper tears."

Though its current appearance is altogether bland and modern, not unlike any other highway, the general thoroughfare I hope to follow all the way to the Smoky Mountains (a linked collection of several roads) is much older than any of my multiwheeled fellow travelers likely would surmise. When, several hundred years ago, the supply of beaver dwindled in what is now upper New York State, Iroquoian-speaking tribes began to bicker among themselves. In search of furs and influence, warriors of the Iroquois, among them the Seneca, raided and did battle with the Conestoga of Pennsylvania and Maryland, as well as the Souian tribes of Virginia. The route they followed southward—*Athowominee,* the "warrior's path"—took them through central Pennsylvania into Maryland, where the trail passed through what became Frederick County, following the eastern slope of the Catoctin ridges and the Monocacy River, on down to the Potomac and into the Shenandoah Valley, a venerable hunting ground for many different tribes. In 1739 the Maryland portion of the route was widened by local settlers to better accommodate wagon travel; by then it was known as the Monocacy Road. From the 1760s through most of the 1770s an ancestor of mine named John Clabough held a position in the northern part of the colony called "master of the roads," which likely required surveying as well as the recruitment of his neighboring farmers for the purposes of adding rock, corduroying muddy places, grading, and other such tasks. It is an odd enough feeling to tread along such an ancient route, but the sensation becomes stranger still knowing that an ancestor was partially responsible for maintaining it nearly two and a half centuries ago. Yet, even as I dwell on the antiquity of the avenue and its relation to myself, I am simultaneously struck by the immense insignificance of that personal connection in light of the many people and animals who had used the route before my ancestor's arrival and the multitudes who would follow it in his wake, including those with whom I share it now, and the future travelers yet to embark. Southwest of here, the main section of *Athowominee* that would come to be variously known in history by an assortment of names ran from Wadkin's Ferry southward up the valley system of Virginia and, bearing west near the present-day city of Bristol, on into the Holston River Valley and then southward again, west of the Smoky Mountains. The age and history of *Athowominee* are immense, yet, for all the entirety of its antiquity, the years of its use dwarfing the long miles it spans, it remains an ongoing journey itself—a trail always in the process of becoming, forever new.

Despite its historical importance as a great highway, *Athowominee* is now by and large, with the notable exceptions of certain congested stretches, a route obscure and lonely, a network of paved secondary highways rendered quaint by the massive twentieth-century construction of interstates. Despite the comparative lack of traffic, however, such derelict roads still do not lend themselves well to foot travel. Although trail hiking carries with it considerable risks, road hiking, while generally offering more accessible terrain and better opportunities for resupply, remains considerably more challenging and dangerous. Trail hiking, after all, usually has its own peculiar support network: people often shed food and supplies for a later wanderer to use (these folks are sometimes referred to as "trail angels"); hikers generally communicate and share information with each other concerning terrain, weather, the nature of the nearest town, and so on; and the locals of hiking towns often are friendly to hikers, providing them with rides to stores or perhaps a simple drink from a garden hose. Trail hikers usually are viewed romantically by the general population, striding over wooded hills or across grassy meadows that resemble in our imaginations Pindar's Nemean fields. By contrast, people walking along roads for the most part are labeled and dismissed as bums and vagrants. If you are a road hiker, it is not uncommon to be heckled, bombarded with trash, or even run into a ditch by a vehicle swerving toward the gravelly shoulder you happen to be walking on. Police and other motorists view you with suspicion or irritation, if they think about you at all. It is altogether possible that if you were injured, lying motionless, or dead, no one would stop, save perhaps the curious policeman or the passing motorized scavenger, bent on sifting quickly through your pockets and backpack.

However unpleasant these phenomena may sound, they remain, after all, literal contingencies one may expect and prepare for. Of much greater difficulty and importance for my own journey are the abstract challenges—my uncertain, yet necessary, interactions with the shadowy specters of history and experience. Even covering the same or similar terrain on foot, I am not so presumptuous as to believe that I can imagine, even remotely, what travel must have been like for my ancestors—the slow laborious procession of all one's possessions, the terrible quality of the road, the utter absence of a doctor to treat the unlooked-for illness or injury, and so on. Doubtful too is the extent of my specialized knowledge of this region's many collective, complex qualities—especially geological, biological and botanical, and anthropological: that which is learned, as the writer James Still said, "by convulsions of earth, by time, by winds, the water's wearings, and minute shapings of man." But when and where the wise and distinguished are unable or unwilling to embark, it must fall to the lesser to go. Which may lead one to the vast and perhaps unanswerable question of what knowledge and wisdom truly are. The German writer Johann Wolfgang von Goethe once had a character of his proclaim, "For all our science and art we can know nothing." The brilliant academic specialist may limn the detailed workings of even the minutest object or subject in his field, but does this make him a wise human being, or even a knowledgeable one? I have always had my doubts. A knowledgeable person possesses a capacity for prescience that consists of much more than the patterned bulk of abstract memory. People come to be known as knowledgeable often precisely because they acquire or make connections between things that are not taught or shared by others: sensibility, visceral experience, and the mysteries of the individual mind, the magic of the personality, then conspire to transmute clinical data into something more than what others see in it, which is how invention happens. The wise are those who possess the ability to relate this kind of knowledge both to our lives and the grand story of existence, often in astonishingly simple, completely nonintellectual terms. Wise people need not command endless lists of facts, since for them proofs always give way to truths. A woman pushes her computer through the window of a twenty-three-story office building; a girl throws her softball high in the air. A physics professor calculates the velocity of these objects; a wise man like the philosopher Heraclitus tells us, "The way up and the way down are the same." Heraclitus was a Greek thinker who lived roughly twenty-five hundred years ago, before knowledge was hacked into the various regimented specialty areas familiar to us today. He and other early thinkers who preceded Socrates, such as Anaximader, were interested in things that exist beyond experience, but because there were no separate disciplines at the time, they were able to make unorthodox connections that seem wholly foreign to us now. Abstractions that eventually would become organized into distinct things like poetry, math, biology, history, and psychology remained overlapped and indistinct in their thought. Anximander, for example, believed there was something ineffable from which all things come forth and return to again; Heraclitus saw everything in flux, what the despairing fictional intellectual Cotswaldo would later call "that depressed and depressing world of chance." This would include knowledge and wisdom, both of which we attempt to journey toward but are themselves journeys, the navigation of the unknown soul through its sorrowful maze. Steinbeck believed, "A journey is a person in itself; no two are alike," and my own trip, several centuries and many lives removed from my ancestors, experienced in a different culture and rendered in another tongue, must necessarily remain foreign to theirs, the whoosh of traffic and the grim jolt of shoes on summer asphalt a hardly imaginable fantasy in an era of the slow, laborious creak of a wagon wheel, half-sunk in mud, turning slowly in the rain.

In Frederick, which the French botanist André Michaux described in 1789 as "little but well-built," I switch over to Highway 340, the heavy oncoming traffic keeping my torpid mind wary beneath the unceasing afternoon sunlight that throbs down upon it. The air is still, heavy, and vaguely brown, slightly dingy and disturbed only by the passing vehicles, the hot wind gusts blasting my body with the strong relentless fumes of burnt fuel, hot rubber, worn brakes. This is the mechanized odor of waste, of spent industrial energy discarded, of, in a sense, death. Yet, for all the terrible smell and difficulty breathing amid the heat, I remind myself that it is actually healthier to inhale fumes along the hot open road than in the closed, cool sanctuary of one's automobile, which functions, in respiratory terms, as a kind of smallish, subtle gas chamber, filling gradually and becoming increasingly toxic with the chemicals of other people's automobiles the longer one drives with the windows closed and the air-conditioning on. Many people of the twenty-first century spend most of their lives literally shut off from the outside world: in their homes, in their cars, at work, even in a tent; and Americans in general probably breathe more stale air than any human civilization before them, the industrial gasses of the outside sucked into the shiny climate-controlled building, only partially filtered, where they are trapped, inhaled, and regurgitated room to room—an invisible process that goes all but unremarked, save the self-conscious sneeze or sudden shortness of breath. Whereas earlier humans depended on their ears and olfactories for essential things such as locating food and water, and predicting weather, our own sensory-worn culture is most notably a society of gazing: at synthetic electronic images on plastic boxes, at signs telling us where to go, at shiny manufactured objects amid the bright decorations of cavernous malls. It is hardly surprising that most of our senses, no longer critical for survival, have begun a slow decline toward atrophy. That which we hear must be ever louder, what we smell ever stronger—the booming stereo, the reeking cologne hardly attracting our attention, as we hurry through the crowded parking lot, more or less conditioned to the industrial odors on the vaguely shifting air, eyes fixed on the ground or set on a particular parking space, the dark clouds looming behind, on the southwest horizon, a minor irrelevance, something to be ignored, if noticed at all.

I also know that, in addition to frequently filling my lungs with large volumes of tainted air, I will be, over the course of my journey, indiscriminately drinking plenty of bad water, especially in remotely urban places like Frederick, where the treated water likely is flushed with a chlorinated compound that gives rise to carcinogens and turbidity. When, as a boy, I would sip cold water from a spring, I was told to be careful not to disturb the sediment with a clumsy hand or to knock nearby leaves and debris, likely trodden upon by thirsty animals, into the water. The water itself was good, mostly devoid of run-off, mineral rich, but naturally filtered and refined as it welled up out of the ground. In the case of much treated water, it is the water itself, a formulaic combination of what has been interpolated into it and what it lacks, that sometimes comes to constitute a problem, its natural contents, good and bad alike, purged utterly by the chlorinating agents functioning not unlike some powerful antibiotic that annihilates all bacteria from the body. Ironically, even as we believe we are refining health and medicine, we compromise and impair ourselves in new ways.

Early settlers around Fredericktown, as it was then known, despite or perhaps because of their vigorous subsistence lifestyle, enjoyed unusually long and healthy lives, more than two-thirds of them living past their sixtieth year, a generous span of existence for that era. My ancestor who came to the area in 1742 would die in his sixties and one local gentleman of the period is on record for having made it to ninety-four, a birthday I'll probably never see. The proximity to the mountains, the lack of low marshy places, also conspired to spare inhabitants from the widespread colonial menace of malaria that periodically struck eastern villages and towns, and for which treatment was decidedly wanting. All in all, people living around Fredericktown in the late 1700s enjoyed a standard of living considerably higher than all but a few of their fellow North American colonists. By twenty-first-century standards, their physical trials were extraordinarily strenuous and mortality's toll on infants and the elderly was high. But for those who made it beyond the compromised conditions of the crib and avoided serious injury or infection, life generally was long and hardy, a robust existence, the fullness of which was occupied mostly by constant outdoor labor, but notably defined, rewarded, punctuated, by those with whom it was shared—the people who worked with you, the person you slept with, the child to whom life was passed, asleep at the foot of the bed or in the next room.

As I leave Frederick, Catoctin Mountain, which had been obscured amid the suffocating traffic patterns and overpasses of Frederick, opens up before me, rising gradually on the horizon. At Catoctin Point, amid the simple pleasure of having arrived at the ridges I'd glimpsed from afar, I see the hills crowd up around a pass to the west. The Catoctin Mountain Highway continues south along the ridgeline, a divergent artery of the great Indian path that led down into the Virginia Piedmont, crossing the Potomac into Loudoun County, and spanning across red clay tobacco country far southward into central North Carolina. This is an ancient crossroads, a good place to pause and sit, below the highway, along the northernmost branch of Tuscarora Creek, named for an Iroquoian-associated tribe forcibly driven by the British from their ancestral lands in eastern Virginia and North Carolina to this area, where they briefly established a village in the 1720s, only to continue northward soon thereafter into the regions that are today New York State and Ontario. Another of history's anecdotes of displacement—a tragic, minor one—but a story destined to unfold many times more, in much larger terms—a tale of sorrow that eventually would become familiar to nearly every North American tribe, a brutal repetitive drama performed across the continent: the bloody opening act of American civilization, of a nation yet to be.

Though frequently robbed, slaughtered, lied to, maimed, and otherwise disenfranchised by the newly arrived Europeans, Indians often took pleasure in and payment for leading their new neighbors across the region that was their home, ironically supplying the foreigners with much of the geographical knowledge necessary to colonize it, which in turn would lead to their own eventual removal. On the other side of the pass that runs beneath Catoctin Point, on a rise above Catoctin Creek, I glimpse the elder peaks of the Blue Ridge mountains for the first time, the smaller summits of South Mountain and Short Hill Mountain in the foreground, divided by the Potomac, with the chain proper rising behind them, dark amid late summer's white-hot haze, great shadowy giants shrouded in pale mist on the horizon. My initial view of the ancient chain I will be skirting for hundreds of miles calls to my mind perhaps the earliest written description of the mountains, which, of special interest, also records the reactions of the Indian scouts who were present at the time. Writing in 1669, John Lederer spied the Blue Ridge from afar and "could barely discern whether they were Mountains or Clouds," until his native guides knelt suddenly in worship and "howled out after their barbarous manner, 'Okeepoeze! (God is nigh!)'" Though Lederer, like nearly every other European, generally painted the Indians of his acquaintance as savages, his description nonetheless captures the sheer enthusiasm, the worshipful admiration, experienced by them at the prospect of the grand peaks they considered holy—an unfeigned joy that translates across time, culture, and language (from their native tongue, to Lederer's recording of it in Latin, to our reading of it now in English). What makes this account strangely powerful likely stems from the fact that at their most fundamental and archetypal level, there is something inherently, unspeakably, and universally majestic about mountains, any mountain, rising as they do out of the landscape, crowned by rock and wind-stunted branches, pointing heavenward, worn but defiant against all weather and time. The Blue Ridge chain is not an especially large orogen, but its distinctive mountains, being the oldest in the world, project a unique regal quality born of ancient being, long experience wrapped in a ghostly, shifting cloak of azure—an indistinct token of their peculiar living force, the process of hillside trees trapping generous portions of the water that accumulates on the mountainsides, which is then released during warmer weather through transpiration, resulting in the curious blue haze described by Lederer as cloudlike and admired in spiritual terms by many who have glimpsed it, both before and after him.

One of the first Europeans to travel in the Blue Ridge, Lederer, a German doctor turned mapmaker and explorer, found the mountains alien and wonderful, perhaps even altogether overwhelming, recording as he did their qualities in arcane, outlandish terms. Among his eccentric observations are claims of having encountered lions and Amazons. Probably he lacked sufficient terminology to describe bobcats, mountain lions, and Indian women who appeared uncommonly active by European standards. When he returned to Williamsburg, his sponsor, William Berkeley, scoffed at his findings and refused to compensate him for his journey. Undeterred, Lederer would go on to explore the Shenandoah Valley the following year with the support of Maryland's Lord Calvert, who thought him "a modest ingenuous person, and a pretty scholar." Though it is perhaps easy now to find humor in many of Lederer's wild interpretations, his observations, for all their shortcomings, were, like my own, made in earnest, the strange fruit of a naked desire to know and experience his surroundings, and even now—for all we know, for all the time we have lived here—there remains much that is indistinct about the region, its constantly changing qualities and fluctuations ever humbling our comprehension, our vain suppositions that this place may be wholly known in its entirety.

By the names we know today, Appalachia spans from Newfoundland to Mississippi, the Blue Ridge—its easternmost flank—from North Georgia to the small mountains of eastern Pennsylvania and western New Jersey. It has been that way for what humans consider to be, if we can imagine it at all, a very long time, though not since always—a vague history only roughly understood, approximated at great intervals by human standards, in estimates of tens of millions of years. Most current earth historians trained in the scientific arts surmise that between 900 million to 1.25 billion years ago the areas we identify now roughly as North America and Africa, along with Siberia and an indeterminate northern section of Europe, were joined as a gigantic land mass called Rodinia. It is generally believed that this huge continent began breaking up about 600 to 800 million years ago. When, around 550 million years ago, Africa split off, the section of Maryland I am currently standing on, altogether unrecognizable, would have been located on the equator. About this time, or perhaps 50 million years or so thereafter, North America developed a continental shelf. These long gradual driftings and natural constructions of enormous stray fragments also resulted in a number of violent, land-shaping collisions and upheavals. When, roughly 450 million years ago, a volcanic island string hit North America, the collision resulted in the development of mountains in the Appalachian region, beneath which rest many of North America's current inland coal fields. Fifty million years later the Blue Ridge was a desert and another 50 million years after that an inland sea stretched from its western reaches to the Mississippi, a geological occurrence that would later result in salt deposits. About 300 million years ago a large continental fragment known as Gondwana—made up largely of what is now Africa and South America—collided with North America, the colossal impact forcing the land to ripple, producing massive ice-capped mountains as high as twenty-five thousand feet. Around this time, all of the continents had come together to produce the great land mass known as Pangaea. A hundred million years later the area, still in the early process of becoming what would look to us like Appalachia, was undergoing a gradual process of extension and erosion, the immense stretching of mountains and hollowing of basins. As Greenland broke away and Africa moved farther east, the Atlantic Ocean began to form, the sea in its infancy fed and deepened by the slow recession of continents.

About 60 million years ago Appalachia finally began to take on what we might consider a somewhat recognizable form, the millions of years leading up to our own time a long era of orogeny and erosion—ever shaping and refining the terrain, while the sea retreated eastward, and the first flowering plants began pushing their way tenuously upward through the soil, clinging precariously in the water-rich low places. Humans, late arrivals to the scene by any measure, moved into the Appalachian region no later than 10,000 B.C.—whether coming via arctic voyage, led by the stars and the winds over the Atlantic from Europe, or from northern Asia, bearing their Clovis spearheads across a land bridge, remains a cloudy point of dispute among loremasters of the species' early history. Although they passed through the vicinity in pursuit of game, it is unlikely that these initial nomadic humans would have settled or tarried long in the Appalachian region. Though gradually warming, the environment remained much colder than today, leading human groups to spend much of their time farther east, in the Piedmont and Tidewater areas, whither permafrost receded, game assembled, and the gathering season lingered.

By 2500 B.C. humans were beginning to wander less and settle down more, forming small villages along rivers, creating primitive pottery, and periodically burning the forests in order to expedite the gathering and growing of various plants, including corn and beans, both of which gradually were introduced from southern areas of North America over a period of several thousand years. Around 2000 B.C. came a major technological breakthrough: the development of the bow and arrow, which revolutionized hunting and transformed animal meat and hides from a sporadic luxury into a reliable and regular commodity. The strange and sometimes large Indian burial mounds in the Appalachian region date from around this time up until about a thousand years ago, but apparently little was known about them among the succeeding tribes—those that would be recognizable to the first European explorers—which began to form only several hundred years ago. Being close to bodies of water was important to these early peoples in terms of game and crop growth, and rivers were reliable resources for navigation—natural avenues along which journeys were made, their loping curves bearing travelers away, welcoming home the long departed.

I make a gradual descent toward the Potomac, around which the Blue Ridge rises, by turns, gradually and jaggedly, its diverse topography shaped by the confluence of the mountains and the Potomac and Shenandoah rivers. This natural intersection is echoed in contemporary geopolitical terms by the coming to-gether of the states of Maryland, Virginia, and West Virginia. However, the river's history as a natural boundary is much older, defining, for instance, the demarcation where the Iroquois and Algonquins would meet and trade—one of their linguistic connotations for the Potomac being "the place to which tribute is brought." Pockets all but empty and backpack stripped to a bare minimum, I have arrived here with almost nothing to exchange or offer, though it will not surprise me here to encounter other wanderers on foot. Settlers would have taken the valley road, from the highway I am walking along to the ferry and on to what was then Shenandoah Falls, not far from where the Appalachian Trail now passes over the Potomac. In fact, the celebrated continuous footpath of southeastern North America, curving back and forth, crisscrosses the road I am following three times over the course of four miles. Behind me, to the east, at a point I have already passed, it heads due north up South Mountain and along a series of ridges toward Pennsylvania. Here, at Sandy Hook, near the banks of the Potomac, the AT curves west with the river before passing over into what is now Harpers Ferry, the village named for Robert Harper, a millwright and carpenter. At the last crossing, below old Shenandoah Falls, it bears south into the Virginia Blue Ridge.

Where the Appalachian Trail crosses the highway, just before the bridge and the river, my glance draws me astray, luring me into the deep shade that encom-passes the popular twentieth-century footpath, so different from the parched roar of the hard summer highway. Beneath the cover of green canopy, the air cooled noticeably, the whoosh and grind of traffic recedes, replaced by overlap-ping birdsong, the distinct tapping of a woodpecker, the vague drone of insects. Straying a few feet from the trail, I remove my pack and lean against the trunk of a hickory for a few moments, nibbling dried fruit and sipping water, the bark grooved and cool through the sweat-laden shirt on my back. The trail appears worn and eroded but the woods are silent and dark; no fragment of conversation or footfall approaches. After resting a few moments longer, I heft my pack again and return, not without reluctance, to the path I have chosen to follow—the suffocating din, the inferno that is the highway—just above the bridge that spans the rough waters of the Potomac.

Stepping onto the bridge, pressing against a concrete rail, as far from the traffic as possible, I try to concentrate on the Potomac, which rushes beneath as well as flanks me, stretching east and west—a wide immemorial conglomeration of rock and current, rapids and pools, carved through the mountains over the immense duration of centuries. Pausing, turning to gaze downriver, I remove from my pocket a hickory leaf—veined, oblong, pointed, green—plucked from the lowest branch of the bough I had rested against in the woods. Arm stretched out over the railing, I release the leaf, watching it flutter as it falls, suggesting in its motion the flight of some fantastic, deciduous butterfly. Touching the water, it vanishes immediately, current and rock conspiring to pull it under, though beneath the surface—among sand, darting living things, the organic matter that makes its home below the waters—I imagine the leaf swept downstream, jerked and then tumbled by the current, pressed flat for an instant against a rock, torn slightly as it slips free, borne via dim, chaotic avenues—the slight puppet of liquid energy—along the bottom. The last river I had crossed, the Monocacy, had appeared brown and murky, contemplative and secretive; the Potomac is passion and fury, the ancient Blue Ridge and the hydrological physics of mass drainage contending with each other, hard matter beset by motion and froth, the stolidity of stone held fast while the Chesapeake Bay, watery gateway to the Atlantic Ocean, beckons, nearly two hundred miles to the southeast.

I am in motion again, walking along the bridge, reminding myself that it remains within our power to plan and predict the routes of our journeys, dates of departures, and points of arrivals, while the manner of our passing, the collective untold variables of the path's unfolding, ever dances imperceptibly somewhere on the horizon, evading the gaze of even the most lengthy foresight. Whether having chosen or been pressed to embark, we lay ourselves open to the vagaries of the journey, floating precariously like leaves on the river: by turns submerged, pummeled, torn, pushed, pulled, swept continuously by the erratic overwhelming energy that shapes being in the world. In the midst of our mad journeys, unpredictable wanderings—events wearing upon us, shaped as they are by forces beyond us—the accuracy of observation remains only intermittent: the blur of passing landscape, the memory of spent action, bloomed before its time into colorful suspect meanings, indistinct rumors. Knowledge and theories of knowing, understandings and suspicions of life in the present, ultimately give way to idle wonder at the happenstance of our passing and all—only partially imagined—that has passed before. We are left then at last with questions, most of them unanswerable, though it may be, after all, the asking that is of greatest importance—inquiries that expect no answer—for which the answers remain debatable, perhaps unknowable.

I am nearing the end of the bridge, departing the river from above. If, for centuries, humans truly knew the Potomac as "the place to which tribute is brought," it would please me to leave something for it—a token of my respect, of my own minuscule passing. But then what does a river need? Another question whose answer evades me, the empty circumstance of which reluctantly concedes the form of an answer unlooked for. Because they are all I have, because I am rich in them, the recipient of a vast wealthy inheritance, I will offer then, in parting and tribute, my questions to the river: to be borne away, drowned, salvaged as debris by others. The fact that I am not the first to do so an assertion that is less a fact, less an answer, and more yet another invitation to inquiry. They arrive even as I depart, these questions, floating from upstream, over washboard rapids and around jutting rocks, faster than I can offer them up:

> How many dawns, prying through eastern clouds,
>   have glanced off these waters flowing into them?
> How many leaves has the river borne away?

WEST VIRGINIA

Some flee the memory of their childhood's home;
And others flee their fatherland. . . .
          —Charles Baudelaire, "The Voyage"

In the great American asylum, the poor of Europe
have by some means met together and in consequence
of various causes; to what purpose should they ask
one another what countrymen they are?
          —Michel-Guillaume-Jean de Crévecoeur,
                    Letters from an American Farmer

C rossing the Highway 340 bridge over the Potomac River southward into
Virginia, near the place called Harpers Ferry, it is easy to be reminded of
Thomas Jefferson's paradoxical description of this unique confluence of mountains and water in *Notes on the State of Virginia:* on the one hand, "placid and
delightful" and, on the other, "wild and tremendous." Above me the slopes of
the Blue Ridge are mild and green, stoic where the summer trees give way to
pale, bald outcroppings of rock, while behind me the river ceaselessly courses
and froths, orogeny in motion, ever wearing upon the stone foundations of
mountains. Harpers Ferry itself, the minute river-crossing town destined to
become familiar to Americans of the mid-nineteenth century, lies off to the
northwest of where I am walking, its initial history as a peopled habitation—the
how of European arrival—a vague affair steeped in legend. Long before the
mid-eighteenth-century appearance of Robert Harper, the man for whom it
would be named, the site was commonly known among frontier folk simply
as "The Hole," an apt summation of its humble geological location beneath

towering ridges of stone. The first settlers to take up permanent residence there were a family of Germans from Pennsylvania led by Peter Stephens, who would operate a small ferry operation at The Hole throughout the decades of the 1730s and 1740s. Lost or foreign wanderers in the region inquiring after his place, desperate to gain the opposite bank, would ask for "Peter in the Hole." When Harper bought the Stephens property in the late 1740s, the ferrying continued, the operation enlarged, and the groups of settlers—arriving in late spring with the hardening of the road's winter mud—growing more numerous with each passing decade. When my own ancestors, bound for the Smoky Mountains, reached the crossing at the end of the eighteenth century, they likely would have waited among others for their turn: checking and tarring their wagon, watering and comforting the animals, resting—as I have—amid the moist welcome cool of river-bottom shade.

For my ancestors and for me, walking in their footsteps two centuries later, the Harpers Ferry area constitutes a special region of chronology: of passage, crossings—through mountains, over water, and across the arbitrary boundaries of humans— accompanied by the persistent and ubiquitous specter of time. Over the course of perhaps three miles I pass through as many states, having bridged the Potomac from Maryland into Virginia and now walking westward, over the Shenandoah River into West Virginia. I am disappointed that I cannot relate precisely how long this condensed interstate progression took, for time has always revealed itself to me more reluctantly than distance, the interval passed and forgotten with greater alacrity than the terrain traversed. Since the outset of my journey in western Maryland, I have walked, for the most part, not out of space, but out of time, generally neglecting to mark the phases of the day, only noting periodically the general position of the sun, the length of roadside shadows. For the first time, I miss my watch, left at home by conscious design. Clock time, the invention of European monks, quickly secularized for the purpose of harnessing the population to the regimented tasks of commerce and industrialization, has never held much meaning or appeal for me beyond the necessary and obligatory adherence it continues to command, like so many other synthetic things, in twenty-first-century life. As the English poet W. H. Auden remarked, "Clocks cannot tell our time of day," and at home I can generally determine the measure of light and organize my outdoor tasks within a few minutes by the relation of the sun to several prominent natural features: the top branches of an immense red oak in a field, the jagged line of dark Virginia pine along a mild sloping ridge, and so on. Without really thinking about it, I seem to leave my watch in a drawer at the slightest convenience and on a number of

occasions have lost it altogether, missing it only a day or two later when I discover myself tardy for or forgetful of and absent from some scheduled function
involving clocks and other people.

Far more interesting and important to me than watches and clocks are the
workings of compasses—in my particular case, the small bobbing, water-locked
direction indicator strapped about my left wrist. Whether stationary or en route,
I have always been fascinated by the compass—watching it gradually rotate as I
shift in my chair or slowly traverse the curved road—my persistent interest likely
stemming from the conviction that it is less a mechanism, less a human device,
and more a kind of harnessed indicator of something that naturally permeates us
at all times: the earth's magnetism—that oft-forgotten immense energy, surging
and receding with deep molten iron lava flows at the earth's core, invisibly dic-
tating monumental occurrences on the planet's surface. Delightful to me too is
the idea that the north magnetic pole to which the compass responds changes its
position from day to day and actually has been *moving* in a northwesterly direction for several centuries. True north then is never really true north but merely
true north for that particular moment: only an idea of position and direction for
the time being. Of even greater interest is the possibility that the poles may be
well on their way to reversing entirely, something they have done before, meaning, among other things, that on some strange future night the high-energy
solar particle trap that creates the ghostly *northern* lights will appear, glowing and
fading, a curtain of flickering color, against dark southern skies.

Another aspect of magnetism, of direction and event in the midst of time,
that has always fascinated me is the moon's relationship to the sea—the fact that
tides are created because the earth and the moon are magnetically attracted to
each other, not unlike desperate lovers: the moon attempting to clutch at anything on the earth in an effort to bring it closer; the planet we live on chastely
managing to hold onto everything that covers it with the exception of its water.
The moon's constant tugging of the oceans results in the patterned tides studied so closely by fishermen, surfers, and other sea-minded humans—the daily
temporal structure surrounding the event as important for these people as the
tides themselves; while, by contrast, the history of time and the tides remains
altogether arcane, irrelevant and indistinct in its immensity. Yet, 550 million
years ago, the Blue Ridge—here, where I am walking—would have been
shoreline to an ancient sea, and our own Atlantic Ocean—a mere 180 million
years old—is now making its way inland, its current rate of progress roughly an
inch per decade. So it is that all of this—magnetism, compasses, the shiftings
of seas—remains pressed close to, hopelessly entangled with, the interminable

phenomenon of time, which ever imparts its inscrutable mystery to the natural laws we are told we know. Can we really conjecture, after all, or even begin to imagine, the Blue Ridge and the sea *half a billion* years ago, a span of counting, of knowing, that is perhaps beyond the frame of short-lived human understanding? Or, to relocate context altogether, was that time *only* 550 million years ago, a brief moment in the chronology of existence—not ours but everything's? Like other unforeseeable things, our notions of time undoubtedly will continue to change in the future, provided that we or some version of us continues to exist in those indistinct days to come. Though clock time may perish altogether—our dusty watches and digital alarms left to canker in remote antique shops and museums—likely our descendants will remain deeply preoccupied with temporality on some level since it is, in the end, not without its uses. Remember, we *only* have about 3.5 billion years before the sun burns away the oceans and makes life for us on earth (at least in our current forms) impossible. And this place—this vicinity of The Hole or Harpers Ferry, where ancient mountains and rivers converge and overlap each other– evokes, has something to do with, these things: enduring with the patience of stone, both before and beyond us, ranging and flowing across spans of time unimaginable.

I depart the Blue Ridge for now, crossing over into the Appalachian Valley, which consists of a chain of relatively flat land that stretches from New York to Alabama, cradled much of the way between the Blue Ridge and the Appalachian mountains to the west. It is a long, smooth, steep ascent, walking upwards from the river bottom, climbing my way slowly out of The Hole, the traffic heavy, likely swollen by late summer tourists rolling toward and returning from the Harpers Ferry National Historical Park, heat and exhaust fumes conspiring to make the gradual slope more of a labor than it should be. At such times—leaning forward, breath short, clothing thoroughly dampened with sweat—one is apt to resort to remote abstraction or meditate with myopic optimism, attempting to slight discomfort, turning repeatedly in one's head, for example, as a means of solace, the old hiker's motto, "Where there's an uphill, a downhill must follow." Of course, devoid of a topographical map, the wanderer will have no idea when or where the terrain will level out, or even if it will at all—as on certain geological rises or inclining fault lines that extend for miles. But he reassures himself nonetheless, as most humans will—salving our present dysphoria with the indistinct anticipation of what lies ahead: a pleasant descent, a fine view, a better life.

I arrive at the crest of my particular slope greeted by a prominent blue sign, the white lettering of which blandly reads "service road," yet beyond which, in

astonishing contrast, stretches a stunning vista of the West Virginia plain, a generous portion of the eastern panhandle of the state, its section of the great valley
system, set in limestone and shale. As if dispatched from the valley or the far hills,
a cool wind greets my sweaty face while I take in the panorama, and I drink
in the air as it curves caressingly about my brow. Notwithstanding all the disappointment and destruction it may wreak when misplaced or overly indulged,
optimism occasionally carries out its promise—those precious times when the
other side does actually turn out to be nicer, the next day a better one.

However, for all this invigorating comfort and hope realized while peering
across the West Virginia plain, I know that I am much changed already, both
in appearance and substance, since the outset of my journey. In the reflective
glass of a service station window I glimpse the face of a stranger, even though it
is my own. Despite having wandered only a few days, the heat of late summer
and the toil of the journey have conspired to effect a significant transformation:
strands of damp blonde hair blown haphazardly around and across my face, the
lower part of which is broken out in stubble; skin browned by the sun, fore-
arms darkest of all; clothing alternately damp, wrinkled, sticking, and hanging,
though the shirt is drawn snug across my chest where the straps of the backpack
hold tight; socks and shoes streaked with dirt and residual asphalt, the soiled
base of a grimy image. By the cosmetic standards of our time, I look terrible,
though probably that is fitting enough, the appearance of my body reflecting
the journey even as it is borne by it. The French writer Montaigne once said
of himself and his writings, "If I had written to seek the world's favor, I should
have bedecked myself better, and should present myself in a studied posture. I
want to be seen here in my simple, natural ordinary fashion, without straining
or artifice; for it is myself that I portray. My defects will here be read to the
life, and also my natural form. . . ." Fine words to excuse our many wantings
and shortcomings, both on the surface and within, which become increasingly
exposed anyway—an unintentional and unconscious striptease, slow, inexorable—the more we attempt to dress them in fashionable threads of artifice.

So it is a dirty, unattractive figure who emerges slowly, not without reluctance, from the air-conditioned service station in whose window he had glimpsed
himself, holding a bottle of water in his left hand, squinting at the white glare of
summer sun, the author of his torrid suffering, but also of his being: the moving
center around which we are all constantly journeying, though it too and the
planets that attend it are themselves assiduous travelers, collectively propelled in
their galactic paths by even greater and more remote forces. Relating our particular centering star to a journey, the Japanese writer Yukio Mishima professed
that for him the sun was a symbol for "the main highway of my life," and so it

may be for me, at least for a time, accompanying me, a tireless companion even as it tires me, casting light and heat on and about me on every road.

Still dwelling upon the sun, I find myself near Charles Town, walking in the evening with the traffic, so that I may be granted the illusion of approaching our star: not staring into it, but walking toward it, devoid of questions, eyes cast down. It is in the midst of this bright plodding, blinding limbo, that I am struck suddenly with a heavy weight just below the back of my neck—an impact that sends me stumbling forward. As I regain my balance, the horn of a red pickup honks even as the truck disappears, evanescent, not around a curve, but literally straight into the sun, into a glare that is stronger than my eyes. I turn away from the brightness—eyes averted to the earth, purple spots before them—vaguely holding my neck with my right hand, stunned but uninjured, the top part of my backpack having absorbed a portion of the impact. Eyes recovering from the glare, they focus on a bright aluminum object in the ditch, the apparent implement of my assault: a can of Coors Light beer. Retrieving it from the highway gutter, I discover that the can, though dinted slightly near the top, remains sealed and quite cold. When I instinctively press it against my forehead an idea springs from the cool of the metal and, chuckling suddenly, I remove my backpack and pull out my foam sleeping pad, unrolling it and then placing the beer inside in an attempt to preserve as best I can its algidity. Farther down the road, toward the diminishing sun once more, I resolve that when the day is over I will toast my assailants and, for good measure, the sun as well, since the same light that blinded me may very well have impaired the red truck beer hurler, forcing his aim awry, guiding the airborne alcohol to my back rather than my head, perhaps even saving my life. Later, in the evening, when the day is done, shadows long and the sun nearly departed, I raise my tepid watery beer to its dim passing: I drink to the sun.

I decide to skirt along the edge of Charles Town, which was initially settled by French Huguenots and the English and later incorporated by and named for the brother of George Washington, Colonel Charles Washington, who had built his home, "Happy Retreat," nearby. Turning south, away from the town, the highway traffic lessens, and the Blue Ridge, which I had missed, reappears in a haze to my left, the eastern position it will maintain for some time. The land here is open and rolling, more cattle and less produce than in western Maryland, though much of the farmland lies, by turns, fallow or overgrown with sporadic new housing developments—plowed furrows flattened, graded soil layered with suburban sod, young hybrid ornamental bushes and trees sprouting from old fields that for centuries have known only fescue, wheat, and corn. When the highway becomes two-lane, more of the land that flanks it remains sown in these venerable crops, which, incidentally, also makes for sparser traffic and more peaceful walking—the quiet familiarity of your skeleton in motion, silent in a solitude that is not loneliness, since there exists nearby, even underfoot, much that is invisibly unfolding. Though the land appears still, in the fields, along the road, as well as beneath it, amid warm gravelly soil, the old dance goes on: the dead things breaking down, fully returning to the ground from which some measure of the energy that sustained them will emerge again—in the crops, but also in the things not planted by us: the fragile loblolly seedling just come up this spring or the mushrooms there beyond the wire fence in the shade, recently sprouted from the decaying pile of cow manure. Life—diminished, consumed, returning, proceeding, taking on new forms.

It is a hot wind that blasts my face as I proceed south, generated by temperatures colliding far to the southwest, the ethereal springs of rivers of air below the atmosphere, flowing to me. In our time the breezes generally are not known by names—save to those who rely on them for the sailing of vessels and navigation of light aircraft—but in ages past they, like most other manifestations of nature, were possessed of distinctive identities and personalities. Among the Greeks, the prevailing winds I will be encountering, those arriving from the south and the west, were known as Auster and Zephyrus, respectively: the former the bearer of rain, fog, and mist, and thus a friend to thieves and scourge to seamen; the latter the mild wielder of warmth and humidity. Little else is known of these winged figures, the children of the dawn and the night sky, which is perhaps appropriate, their identities naturally hazy—as invisible as the wind, yet felt—and obscured by their impartial, elemental roles: ever greeting, with the same embrace, good and evil alike, all upon the earth, with hail and high winds, gentle mists and pools of sunlight. I know that Old Auster and Zephyrus, or whatever we might choose to call them, whatever words and myths we might summon to cloud or name experience, will be pushing against me so long as this journey lasts, all the way to the Smokies—a thought that comforts rather than menaces me, for the wind is the companion of the traveler.

Later, resting in the shade of an apple tree, the wind still with me, fluttering gently the leaves of the uppermost branches, fruit hanging in near fullness but not yet ready, mind still lazing, drifting in the humidity with Greek and Roman names, I recall part of a poem written long ago by a man called Tibullus which describes the comfort of sitting "sheltered from August's heat in the cool of the apple-tree shadow, hearing the sound of the brook slipping like silk beside me."

I am not so fortunate as to have the gentleness of flowing water nearby—no garment of silk—but I am comfortable nonetheless, the simple pleasure of respite, the rough fabric of my backpack behind me, the thick moss beneath my bottom, fine luxuries relative to the circumstances of my travel—something that forms in me the question of comfort among my own countrymen in our own time: Americans of the twenty-first century, citizens of perhaps the wealthiest country in the planet's history, yet so few of whom are content or even mostly happy, their beds and full bellies perceived only as conditions to be improved upon—a larger bed, a better restaurant. Progressively, what had once been sustenance becomes a symptom of perceived poverty, luxury eroding into need—the creature comforts expanded and refined, made common, yet who is to say what is decadent or necessary when excess becomes the norm? The next thing must be bought and bought now, for it is now believed to be truly needed. I would like for the apple that falls next to be the one that strikes my skull, bearing in the blow an answer. But instead the air is still: no apple drops, no answers come, and I have rested here long enough, probably too long. Still, I would like to wait beneath these shady branches for the apples to fall, putting them to use, leaving enough for the animals that know this tree, slicing and drying the others on rocks in the sun, making them light and then bearing them away with me, fingering, if I am fortunate, the last wrinkled sliver beneath the Smokies, a well-traveled, final piece of West Virginia, imbibed hundreds of miles from the tree that was its creator.

The apple tree and its dry imagined fruit are gone, well behind me, and before me the Smokies are still hundreds of miles to the south, but the wind is with me, curling around my face, more palpable now than it had been earlier in the day, bearing clouds from the southwest that begin to fill the sky. What at first is merely the cool of breeze and cloud cover soon begins to coalesce into the makings of a summer thunderstorm, the falling ground temperature, the suddenly palpable heat of the road, the rich odor of moisture, as the front moves up the West Virginia plain, announced by a mingling of silence and stillness, the birds and insects having sought their shelter, with the vague distant rumblings of approaching thunder. As the darker clouds draw near, they are borne on a breeze that forces high-blown leaves to shift their pale faces upward, as if turning suddenly and expectantly for the purpose of beholding something not yet arrived. When the first bolts of lightning vein the sky, followed by the booms of thunder and the smaller splintering of air that comes with the first drops of a hard rain, I feel the animal press of my own instinct for shelter, despite the mind's knowledge that, except for the ditch, there is no place for me along this road, where I am little more than a diminutive lightning rod in motion, an attractive moving target, constructed mostly of water, of which lightning is very fond.

I am becoming wetter, more watery, by the instant, the salty sweat about my head and hair washing into my eyes, burning them, though, collectively, the cool rain on my body is an overwhelming refreshment and delight. But the lightning is difficult to ignore and my earlier recollection of what it actively seeks out is followed by my perception, through squinting eyes, of a nearby poplar in the field off to my right, its canopy small, a jagged dead streak, electricity's scar, working and twisting its way down the long, straight trunk. Though considerably taller, poplars, like us, are uncommonly upright objects, especially rich in water, making them frequent casualties of the summer's periodic electrical wrath. As the German poet Gottfried Benn asked, "Who ever saw a wood of poplars?"

I feel fortunate and calmed when the lightning passes quickly, giving way to an earnest, steady, soft, rain—the kind that gradually soaks the soil, causing gardens and all growing things to erupt in prodigious activity when the sun returns. For a human too these are favorable, gentle conditions, welcome to the traveler on foot—shoes and clothes noticeably heavier but balanced, offset, by the cool temperature, the soothing moisture: the absence of sun and sweat. Less traffic along the road too, cars more occasional, lights on, driving slightly slower—with a measure of greater care that is perhaps illusory—toward the places of their drivers, the where of lives not mine.

I spend a rainy night not far from the road, showers coming and going, alone with the darkness and the wind in a dilapidated outbuilding with a dirt floor and a rusty, brown tin roof. Probably a defunct tool shed, though it might have been converted to that purpose after serving as a cabin for many years, the kind of one-room building a tenant farmer of the twentieth century might have once called home. It is now the domain of wasps and mosquitoes, the former huddled together, bodies hanging, resting uneasily, beneath their nests along the ceiling beams; the latter hungry and nocturnal, droning about me in the dark. I have eaten half a small clove of raw garlic and rubbed the juice of a cross-section on my exposed skin, but still the remarkable insects hover close, an occasional sting belying a place the garlic missed or an especially acute hunger. Worn out but not yet drowsy, too warm to get into my sleeping bag, I listen to the rain and sing softly, plucking the damp laces of a removed shoe as if they were the strings of a lyre, the whimsy of tired consciousness that precedes slumber.

Eventually, I get into my bag, the unzipping of which is met with a rustling from above. Training the flashlight on the sound, I discover that the wasps and mosquitoes are not my only neighbors, the beam capturing the greenish-yellow glimmer of bright eyes, these belonging to a rat nearly the size of a possum, perched on a two-by-four above the far wall. It lingers—apparently defiant rather than confused—and flashes a fanged grin before shuffling fast toward the dark near corner, disappearing by a route I cannot make out, as nuanced a departure as any I have seen on a stage. Anticipating mice, I have hung my food a few feet away from me, in a canvas pouch suspended from the rusty head of a wall-driven nail, sharing space, hanging, with strands of rotten bailing twine—the chords of some forgotten harvest now decades past. Settling into my bag, I am untroubled by the rat, though it will not surprise me if he or his rodent cousins make a play for the pouch later. Killing the light, I give myself over as best I can to the strange night sounds that afflict us all when we sleep in strange places—the disquiet of the unknown Here on the workings of the displaced mind.

Lying in the dark, hot and grimy, my thoughts seek comfort, as our thoughts often do, in the familiarity of the past, though the image of the rat stays with me. Where I grew up there lived an old retired farmer who practiced woodworking in a tin-roofed building that stood in better repair than the one I find myself in now. Sometimes my mother would help him make axe handles, bookshelves, or birdhouses—whatever might be needed or sold. At the end of one particular cold rainy day, during which they had been running an electric saw incessantly, my mother noticed that when the machine finally was silenced, a vague, soft droning sound persisted somewhere inside the shed. After years of running power saws and tractors, the old farmer could not discern the gentle noise. But my mother stubbornly insisted on what she was hearing and eventually honed in on the sound, which derived, to her surprise, from a large brown rat snoring on a beam high above them in a dark corner of the shed. Upon having the slumbering varmint pointed out to him, the farmer made as if to fetch his .22 rifle, which my mother eventually talked him out of. After all, it was the constant sound of the saw and the drowsy, metallic cascade of rain on tin, as well as the dry heat of the wood stove, that had put this creature to sleep. Would it not be wrong, she reasoned, to blast him from his comfortable beam, to murder him in his sleep? The old farmer, a World War II veteran from Bedford County, Virginia, who had been wounded at Anzio and watched Vesuvius erupt from his hospital bed, before returning to duty and taking a couple of wooden German bullets during the Normandy invasion, rubbed his chin on this for a moment before resolving at last to let the drowsy rodent live, at least for that day.

It is comforting and easy to recall these things here, falling asleep, not un-like that rat must have, to the sound of rain drops tapping an old tin roof, the stale smell of dust pressed close and the decades-dried dirt on the ground cling-ing to everything it touches. Filthy, dark survivors and some of history's greatest carriers of disease, rats produce in most of us feelings of malignant revulsion, yet in my imagination—the fancy of the self, imperfectly shaped, like all our knowledge, by experience—they remain ever sleeping, hungry, and somehow vulnerable: the furry inheritors of old farm outbuildings.

Dawn nearly always carries with it hope, but the sun of a pale new morning after a night of rain bears a unique bright, clean vividness—a clearness of possibility, however illusory, that arrives with it and springs both from it and the dripping and glistening things that greet and reflect its light. This is a precious energy to be absorbed, yet also tempered and stowed, prolonged for as long as possible, against the unforeseeable trials of the day. Shoes still damp, I have covered cer-tain places on my feet in preventative Band-Aids, anticipating blisters, but on this morning my feet are light and untroubled, the ground rolling beneath them, returning the energy of calf, ankle, Achilles: stretching and contracting, body in motion, devouring miles.

Beyond a family restaurant along Highway 340 where I had stopped to eat, the ground rises to offer an especially fine view of the Blue Ridge, fore-grounded by fields of hay and corn and the occasional lonely silo. With this peaceful prospect flanking me, I approach a large highway sign that announces the boundary between West Virginia and its mother state. Here, I slow and then pause, wavering—belly full, shoes nearly dry, body full of energy—yet somehow reluctant, hesitant, to pass over into a new domain, though I know too the idea of "state"—the notion of geographical area shaped by human political history—is as arbitrary and ridiculous as anything else in our existence. No, it is less the idea of "state" that halts me and more my relation to area itself, the immediate domain of the "what is" that surrounds me—the troubling notion of the surroundings we perceive. My time in the place called Maryland had been brief and the interval in West Virginia, which was part of Virginia when my ancestors passed through it, still briefer; but Virginia—however I might embrace or explain away the idea of it—would mark the dominant portion of my journey, the longest trail and trial of body and understanding, more than 350 miles of roadside hiking. Having removed my backpack, sitting now cross-legged upon it, gazing at the sign that announces its grand established domain, I find that my mind teeters, wavering, a little erratically, doubtfully, backward and ahead, grasping at the whole nature of my journey: how much I have really learned about these small sections of Maryland and West Virginia, despite having traversed them so deliberately and openly to the best of my ability. Beyond what might pass for simplicity, they already appear partially blurred and whimsical in mind and memory, in motion and indistinct, like children playing hide-and-seek at twilight.

It follows that even the smallest of places, the most minute of sites, contains an immense identity and history, and, for all its provincial uniqueness, one that usually is shared with others across time and place. The philosopher Martin Buber warned, "He who, with his eyes on the two-fold principle of human life, attempts to trace the spirit's course in history, must note that the great phenomena on the side of acts of distance are preponderantly universal." As is the case with most philosophers, Buber's words have different contexts and meanings than the ones we might suspect or prefer. However, even taken in the most conventional sense, what he says provides much to think about. Especially the ideas of distance and universality. Not only the distance I am walking, the spaces between arbitrary places or geological locations that become acted upon, traversed, amid direction and time; but the spans, temporal and real, between the different events, recent and long ago—the universal happening—we experience, summon, and attempt to imagine. Somewhere in here lies the spirit flown forever or impulse of history, the why of the telling, which is different from history itself.

With this, I remember a fragment of something else, read long ago, from the late-eighteenth-century French traveler Michel-Guillaume-Jean de Crévecoeur: "In the great American asylum, the poor of Europe have by some means met together and in consequence of various causes; to what purpose should they ask one another what countrymen they are?" A question of identity posed to the various Europeans who suddenly found themselves Americans, the haphazard populace of a fledgling nation; yet as relevant today, perhaps more so, in light of our vast international populations. Along with Crévecoeur's probably unanswerable question—unconsciously neglected until now, prodded into thought, ironically, by an invisible physical boundary, the state line before me—comes a revelation with regard to places and people both now and long ago: those experienced and imagined. I realize then that if I am to follow further these footsteps, to imagine these places as the dead once knew them, I must first attempt to answer, to remember and evoke, here by this roadside, on the threshold of yet another place, both for myself and those who have chosen to travel with me, Crévecoeur's question on behalf of my long-departed ancestors, whose identity both is and is not mine, but must serve partially, in some sense, while you travel with me, as our own.

My own family and many others like them arrived in the colony of Pennsylvania in the early 1700s after having lived for several centuries in the eastern area of the old Palatinate section of what would become Germany, thus Benjamin Franklin's disparaging description of Germanic immigrants as "Palatinate boors." The name of the small area, derived from the word Palatine, is attributed most often to the historical presence of imperial Rome in the region or to a judicial post connected with the Merovingian lords of France. Long a territory of dispute and route of invasion among French rulers and the princes of various Germanic states, the Palatinate and its population suffered a number of staggeringly intense episodes of destruction and privation from the twelfth through the seventeenth centuries. Throughout the seventeenth century the people of the region had been forced to change their religion three times, and their religious oppression was complemented toward the end of the century by the military variety. Among the worst of the conflicts that passed over these lands were back-to-back wars spanning from 1684 to 1713: the War of the Grand Alliance and the War of Spanish Succession. Both struggles stemmed mostly from the ambitions of Louis XIV of France, who, like several of his predecessors, hoped to establish a permanent French border along the Rhine river. Throughout the 1670s he orchestrated a number of raids into the western part of the region and in 1685 claimed the territory on behalf of his brother, following the death of the Elector Palatine. Outraged, the German princes formed the League of Augsburg and were later joined by Holland and England. However, before these allies could organize their forces, Louis, hoping to make the land unfit for occupation by the allied armies and also to exact acute suffering upon the Protestants who dwelt there, dispatched a host of fifty thousand soldiers under an officer named General Montclas in the dead of winter with orders to annihilate the province. Montclas enjoyed considerable success in carrying out his task, driving men and their families out of villages, the heat and acrid smell of their burning homes at their backs, and onto bitter, snow-filled roads where many died of exposure and starvation. Some were taken to France and forced to recant their religion, while others were merely raped, maimed, or otherwise butchered—the veritable old footnotes of war. In Mannheim citizens were forced to help destroy the city's defenses before being herded out into the barren countryside; corpses lying stiff and frozen in the fields were not an uncommon sight. Later, during the following summer, farmers in some areas were made to destroy their crops, plowing under the very stalks of corn that had sprouted from the seeds they had planted. In 1689 the Diet of Ratisbon banned all French officials from the German states, but by 1692 Louis's forces were back again, looting and burning, reducing Heidelberg's celebrated castle to rubble. With Louis's coffers nearly exhausted and the allies bickering among themselves, the 1697 Peace of Ryswick finally was established, which returned all lands of the Palatinate region to their prewar status. A bitter irony, familiar in our own time, that after more than a decade of slaughter and privation, the geopolitical situation would return, essentially unchanged, to its original order.

Peace would not last long. By 1701 Louis was panting with ambition again, this time for the throne of Spain. Having declared the ascension of his grandson, Philip of Anjou, to that post, Louis saw Europe rise against him in outrage and arms once more. Complementing these political and military dilemmas was an ongoing campaign of religious persecution. Though Palatines had been directed to alter their Protestant faith throughout the 1600s, they had been spared a return to Catholicism, the church of their French invaders. All of that would change under the successive electorships of Johann Wilhelm and Karl Phillip, each of whom pressed their charges, coercively and viscerally, to embrace the religion of Rome. During the War of Spanish Succession the Palatinate and Bavarian regions suffered bitterly, the French armies periodically cutting swaths through those areas, advancing and retreating, deliberately or on the double, but nearly always finding time to burn a few villages and lay waste to fields. In 1707 Marshal Villars brought his army into the Palatinate for the primary purpose of rendering a repeat performance of Montclas's crippling campaign of 1688—an ambition fully realized with overwhelming success.

In the wake of Villars's devastating tour, which corresponded with ongoing religious intolerance and a recent shower of English propaganda celebrating New World opportunity, people began leaving the region in significant numbers—a movement that would become known as *Massen-auswanderung der Pfälzer:* the Great Exodus of the Palatines. The diaspora intensified after the unusually harsh winter of 1708–09, during which it was not unusual to hear tales of wine freezing into ice, and continued for almost the next half-century. The Elector Palatine was furious with the defections—which among other things deprived him of labor, military manpower, and a dependable tax base—and issued an edict promising execution to anyone caught departing the country. However, since death and disenfranchisement had been close at hand for decades, the threat did little to discourage the population; the exodus continued, even after the Peace of Utrecht in 1713. It was probably during the early 1720s that my ancestor,

Frederick Clabough, resolved to depart. Prolonged suffering molds desperate men and almost thirty years of sustained hardship and instability served to make the propagandistic, self-serving declarations of English speculators—known as *Neulanders*—very nearly irresistible.

This is no sad story of the death of kings but a much more humble tale: the long past of the people they trod upon, faceless and poor but possessed of a will born of desperation to take their families somewhere, anywhere—braving oceans and death, all obstacles—where some semblance of life, of personal prosperity, might at last become possible. It is a story that has come to be thought of, claimed, by some as definitively American, yet lies wrought upon a much larger tapestry—more universal, more timeless—an archetype of human history, a song refraining still: of arbitrary boundaries established and transgressed, be they mathematically surveyed state lines or the shifting sandy banks of the Rhine—one more cause and symptom of the ongoing human infliction of suffering upon ourselves.

From my ancestors' life-threatening circumstances and impetuous travel—menaced, hungry, desperate at thread's end—to my own more leisurely wanderings across rivers and mountains, dangerous but freely undertaken and embraced: a long-removed passionate expression, in a sense, of the freedom they longed for. With this feeling, more a sensation than a rational realization, comes the assurance that for all my lackings and shortcomings of perception and being, for all the things I miss and will never imagine or become, my freedom to make this journey, body and mind, and attempt to understand it—a small, brief metaphor for the immense odyssey that is our lives—remains the most important thing, the only thing, and, in fact, all that any of us can ever really ask for.

I pass into Virginia then, as I have entered all states and nations before it, as I came into the world and ever will be so long as I am—imperfect, limited, one more human whose knowledge remains suspect—but with history and experience, existence, mine and others, ours, both at my back and before me, around me, everywhere, unfolding, now.

VIRGINIA

Shenandoah Valley

The Indians left little in the Valley—mounds to be
plowed down, arrow heads, the dust of bones. They lived
like shadows among the trees, like shadows they have
passed. . . .

—Julia Davis, *The Shenandoah*

What is notable about this early landscape is what it was
not. Absent, of course, were the grand houses of a gentry
class of tobacco planters. Missing, too, was any significant
disparity between the houses of the great and the small.
. . . These were the dwellings of families neither rich nor
poor but all owners of their own land. . . .

—Warren Hofstra, description of
eighteenth-century Valley Germans,
The Planting of New Virginia

I

W alking southward into Virginia, having departed the state that once
was part of it, I follow Highway 340 as it curves away from the Blue
Ridge, compelling me to bid farewell to the mountains, cast now in the haze
by which they are known, for the time being. Here, in Clarke County, the road
declares itself early and often the Lord Fairfax Highway, and horse farms, grand
and humble alike, line the road. Much of the topography, however, remains the
same as in Jefferson County, granting a measure of geographical understanding
to the district's reluctance at its unwilling alignment—the bitter legacy of a distant conflict—with West Virginia, its economic and cultural concerns resembling those of the Virginia Valley region, sharing little with the mountainous
Allegheny counties to the west. So it is that the identities of both the places we

inhabit and ourselves often are shaped only partially by us, forged at intervals by forces outside, until the idea by which we are known and even part of what we are appear to others and ourselves, glimpsed unwillingly in life's invisible mirror, as things we never intended to be.

Passing one of the smaller rural homesteads along the road, I hear an abrupt bark from the deep shade of a large oak, followed by the swift advance of a large black and tan dog. It barks as it lopes, tail up, bearing down upon me with bounds and growls. Instead of running, I loose the straps of my backpack and pull it around before me, holding it, elbows bent, as a shield, however ineffectual it might prove to be. When the canine, a well-fed Doberman, gets within a few paces, he stops and dances from side to side, an inimical jig without music, save the barks he continues to hurl at me from deep within his throat. I gradually continue to advance down the road, backing, talking softly to the dog, remaining as still as possible, while trying to work my hand into the top end of my pack. After a few seconds of digging, I find the zipper to the tent pack and am able to pull free one of the folded fiberglass tent poles, hard to break and, when wielded, capable of inflicting intense pain on the sensitive end of a dog's nose. The Doberman follows but seems content to merely dance and bark. Watching him or her, I remind myself that this is no feral, rabid thing, but a fat domestic with a leather collar, dangerous to be sure but a creature that someone surely feeds and dotes upon, probably used to chasing the rare cyclist or wanderer who appears along his portion of the highway. Perhaps sixty feet down the road from the place where our confrontation began, the dog slows as I continue to fall back and then stops altogether, though its eyes remain fixed upon me, its barks becoming intermittent. I retreat a few more feet and then turn and continue, the tent pole slipped back into the pack, the pack reunited with the sweat on my back, torso and shoulder straps reluctantly tightened. A few paces later I glance behind me to see my potential assailant turned away from me, watering a sign post, leg cocked. He completes his marking, kicks up some loose gravel with his hind legs, and trots back down the roadside toward his shady tree, tail high with pride, identity intact, victor of the conflict, lord of his territory once more.

On this day Berryville is a quiet, peaceful town. Sitting in the cool corner of a shaded parking lot, hiding from my loyal fellow traveler, that persistent late-summer sun, and drinking from a cold twenty-ounce can of beer, I sense the presence of a place where folks are forced to make their own fun but are probably altogether content, like the inhabitants of so many small places, to have things that way. Yet, as with many other places, this was not its nature more than a couple of centuries ago, the parochial visage of the mature present grown drowsy and somber in the wake of youth's primal howl. Originally laid out in 1798 as Battletown, the village would alter its name later in tribute to its swash-buckling crossroads innkeeper and games master of the mid-eighteenth century, Benjamin Berry, who had constructed on his tavern's front lawn, not far from where I am sitting, both a bear pit and a fighting ring, in which he was fond of pitting men or animals against each other in the hopes of drawing a bloodthirsty crowd, which he calculated, accurately it seems, would soon seek refreshment at his inn. Set along this well-traveled road, the place was ideally situated to attract fresh combatant and naive victim alike. Among the more storied fighters to pass through Berry's ring was a young Daniel Morgan, then a hard-drinking wagoneer, who bested local champion Bully Davis in a punishing, bar-wrecking melee of more than an hour's duration, which would lead to a rematch several months later that quickly dissolved into a free-for-all involving the entourages and friends of both Morgan and Davis, as well as the more than one hundred spectators who had come to witness the contest. Eventually Morgan's contingent was victorious and the festive rowdies, stoked by blood and thirst, rushed Berry's tavern en masse, much to the innkeeper's delight.

Departing the placid Berryville of the now, falling in with the sun once more, I am reminded that ours is an ongoing savage history—in spite of the en-titled sense of progress for which we congratulate ourselves—one we continue to exact upon each other as well as the other creatures of the world we live in. The latter transgression has always seemed to me the more heinous since the animals who suffer at our hands cannot understand the material, abstract, or perverse human motivations that orchestrate their agonies. I think of the Doberman who had pursued me, wondering if he possibly had been encouraged or trained to go after every foreign thing that approached his owner's domain. Then my image of him, dancing back and forth, nape hair raised—nature made over again by dream—dissolves into that of another such dog encountered years before, beneath a roof of corrugated tin in a nineteenth-century red-brick warehouse converted into a dirty, hot gym, the concrete floor covered in dust and vague stains, the old steel equipment, nearly all of it, wearing a thin coat of orange rust. This grimy place of low grunts and sweaty bodies was owned by a semiprofes-sional football player who also worked as a bouncer and dabbled in drug deal-ing and dog fighting. He was, however, for all these things, not a completely terrible fellow, inquiring after your health and freely offering his mostly hard-earned knowledge of the human body. Following him about the dark, ill-lit building—clammy in winter, ovenlike in the warmer months—was a massive three-legged Doberman, his absent hind appendage mangled and amputated in the wake of some ill-fated distant contest. Yet, despite the needless cruelty to which he had been subjected by his owner, the dog remained loyal to him, ever at his side, a bane to any who might threaten him and altogether terrifying to many of the unoffending weightlifters. On one particularly hot afternoon, not unlike the one I find myself walking in now, as I lay on a rusty bench, pressing weight from my chest, I felt a sudden heavy pressure on my right thigh. Returning the weight bar to the steel frame above my head, I half-rose to find the three-legged Doberman resting its head on my upper leg, its brown eyes fixed on my own in that strange imploring glance of companionship peculiar to dogs. Sitting up, I patted the dog's head and rubbed his ears until he wandered away, probably in search of his master.

The Catholic thinker Saint Thomas Aquinas believed that animals have no souls. One need know very little about them or theology to be certain that Aquinas was dead wrong; yet for all our science, our understanding of dogs and other animals remains so limited as to render our knowing indistinct—the knowledge of the other blurred by our preoccupation with ourselves, our focus fixed closely on our side of the relationship, our own perceptions, and molded by the limited collective assumptions of the time in which we live. Of course, arrogant hypotheses and the uninformed conclusions that inevitably follow them are not restricted to our relationships with animals or our own time. While traveling with a survey team in the area of Frederick County, the district into which I soon will be passing, in the spring of 1747, a sixteen-year-old George Washington noted that the inhabitants "seem to be as Ignorant a Set of People as the Indians. They would never speak English but when spoken to they speak all Dutch." Preoccupied with the importance of his English-speaking survey party, this precocious teen insists that the German settlers he encounters naturally should resort to his native tongue, attributing their reluctance to an inherent Indian-like ignorance and declining to entertain the possibility that they may have been speaking their own language out of preference, perhaps even in order to talk undetected about Washington and his companions. Washington also neglected to perceive his ignorance of the German language as a personal failing, a symptom of his own incomplete knowledge, but then he was, after all, only a boy; and, reminding myself of this, I recall, all too clearly, the thick-headed prejudices of my own teenage years—that dynamic self-obsessed period in which one wishes irrationally for other things, both possessions and circumstances, and believes he is privy to all answers, while the world about him responds too slowly— those who love him appearing merely as obstacles to a better life. It is a phase of development that, unfortunately, fewer and fewer people of our own time appear willing or able to completely outgrow.

Approaching Winchester, the town to which Daniel Morgan retired when his days of brawling and soldiering were done, one perceives against the western horizon Little North Mountain and Great North Mountain, eastern outcroppings of the Alleghenies, the great chain of peaks stretching northward into Pennsylvania and on toward the Catskills. Having longed for mountains since departing the Blue Ridge, I am struck by an indistinct reassuring comfort that accompanies their appearance. John Esten Cooke, born in Winchester in the first half of the nineteenth century and destined to witness the monumental carnage of that century's, our nation's, bloodiest and most tragic conflict, serving in the Confederate army, felt a comparable solace at the prospect of these hills: "I know not how it is with others but to me all sorrows and heart-sinkings come with far less poignancy amid the fair, calm, silent mountains." Cooke, perhaps possessed of some vague inkling of what horrible events lay ahead for his home and himself, also associated mountains with "the great mist-shrouded future," the nature of time as yet unfolded, obscured by the mist that hangs from the hills, resting softly on treetops. Greeting the Alleghenies and thinking of Cooke, I wonder what they may hold for me.

Upon crossing Opequon Creek into Frederick County, I begin a long, gradual ascent toward Winchester. Whereas the Alleghenies had introduced themselves remotely, above the horizon in the distance, Interstate 81, an immense road that will shadow me throughout much of my journey but that I hope to avoid as much as possible, appears for the first time below me, beneath a highway bridge I am crossing. The massive travel artery that replaced Route 11, which in turn had developed out of the wagon road sprung from *Athowominee,* 81 is a swarm of gaseous wind, speed, and thunder, trucks and cars interweaving, packed close, hurtling toward ends and destinations I cannot guess. Though possessed of a generous median and wide roadside shoulders, the large thoroughfare is banned to foot travelers, probably for their own good; but there are places to the south—if I am fortunate enough to arrive that far—where it merges with, or rather absorbs, Route 11, places where I'll find myself reluctantly tracing it, or, without much regret, passing along an alternate route.

The strip malls and businesses that seem to appear with the interstate feel claustrophobic after so much walking in the open, amid agricultural land and the occasional residence. Yet, these are appropriate enough sights to greet me as I enter this place founded and perpetuated on commerce. In 1789 André Michaux described Winchester as "a little town whose Trading with the Settlements of Kentucky is done by land. The merchandise comes from Philadelphia, Alexandria and particularly from Baltimore." A cog in the machinations of westward colonial distribution, Winchester was a place to buy, sell, and haggle—to empty the wagon or resupply, depending on your needs. One notable local merchant whose trade had far-reaching influence was the German gunsmith Adam Haymaker. Following the European German tradition, early gunsmiths in North America had crafted high-caliber flintlock rifles for the purpose of felling animals as large as a mature black bear. However, soon realizing that mobility, and therefore considerations of convenience and weight, was of the essence given the circumstances of travel, gun craftsmen like Haymaker began engineering smaller barrels and stocks, maple and black walnut being the materials of choice for the latter. By the second half of the eighteenth century the typical gun was a .36-caliber rifle, usually fixed with a bayonet for the purposes of possible Indian engagements or finishing a kill. The weapon was lighter, more accurate, and required less powder.

Beyond colonial Winchester, one need look no further than the multibillion-dollar military-industrial complex of today to see that weapons and commerce have always gone hand in hand in the United States, and are still going strong, the path to economic development cleared through military might, though the terminology changes slightly, the bluntness of Manifest Destiny having given way to bleary linguistic blankets such as Nation Building. It is a small semantic irony too that a century or so following the improvements Haymaker and others brought to the North American rifle, a gun called the Winchester, developed by a New Yorker named Oliver Winchester, would come to be lionized as "the gun that won the west," its repeating rounds introducing a new deadly quality into firearms combat. Like other such technological innovations of war, the Winchester was an implement of dehumanization as well as progress, both in terms of the way it impersonally vanquished those who opposed its wielders and the unconscious toll it could exact on those very wielders, as well as on the people involved in its creation. Having come to believe her family was haunted by the restless ghosts of the thousands cut down by her husband's rifle, Oliver Winchester's wife, Sarah, would flee, shortly after his death, from New Haven, Connecticut, to San Jose, California, where she would use her husband's lucrative industry profits to construct indefinitely an elaborate, 160-room mansion, designed haphazardly with the help of a spiritual medium to accommodate the angry ghosts seeking vengeance upon her. As the family necromancer explained to Sarah, "You can never stop building the house. If you continue building, you will live. Stop and you will die." A Rasputinesque hoax perhaps, yet one wonders if modern psychology could have offered Sarah any greater measure of peace, the lives extinguished by her husband's invention having come to be the sole fixation of her own.

Lost amid these musings, I discover that I myself am lost, literally, in Winchester, wandering in a residential neighborhood, evidently having missed the signs that would navigate me through town and onto Route 11, the street I am walking along devoid of a number, bearing an unfamiliar name. Though curious at my misstep and apparent inattention, I am not especially bothered, having found that most people in towns and small cities—at least in this part of North America—usually are willing, if not happy, to give directions. As John Steinbeck noticed decades earlier, "The best way to attract attention, help, and conversation is to be lost. A man who seeing his mother starving to death on a path kicks her in the stomach to clear the way, will cheerfully devote several hours of his time giving wrong directions to a total stranger who claims to be lost." Though I have never attempted Steinbeck's strategy of merely purporting to be lost, his point about direction-givers appears mostly true. Asking directions at the next convenience store, I am not only told where to go but actually taken there by a carload of friendly female students from Shenandoah University, a local college somewhere nearby. Sitting in the backseat of the car, trying to soak up the air-conditioning, my voice sounds to me both tight and sluggish as I converse. Only later, after I am dropped off, do I realize that these are the first people I have talked to at any great length in days. . . .

Since the outset of my journey, I have heard fragments of numerous voices, but used my own very little, though this silence is partially by design. Many scribbling wanderers, especially the journalistic variety, go out of their way to talk to as many people as they can, seeking out, sometimes obtrusively, county officials and influential community people on the one hand, and those they believe to be the local downtroddens and deviants on the other, ostensibly hoping to arrive at a kind of voyeuristic sociological montage of the community at hand. Yet the people on the other end of these questions—rich and poor, educated or not—usually divine exactly why they are being questioned, often because the traveling interlocutor readily and proudly volunteers his purpose and aim. As a result, the people at hand frequently offer only embroidered images of their lives and places—appropriately fabricated responses to forced, synthetic questions. I wanted to avoid a lot of that if possible. I knew I was passing through the environments and spaces of others—*their* lives and places—and to actively seek some kind of connection seemed artificial and presumptuous to me. My attitude was that it would come to me or it wouldn't, and that whatever did arrive of its own accord would be far more interesting and authentic than anything I might actively seek out. The philosopher Buber went fundamentally further, asserting that "the depths of the question about man's being are revealed only to the man who has become solitary, the way to the answer lies through the man who overcomes his solitude without forfeiting its questioning power." Though the twenty-first-century human of the United States finds himself wholly interconnected on the literal, technological level, his fundamental personal state remains significantly cloistered by the very economic and industrial forces that connect him, in the abstract, to the rest of the world. Remoteness then is not something most of us have to work at very hard in order to achieve. As the poet Rilke maintained, aloneness "is at bottom not something that one can take or leave. We *are* solitary."

So I feel myself passing more like a ghost, transparent as the wind, a walking stranger in the night or the day, there and then gone among places and people. It encourages me too that the first European to enter the Shenandoah Valley, John Lederer, traveled in much the same way, treating with the Indians only when invited to do so and remaining ever silent and courteous at the strange things he witnessed, most of which he did not understand and could not hope to explain or even portray—foreigner to a land that did not know him, one of great mysteries. As the poet W. H. Auden said of the wanderer in his poem of the same name, "Ever that man goes through place-keepers, through forest trees, a stranger to strangers. . . ."

The kind Shenandoah students have dropped me off near a local high school on Route 11, a road known also as the Lee Highway and the 11th Infantry Regiment Highway, the history of human conflict asserting itself again in these memorial dedications to distinguished American soldiers of the past. A site of strategic geographical importance in eighteenth-century North America, Winchester was destined to accommodate its share of military personalities. At the beginning of the French-Indian War, long before the town had become a great trading center, Colonel George Washington, having negotiated his teenage years and passed into early manhood, came to the area with orders to raise and train a militia, which in time would effectively transform the village into a kind of garrison. However, even as the newly constructed Fort Loudoun (named by a grateful Colonel Washington for the British general who armed the fort and afforded him the legal authority to hang militiamen for disciplinary infractions) loomed over the town with its 240-foot walls set atop a hill to the north on an ancient burial ground, the basic lack of discipline among young Washington's charges and the imperative need for readiness forced him to resort to draconian methods in literally "whipping" his men into shape. Profanity, for instance, brought twenty-five lashes from the cat-o'-nine-tails, feigning illness fifty, and drunkenness a hundred. Although whipping-post justice was not new to Winchester—in the mid-1740s, for example, a girl received twenty-five lashes for bearing an illegitimate child—the offense of drunkenness, despite the harsh penalty, remained particularly prevalent and difficult to stop since locals had developed as a prosperous side racket selling gin and whiskey to Washington's men. Late in the summer of 1756 the young colonel threatened the townspeople not to allow "the Soldiers to be drunk in their Houses, or sell them any liquor, without an order from a commissioned officer; or else they may depend Colonel Washington will prosecute them." For all this warning and intimidation, threats and whippings in some cases were not enough. In one particular instance, two men were hanged from a newly constructed gallows before the town, shortly after the arrival of a group of new militia recruits—a spectacle Washington felt would "be good warning for them."

It is odd to think of young Washington, for whom so much destiny and distinction still lay in wait, chiding and bullying his men and the townspeople, frustrated at their stubbornness, their lack of fear in the face of verbal and physical intimidation, their indifferent stoicism and strong will when punishment was visited upon them—though it would be these same traits that eventually would transform many of them into fine soldiers and, if they managed to live into the 1780s, archetypal Americans. Odd too that on the site of an old Shawnee camping ground Washington was training a force to help bring about that tribe's destruction, history—even when rooted in a single place—steadily moving toward the next conflict, the next seizure and occupation: the traces of the conquered buried along with their culture, the conquerors having begun already the unconscious journey toward their own indefinite downfall, the vague legacy of the defeated, departed and approached again.

I am glad to get out of Winchester, although the sprawl that emanates from its center makes it difficult to say exactly where it ends. One does not really *feel* the Valley either until Winchester is left in wake, the topography revealing itself again, less impeded and concealed by the deeds and constructions of humans. A long strand of low rich land stretching northeast and southwest, the Shenandoah Valley lies cradled between the Blue Ridge to the east and the western

Allegheny Mountains, their name drawn from an Indian word meaning "End-less." Because the Shenandoah River flows north, general directional travel ref-erences are reversed here: heading south as I am is referred to as "going *up* the Valley." By the eighteenth century, few Indians inhabited the region, though they still passed through frequently on hunting and trading expeditions. When European settlers arrived, parts of the Valley already were open with meadows that could be converted easily enough into agricultural fields, their openness a result of those periodic Indian burnings, purposeful land-clearing forest fires, not unlike those employed by foresters today, set to facilitate crop growth and attract game.

Nearly all of the early forest that remained in the Valley would be cut by set-tlers. This while resting beneath, enjoying the shade of, its most common tree, then and now: a modest roadside white oak—this particular one perhaps half a century in age, its bottom branches hanging so low I can brush the tips of the leaves with my fingers while sitting on the ground, my back against the trunk. Writing in 1796, Isaac Weld Jr. noted at great length the already palpable devel-opment of the Winchester area in the context of the still largely uninhabited Blue Ridge:

> In the neighborhood of Winchester it is so thickly settled,
> and consequently so much cleared, that wood is now be-
> ginning to be thought valuable; the farmers are obliged
> frequently to send ten or fifteen miles even for their fence
> rails. It is only, however, in this particular neighborhood
> that the country is so much improved; in other places there
> are immense tracts of woodlands still remaining, and in
> general the hills are left uncleared.

The wilderness transformed into plentiful fields, wheat became the dominant crop in the Valley during the second half of the eighteenth century and would remain so for more than a hundred years. There are fields of it even now, grown from verdant green nubs into swirling wind-blown oceans, golden with new grain. Both during the American Revolution and decades later, when Virginia seceded, it was the Valley that provided bread and forage for its armies and horses, though great fields of hemp were cultivated as well in the time of the for-mer conflict, primary material in the making of rot-resistant rope and paper.

For all the transformations humans have inflicted upon the Valley, it remains even now an altogether spectacular visual landscape, framed by ancient moun-tains and drained by the numerous rivers and creeks that ever enrich and refresh its soil. In his own time, Weld too was struck by the beauty of the landscape, celebrating in particular the special appeal of those venerable trees fortunate enough to have been spared the axe:

> The hills being thus left covered with trees is a circumstance which adds much to the beauty of the country, and inter-mixed with extensive fields clothed with the richest verdure, and watered by the numerous branches of the Shenandoah River, a variety of pleasing landscapes are presented to the eye in almost every part of the route from Bottetourt to the Patowmac, many of which are considerably heightened by the appearance of the Blue Mountains in the background.

Though the Valley is much changed, there remain places where Weld's visual description is as accurate now as it was more than two centuries ago, much of the land still farmed, rolling—laying well, you might say—and most of the visible Blue Ridge clothed in dense forest, substantial tracts of it owned and preserved by the federal government.

Along the highway again, passing over Opequon Creek, a body of water I'd already encountered once, I am reminded of the well-known expression by the ancient philosopher Heraclitus: that one cannot step into the same river twice. Though bearing the same name, the Opequon beneath me is, for all prac-tical purposes, a disparate body of water—fed by different streams, containing a variant water chemistry—from the one I had crossed to the north. So too both it and the whole Valley are vastly different entities within their respective iden-tities from what they once were in the past—though each occupies the same geographical position and may appear in places similar. I remind myself of this condition from time to time: that this is merely, and can only be, despite the occasional temptation to imagine it otherwise, the Valley of my own era.

More discernible and easier to keep in mind, since they are ever before and beneath me, are the changes to the route I am shadowing: this highway of as-phalt, concrete, and rock as opposed to what once was *Athowominee*—a muddy footpath, overgrown in places by weeds and grasses, cobwebs and sapling branches greeting the face of the infrequent traveler. In the wake of the French-Indian War what had been a modestly traveled wilderness path for Indians and, increas-ingly, frontier settlers was widened and graveled in an effort to make wagon travel easier. Local counties generally shouldered the expense, though the funds they put forth usually came back to them or were surpassed as a result of in-creased travel and commerce along the route. In addition, it was local farmers who performed the labor in the winter months or during the slow time between planting and harvesting. Thus, much of the money expended went to local residents and, by extension, back into the county economy.

Above the village of Stephens City, originally Stephensburg, I climb a plateau from which I can see the Blue Ridge and Alleghenies off in the distance on either side of me, a perspective that reveals a kind of context both for the Valley and my place in it. Unfortunately, the prospect also affords a clear view of 81, the large multiwheeled trucks, the size of toy models at this distance, dwarfing all other traffic. Though I dislike the appearance of the interstate, I am glad it is there for the purposes of my labors—the thought of all that traffic, all those massive trucks crammed onto Route 11, not a very pleasant one. Of course, long ago the route had accommodated a significant portion of the overall commerce in the North American colonies. Instead of long lines of trucks, the late-eighteenth-century traveler would have encountered herds of livestock—cattle, goats, sheep, pigs—being led to market, either in the nearest town or perhaps even to the great livestock capital of Philadelphia. Other essential merchandise—salt, sugar, medicine, tools, gunpowder, manufactured goods—was transported either by wagon or packhorse train. And then there would have been the locals, walking or riding to work or church, and the far-bound settlers, afoot or perhaps sitting amid their possessions in Conestoga wagons. Ironically, many local folk then felt the same way about Conestogas as modern travelers do about tractor trailers, the wagons' heavy bodies and wheels creating deep ruts and mushy holes when the ground was wet, and huge clouds of dust in the arid heat of late summer and early fall. Just as massive truck tires litter the highway with their disintegrating retreads, so wrought-iron nails would shake or jolt loose from the wagons, dropping to wait unseen in the dirt for an unsuspecting traveler—perhaps the next barefoot farm boy, sent to town for a few grams of salt or sugar, and maybe, if he was lucky, a piece of hard candy for himself.

Late afternoon, shadows long, grass already dampening, resting before I strike the tent, having received permission to camp at the edge of a pasture, I hear a cow bell in the distance, and, closing my eyes, try to imagine, as best I can, this time of day for those distant travelers who passed this way before me. Along the road, in the fields, amid the gentle dusk of a Valley summer, the packhorse and wagon teams unhitched and hobbled, the long day's sweat and imprint of harness thoroughly scrubbed away from the horses' flanks by the attentive human master for whom they constitute a livelihood. With bells placed about their necks, they wander deeper into twilight, grazing, until darkness fills the Valley and the drowsy traveler, laid out beside a fire or stretched on a straw mattress in or beneath his wagon, can no longer see them. Yet this does not trouble him as he gradually succumbs to slumber amid the damp grass and all his worldly goods, for across the field there drifts, lighter than air, a kind of lullaby of wind chimes: the soft tinkling of horse bells.

However we modern individuals might choose to imagine it, traveling was no romantic matter for drovers and wagoneers, the livestock and goods they managed a necessary hindrance and burden ensuring their ability to set food before their families. Bent on speed and efficiency, they would have carried little else with them beyond their goods, the bare minimum—an essentialist mentality that still exists today for those who happen to travel long distances on foot or horseback. Next day, wandering here along the road, my wagon on my back—a forest-green Lowe Alpine backpack of polyethylene foam, roughly a foot across and two feet in length—contains everything I deem necessary on a daily basis, though even an experienced hiker may discover over the course of his journey that he is carrying things he really does not require, in which case they are usually left behind, given away, or mailed home. Subtracting weight from one's pack is a fundamental and persistent objective of all wanderers since it increases one's comfort and ease of movement while lessening the unrelenting strain upon the back and knees. Along this road my own material existence is reduced to a two-pound tent, a summer-rated light sleeping bag, a foam pad, a lightweight battery-powered headlamp, a small flashlight, a stove and one-liter fuel bottle with cook pot, a Kabar knife, three twelve-ounce plastic water bottles, one-ounce bottles of disinfectant rubbing soap and sunscreen, a half-roll of toilet paper, a small stainless steel bowl for both drinking and eating, dried fruit, meat, and garlic cloves (to deter insects) in ziplock bags, a clay pipe and tobacco pouch (a nonessential vice), a bandana to keep the sweat from my eyes, a white cotton shirt, one pair of shorts, underwear, a pair of liner socks and two pairs of wool socks, a wool pullover, rain pants, a poncho, moleskin and a one-ounce bottle of hydrogen peroxide, and a jackleg collection of road maps for Maryland, West Virginia, Virginia, and Tennessee, torn from their travel books and held together by a plastic, as opposed to metal, paper clip. Everything else on my body, worn and in use.

Perhaps such lists can only appear mundane, mere corporeal distractions from greater abstract purposes. On the other hand, it may be closer to the truth that they, the visceral and the mental, are intertwined, perhaps even hopelessly tangled. Among all the world's thinkers, probably it was the philosopher Spinoza who pursued most doggedly the confluent nature of mind and body as mutual determinants of human existence. In fact, as my journey unfolds, I find my bodily needs and mental musings increasingly overlapping and giving way to one another: the mind that hungers in the monotony of travel, the body that wonders in the midst of its fatigue. To be sure, there are times when I wish for additional equipment or information, as well as various other things, but these desires eventually give way to the more perspectived and abstract observation that I generally have with me, amid this twenty-five to thirty pounds of mass on my back, all I really *need*. Obscured, or rather drowned out, by conditioned cultural and corporeal concerns, this brand of thinking—a kind of applied minimalism—comes to twenty-first-century Americans with great difficulty, ours being an unprecedented arcane culture of wealth and immense ownership, the frivolous objects in our basements and the ever-appearing, labyrinthine roadside storage complexes hardly necessary to our existence.

By and large, such gluttonous consumption would have been foreign to the local residents of over two centuries ago—homes small and spare, possessing for the most part, only what they made or grew—though there were notable exceptions. Leaving the area of Middletown, I pass the opulent limestone estate Belle Grove, built in 1797 for Major Isaac Hite (Heydt), a descendant of German immigrants from Alsace who attended the College of William and Mary and served in the American Revolution. In 1731 Isaac's father, Hans Jost Heydt, had bought ten thousand acres of land in the Valley and led a party of German families down *Athowominee* from Pennsylvania onto Maryland's Monocacy Road and over into the Shenandoah. Though Jost did not own slaves, his son, years later—grown immensely wealthy through the gradual, efficient, and lucrative sale of his father's real estate—eventually would come to have in his possession more than a hundred, a bizarre anomaly in the region. As Isaac Weld Jr. summarized in 1796, "On the eastern side of the ridge, cotton grows extremely well; and in winter the snow scarce ever remains more than a day or two upon the ground.—On the other side cotton never comes to perfection; the winters are severe, and the fields covered with snow for weeks together." Furthermore, with a few exceptions, the nights were too cold in the mountain and valley region of Virginia for cultivating the less hardy variety of tobacco grown at the time. This and other environmental variations between western and eastern Virginia, along with the inherent cultural differences among western settlers and the Anglican planters of the East, conspired to make the slave plantation an exception and the African-descended population sparse, though the latter would grow steadily in the decades leading up to the Civil War. Frontier Germans in particular took pride in their independence and self-sufficiency, developing small farms that could be run efficiently by the family with occasional help from neighbors during episodes of construction, planting, and harvesting. These lifestyle differences from eastern Virginians eventually voiced themselves through legislation. With the aid of lawmakers like Jefferson, western Virginians—the more numerous Scotch-Irish, as well as the Germans—increasingly pushed for greater influence in government, ultimately disestablishing the Anglican Church and abolishing the laws of primogeniture and entail, which they generally viewed as decadent and unfair.

The influence of the East, however, with all its benefits and evils, did penetrate certain portions of the Valley: on the rare large plantation like Hite's and around Winchester, where nearly everything could be sold or traded, including the labor of slaves and indentured servants. Frontier Germans were especially unlikely to own or acquire slaves as a result of their religious convictions, economic frugality, and their own recent vivid experiences with thralldom. Coming to North America, families that had fled the Germanic states, including my own ancestors, would have endured a hellish six- to eight-week passage across the Atlantic from Hamburg or Bremen. Despite the terrible conditions they had lived under in the Palatinate, few were penniless when they departed their homes, and the southwestern Germanic states were among the least feudalistic, meaning that some individuals actually had owned their land. However, all but a few were quickly exploited out of whatever money or possessions they might have had on them. Frequently, they were purposely detained at ports while local merchants orchestrated a practiced racket of gradually sucking dry whatever money the travelers had brought with them. Once onboard, they often found that their goods were looted by the crew as their physical health began to diminish in an environment highly conducive to malnutrition and epidemics. As Gottlieb Mittelberger remarked, "During the passage there doth arise in the vessels an awful misery, stink, smoke, horror, vomiting, sea-sickness of all kinds, fever, purgings, headaches, sweats, constipations of the bowels, sores, scurvy, cancers, thrush and the like, which do wholly arise from the stale and strongly-salted food and meat, and from the exceeding badness and nastiness of the water, from which many do wretchedly decline and perish." Mittelberger, like many others, traveled on a cargo ship haphazardly altered for travelers through the construction of a makeshift deck built between the upper deck and the hold. Since it would be collapsed after disembarkment to make cargo room for the return voyage, the deck was loosely built, primitive, and uncomfortable. The ship's hatches provided the sole ventilation and were clamped shut whenever the weather turned foul. Latrines were scarce and the middle deck was entirely open, affording little privacy for women, who sometimes found themselves molested by the ship's crew. By the mid-eighteenth century shipping tactics and conditions, particularly on vessels owned by an especially nefarious English company called Stedmans, had refined themselves nearly to the point of rivaling the Atlantic slave trade in overall cruelty and dehumanization. Between 1750 and 1755 two thousand passenger corpses were cast into the ocean.

Onboard, travelers were expected to provide their own meals and, having little or no prior knowledge of sea travel, they usually misjudged their provisions; if their supplies gave out they had to buy food from the captain, for which they were charged exorbitantly—a calculated measure to bury them deeper in debt. Those who brought with them chests full of dried meats and fruits, brandy, and medicine often were forced to leave them behind or store them on other ships, which again placed the traveler at the mercy of the ship's commanding officer. If a passenger died during the passage, family members were charged the individual's fee, a particularly tough blow if the sole survivors were women and children. If a child's guardians both died, the minor would become the property of the captain, who would then sell the child as a means of exacting payment for its parents' fare. Plummeting into debt meant having your family become servants in the New World. The going price for a man was ten pounds for three years of servitude; some were bought for up to seven years; and children were owned until the age of twenty-one. In return for this specialized variety of slavery, the owner would pay off whatever debts the traveler owed the captain; the process was called the "redemptioner system." The eighteenth-century German immigrant arriving in Philadelphia harbor would have been allowed to disembark only if his sea passage was paid and he had no outstanding debts. Those who owed money waited to be sold off, the healthier going first and the sick and the weak sometimes dying onboard, too useless for purchase.

Being bought by a master carried with it no guarantees of fair treatment or extended care. People could be swapped or sold if they did not fit the owner's plans. As one period advertisement read, "For sale, the time of a German bound girl. She is a strong, fresh and healthy person, not more than twenty-five years old, came into the country last autumn and is sold for no fault, but because she does not suit the service she is in. She is acquainted with all kinds of farm work, would probably be good in a tavern. She has still five years to serve." As horrific as this process might sound to twenty-first-century readers, the sum and utility of a human being set in the bargain-value context of a newspaper's classifieds section, we must do our best to keep it situated in the context of the time, during which such prospects did not seem completely unpleasant alternatives to the mauling periodic violence and ongoing deprivation of early-eighteenth-century life in the Palatinate or Bavaria. Furthermore, as with all slaveholders, there were good masters and bad ones, and the degree of one's youth, strength, and potential knowledge of a trade affected the manner in which you were treated, the adept learners and hard workers quickly becoming indispensable to their masters, the weak and the slow loathsome burdens. Difficult for the modern thinker to grasp, it was a system devoid not only of civil rights, but of any rights at all; and though it is said to have been increasingly "humanized," the practice was not abolished altogether until the 1820s.

I make a long descent toward Cedar Creek, on the other side of which once rested Fort Bowman, or Harmony Hall, the former epithet drawn from George Bowman, son-in-law to the aforementioned Jost Hite. Built in the 1750s, the structure was known as a particularly fine exemplar of Pennsylvania German architecture in the Valley. Although the word "fort" implies a military fortress, eighteenth-century frontier forts were simply houses, though sometimes especially sturdy and centrally located ones, where families could gather in the event of an Indian raid or other disaster. Fort Bowman is only the first of several humble strongholds along the route I am following, nearly all of them springing up during the French-Indian War as the English sought to protect their dominant frontier thoroughfare and, of secondary importance, the settlers who lived along it. Familiar, as we have seen, with life in the Valley, Colonel George Washington considered the forts impractical, noting that the manpower required to build and occupy them would have to be drawn from local men already burdened by agricultural subsistence, militia duties, and road maintenance. Yet defending themselves increasingly became a necessity, as a number of Indian war parties, resentful of "the Great King Across the Water," as they called England's ruler, and stoked on by the French, embraced the struggle as a means of exacting vengeance upon the encroaching Europeans.

Stemming mostly from their religious convictions and horrendously vivid experiences of warfare and abuse in northern Europe, German settlers generally were slow to resort to violence and reluctant to take up arms, a disposition that sometimes led to their being labeled cowardly or lazy by their more hawkish English-speaking neighbors. However, the proximity of the French-Indian struggle to their land and families made their participation more or less unavoidable. In the wake of a British army's defeat near Fort Duquesne in 1755, Indian raids would intensify along the frontiers of Virginia and Maryland, a development with which the governors of those states remained generally unconcerned. Virginia's lieutenant governor, Robert Dinwiddie, for example, scolded frontier leader John Buchanan and attributed his misfortunes and those of his neighbors to their failings as capable defenders: "If Yr. People will dastardly give up their Families & Interests to a barbarous Enemy without endeavoring to resist them, they cannot expect to be protected." To the north, Frederick County, Maryland, equally isolated and unaided, would receive its share of the suffering in early 1756: three boys scalped, the Lynn family abducted, the Matson farm burned—its sheep cast upon the flames alive. Not long after this raid, my ancestor Frederick Clabough Jr. would join Captain John Middaugh's Maryland company, mustered in Frederick, the visceral realities of a broad European and North American conflict having finally touched the lives of his neighbors.

Highway and horizon simmering in the heat, I am nearing a figure along the roadside. A few feet off the highway, on a rise above the ditch, an elderly man works on a fence—patching the holes, shaping bent cow wire with his gloved hands, nailing it into treated wooden posts. I pass nearby, inadvertently startling him. When he looks up suddenly from the strand of wire his hands have been twisting, he blinks at me in the hot white light of early afternoon as if not entirely certain whether I had risen up out of the dusty roadside gravel or materialized out of the heavy summer air. Though it may have occurred in his perception, I am more or less certain my body never disappeared and reappeared again after an interval. While I apologize for surprising him, he recovers quickly and comments on the weather—a mundane, obligatory subject coming from most people, but not from farmers, for whom it dictates so much, sometimes everything. He finishes patching the hole before him while explaining that he hates to be working this time of day in the heat, that his doctor had told him not to, but the cows had kept getting out this week, the smaller north pasture grazed to a nub, and he was afraid they would escape again and wander onto the highway. He carries his fencing tools in a metal bucket as I walk along with him to the next slack section and, slipping off my pack, stretch the wire for him with a mini-crowbar while he ties in the new strands with the old and hammers steel staples into the post. I help him do a few more sections without much talk and when we are done he invites me to dinner. Declining this offer as gracefully as I can, I tell him I want to travel a few more miles but am not interested in getting a lift. He remains wholly unrelenting though in not letting me go without some kind of reciprocation. As if remembering something, he motions me over to his truck, parked between the highway and a heavy metal gate leading into the pasture. From the passenger-side floorboard he pulls forth a shoe box and sets it on the hood. When the brown cardboard lid is removed, I see that it is half-full of arrowheads.

The poet William Carlos Williams had written of Virginia, "In the corn-fields almost anywhere you'll pick up Indian arrowheads of quartz," and here I am, standing next to a pasture, absorbedly sifting through a shoe box full of them, like a child discovering history for the first time. My naked excitement at such things, at discovering unlooked-for pieces of the past, has led to my occasional embarrassment among others from time to time, but I recall too that the Chinese philosopher Chuang Tzu, writing around 300 B.C., asserted that the "True Man" retains in part the unspoiled simplicity of a child. The old farmer is pleased at my obvious interest in the arrowheads and urges me to take some. Possessing the gift some people have of spotting unusual objects on the ground, he had collected these from his land over the years, not for history's sake but rather as a kind of game—a pastime to liven somewhat his unrelenting daily chores. Some farmers, he explains, are equally adept at spotting and hoeing in-vasive weeds, glimpsing them in pastures from moving trucks and tractors and stopping impulsively to eradicate the menace. I select an arrowhead that is not too large or too perfect, one that had been overused or perhaps not fully com-pleted, but he presses me and I take a few more, zipping them away in a small compartment of my backpack.

Bidding farewell to the farmer, I cannot help feeling that this is a happy omen, trail or road magic of the best kind, centuries-old implements passed into my hands, available to be used by me. Or perhaps this is the wrong reaction to have, bumbling along again with my brain half-cooked, fanciful in the summer heat, happy at the idea of a few new pieces of rock adding weight to my pack. Livy, one of modern history's fathers, strongly believed that there is no reason to object "when antiquity draws no hard line between the human and the super-natural: it adds dignity to the past." But what of those occasions when the fantas-tic or whimsical (those loosed and often indistinct metaphors of expression) come to neglect experience or the stories and so-called facts known to many? This is a tension less familiar to scribes but intuitively felt by poets, for whom metaphor and whimsy serve as both the indirect sorcerous wielders of unmatched human insight and those chaotic imps that cloud, mislead, and torture the mind. The thinker Bertrand Russell asked, "Is it possible to preserve the lover and the poet without preserving the lunatic?" The answer to this question, glimpsed only partially, as if from behind a curtain, never reveals itself to me fully—heat pounds my skull, the train of thought evaporates.

Magic still vaguely on my mind, I am aware that a more enormous, yet subtle, road magic lies in the very layout of the Valley towns along this road, each roughly separated, purposeful in their eighteenth-century spacing, by a day's wagon journey or, in my case, a day of vigorous walking. I pass over 81 again, the interstate not troubling me this time, before entering Strasburg, a frontier town founded by German settlers in 1740 and named for the old capital of Alsace. There is a fine view here of ridges jutting out into the Valley toward me, the most prominent series of which constitute Massanutten Mountain, the beautiful middle range of the Shenandoah.

The eighteenth-century settlers who lived in this area were known for their skilled crafting of earthenware objects and *fraktur* etchings, which began with the arrival of Brother Sirone, a gifted Dunker potter from Pennsylvania, in the early 1760s. In Strasburg I pass the Hupp Homestead, built in the 1750s and, like Fort Bowman, one in a series of forts constructed on Cedar Creek for the purpose of withstanding Indian attacks along what was then considered the frontier. The traveling Englishman Andrew Burnaby had said of mid-eighteenth-century Strasburg citizens, "If there is such a thing as happiness in this life, I think that they enjoy it." However, the word Massanutten translates as "the Indian Old Fields," and the traditional proximity of various Indians to the area would have tragic results toward the end of the French-Indian conflict, the Shawnee orchestrating raids in the summers of 1763 and 1764, abducting or killing and scalping all they encountered. Most of the victims were locals surprised while traveling along isolated roads or working in the fields—too remote to seek shelter in the Hupp fort or the nearest house.

Crossing Tumbling Run I begin an ascent toward what amounts to a relatively uneventful portion of my journey—to and beyond Toms Brook—peaceful and blurry, the weather fair, road open, rolling beneath me, myself hot and fatigued but not wholly uncomfortable, feeling my skeleton pounding against the asphalt or partially absorbed by the cooler and more forgiving grass alongside it, the whirling fields of hay and broomstraw, dancing to the invisible tune of the wind, beyond fences of wood and barbed wire. Before heading uphill to Woodstock I cool myself in Pughs Run, lying down in a little rapid, where the water quickens before a narrow channel, feeling the current pass around me. To experience the water of a shallow natural watercourse flowing over, under, and about you is to sense vaguely the body of the landscape come alive in motion, not unlike feeling, only half-awake, the pulse of the woman sleeping next to you, your curved palm resting upon her neck, half-aware, dreaming.

It is said that Woodstock and Winchester were both founded by James Wood, a hard-drinking English surveyor come down from Oxford and a veteran of the Royal Navy, but since both towns were constructed on old Shawnee campgrounds, the credit for choosing the sites must rest with that tribe, or perhaps the people who preceded them in inhabiting these places, whose ancient burial mounds rest nearby. Woods was an Englishman, but Woodstock's population, like that of Strasburg and many other Valley towns, was predominantly German, the sound of high Deutsch, if we can even imagine it, like strange music inside a dream, echoing in the streets well into the middle of the nineteenth century. Woodstock is home as well to the oldest courthouse west of the Blue Ridge, established in the 1790s, but the area stands out to me more for its natural features: the seven great bends in the Shenandoah River, flowing nearby, and a number of fine views of the Massanutten collection of ridges. However, its close proximity to both the Blue Ridge and Little North Mountain and the Alleghenies, along with the unfortunate absence of a fort, made the village an attractive target for Indian raids. In 1757 a war party of the Shawnee came over the western mountains, falling upon the town without warning. Locals took shelter in George Painter's stone cellar, which the Shawnee immediately set afire, the structure quickly engulfed in flames, forcing those inside, suffocating amid the intense smoke and heat, to surrender. Painter himself had been shot fatally trying to flee his home, and when the townspeople were brought out, several infants were taken from their mothers, suspended from tree limbs by taut grape vines, and dispatched with rifles as their parents looked on. After lingering long enough to burn an outbuilding with several sheep and cows inside, the Shawnee war party retired back into the Alleghenies, carrying with them their forty-odd prisoners and other spoils of war. Though nearly all of the hostages eventually were allowed to return home via ransom, a few would remain with the Indians, including three of the late George Painter's daughters, who in time took men of the tribe as husbands. In 1766 Woodstock was home to the Valley's last recorded Indian attack, again administered by a group of Shawnee, some of whom, if they were fortunate enough to have survived the French-Indian War, might have taken part in their favorable raid of nearly a decade before. Their assault on the home of minister Hans Roth took the lives of the preacher, his wife, and two sons, the woman and her boys tomahawked in succession after the father was shot down in his doorway while seeking to negotiate with his attackers. Roth's daughter escaped into a dense nearby hemp field with the family infant, where she remained hunched and hidden, listening to the sounds of slaughter and the cries of her dying family, trying to keep the baby quiet until at last she deemed the conditions safe enough to run for aid.

Though life in Woodstock beyond these horrible isolated incidents generally was peaceful and uneventful, tragic human conflict would continue to shape and define the destinies of the village and its inhabitants, for it was also in Woodstock, at the outset of the American Revolution, that the German theologian Peter Muhlenberg stood before his congregation and tore off his preaching gown to reveal a military uniform. Having urged his Lutheran flock to fight for Virginia, Muhlenberg assembled and led a rebel contingent known as the German Regiment and proceeded to serve with distinction, rising to the rank of brigadier general. Though slow to resort to soldiering, German settlers, their victimization in Europe only a few decades removed, were quick to comprehend the hardly veiled injustice of British taxation. Back in western Maryland, the Frederick area tax collector was burned in effigy. Shortly thereafter, John Clabough, already a veteran of the French-Indian War, took the oath of allegiance and returned to service as a sergeant in Captain John Carmack's company, for which he received a salary of eight dollars a month. J. F. D. Smith, a Scotsman and spy for the British who was captured and imprisoned at Frederick, would later remark that the locals "were always very liberal of insults and abuse," a testament to their passionate partisan involvement in the struggle. Honed and hardened both by their northern European past and conflicts with Indian war parties, and fiercely protective of their newfound personal freedom, German settlers in places like Winchester and Frederick remained largely unperturbed by the darkening shadow of British oppression and military might—the threat for them an old and familiar one, certainly an ominous song but one to which they already knew nearly all of the words.

On the other side of Edinburg—despite its Scottish connotation, another village originally peopled by German settlers—I stay at the Mountain View Court, one of many hotels built along Route 11 in its heyday as a major thoroughfare and now either run-down or lying in ruins. In another of history's many arcane twists, the hotels that exist today along 11 collectively resemble the original taverns that lined it in the late eighteenth century: a wide assortment of stop-offs, from the dingy and near-condemned to the clean and efficient—most of them bearing symbols on their signs in an effort to convey to illiterate or non-English-speaking travelers what the inn offered. Whereas German-run hostelries in the North generally could be depended upon for good food and clean accommodations, taverns in the South were a mixed bag. On a given night one might come in from a long day or two on the road only to find a drunken brawl à la Battletown in progress or every room taken—in both cases the custom was to retire to the stables, where one could at least sleep on dry hay with a roof overhead. After hours or days on the road, tired travelers, melancholy for the places they had left and uncertain of what might lie before them, naturally would be attracted to a tavern—even the worst sort—in the hopes of receiving at least some semblance of food, shelter, and news of significant events, as well as the nature of the upcoming stretch of road. As Johann Schoepf noted, the traveler who stops at an inn "can inform himself as to where the taxes are heavy, where wives have run away, horses been stolen, or the new Doctor has settled." The prospect of such information, seen in light of the road's formidable loneliness and deprivation, led many a wanderer to risk robbery, abuse, and bedbugs in the darkest and most humble of roadside dives. Especially disturbed by the nature of tavern beds, André Michaux wrote, "Happy the traveler who arrives on the day they are changed." Though the sleeping arrangements could be most wanting, many Virginia inns had good menus of pork, eggs, and hominy (boiled Indian corn), as well as rum, wine, brandy, whiskey, beer, and cider. In the evening's later hours one could seek fellowship playing cards or drinking by candlelight, though these pastimes could devolve rather suddenly into disagreements and blows. Before courthouses were established, inns also served as meeting places for local political events, trade, and betting. Outside the inn, on a lawn or in a field, it was not uncommon to witness simple festivals and athletic events on weekends and holidays. Men would wrestle, race, bowl, and even introduce their most vicious rooster in the hopes of winning a little extra money from a cockfight or two. Taverns also provided the first highway distance signs in North America, posting how far it was to the next inn or town, the nearest civilized resting place on the long road ahead.

Before leaving Mount Jackson I rest in the shade against the cool surface of a thirty-foot stone wall, not far from Mill Creek, the dark rock a salve for shoulders both sweaty and sore. When I step into brightness from the shadow of the wall, my feet too are cool and light, and remain that way for a time. Just as I am becoming uncomfortably warm once more, coolness greets me again, this time upon the air, rising from the north fork of the Shenandoah River over which I am passing—generally narrower, deeper, and flowing more sluggishly than the south fork, which runs fast and clear on the other side of the Valley, beyond the Massanutten range. The French-American writer Julian Green described a stretch of the north fork on a sunny day in June 1941 as shining "like a great sword laid on the grassy meadows," while above it he felt "a spiritual majesty about these Virginia horizons that cannot be expressed." The river had also touched the imagination of the German explorer John Lederer nearly three centuries earlier, who believed he had found in its current the flowing passage to a great inland sea—the same misguided theory that would lead to Henry Hudson's disappearance into that larger, icy northern river which now bears his name.

South of New Market, though no structure stands, history invisible, is the birthplace of John Sevier, the son of a local Huguenot innkeeper born in 1745 and fated to have an enormous impact on the area of East Tennessee that is my destination. That region remains distant yet, though it is interesting to gauge in advance, walking along the road that would bear him south, how far destiny carried Sevier, from the occupant of a humble crib in the Valley to a flamboyant leader and slayer among men in the wild country that would become the state of Tennessee near the end of his life.

It is while dwelling on Sevier that I soon encounter another invisible piece of history that immediately suggests distance to me, albeit much more literally: the southern boundary of the Fairfax Line, a surveyed collection of lands that once consisted of over five million acres and spanned, south to north, from the present-day Rockingham County line to the Maryland border. In September 1701 the Virginia Burgesses had introduced an act "For the Better Strengthening of the Frontiers and Discovering the Approaches of an Enemy," which enabled the governor to allot ten thousand to thirty thousand acres of unclaimed frontier land to any suitable "society." The provision generally was ignored until William Gooch became governor in 1727 and, under pressure from London officials who feared French expansionism, vigorously pressed for settlement of the Valley. However, the effort among Virginia lawmakers to people the area was impeded by the fact that hundreds of square miles of the northern Valley already were claimed as private property by Thomas, sixth Lord Fairfax, Baron of Cameron, a flabby, ill-mannered, eccentric bachelor and huntsman who spent most of his time at his castle in Kent—the countenance of his extant portrait adroitly described by Jefferson County writer Julia Davis as "a young, pouting, corpulent face, wearing an expression of petulant astonishment."

King Charles II, exiled in 1649, had bestowed the entire Northern Neck of Virginia—the great stretch of country between the Potomac and Rappahannock rivers—upon his "right trusty and well beloved" companions, and the rights to much of this immense tract had reached Fairfax through inheritance on his mother's side. Robert "King" Carter, Fairfax's land agent in Virginia as well as an influential member of Governor Gooch's Council, aggressively fought Gooch's intention to develop Fairfax's lands in the Valley. However, the Lords Commissioners in London, mindful of the French menace on the western frontier, pressured Gooch to facilitate settlement of the Valley as a kind of buffer for the wealthier and more established English settlements in Tidewater and the eastern Piedmont. Between 1728 and 1736 the governor signed several Orders in Council that dispensed immense sections of Valley land to individuals referred to as "applicants," most of whom consisted of Gooch's friends and powerful acquaintances, such as William Beverly and William Byrd II of Westover. These successful "applicants" generally doled out roughly ten shillings for every ten acres while also pledging to settle a certain number of families on the land. The default loser in all of these proceedings was Fairfax, though he remained comfortably wealthy and still in possession of thousands of acres, much of which he eventually would sell off to settlers.

From history's image of the larger-than-life holdings of Fairfax, abstract comprehension of nearly inconceivable individual ownership, to another vision, lingering in our time before my very eyes, large in its own setting, purporting to both claim and name: just south of the now-defunct Fairfax Line I glimpse what I initially take to be peculiarly patterned rock or a mirage, but what is, in fact, immense white lettering in the distance off to the left, lying against a mountain of the Blue Ridge over a span of several hundred yards, reading, "Endless Caverns." This massive advertisement, grand in its gaudy manner though it disrupts and cheapens the rock against which it rests, harkens back to a time in the twentieth century when Route 11 was a major North American vacation thoroughfare, and families, children eager for diversion, frequently sought and found themselves waylaid by such roadside attractions. The construction of 81 made this particular venue out of the way and remote, perhaps seven miles from the nearest exit, though doubtless it continues to attract its share of vacationing tourists, lured away from the long rolling miles, the bland efficiency, of the interstate.

Although something inside me intensely dislikes the marketing of these caverns, the enormous sign does bring me to reflect on an idea that had not occurred to me for some time: the concept of existence inside and beneath the mountains. As I walk here in the heat, I find it soothing to summon the prospect of summer caving—the simple act of arriving at the subterranean opening you've chosen, humidity giving way, the cool underground air encompassing your body as you check flashlights for the last time and, if you are particularly cautious, don a helmet. Entering a cave that descends oft has been likened to peeling back the layers of the earth's history, the changes in soil and rock as one proceeds deeper amid failing natural light. Life too, at least surface life, undergoes a kind of diminishing, bat guano and other organic matter becoming less and less frequent the farther you proceed. Such literal regression possesses a peculiar sense of fascination—rewarding to absorb. One of my favorite things to do at some point over the course of such a journey is to go off down a side passage, away from my companions, if I am with a group, and extinguish my headlamp. After a few moments, footsteps of your friends growing fainter, a curious sensation begins to set in amid the utter absence of light, no sound save your own breathing and perhaps the dripping of water somewhere far off—a kind of natural sensory deprivation that plays upon the mind until, after a time, the mind begins to make its own company, inventing sounds and shapes in the dark. On one occasion I was wading with some friends in a wide, slow-moving underground stream that continued to deepen the farther we proceeded, from our knees to our waists and up. The summer had been an unusually rainy one and the water table was high, so much so that we eventually found ourselves awkwardly splashing and treading with water about our necks, feet slipping on the slick rock bottom, the way ahead, floor to ceiling, occupied utterly by the stream now swollen into a dark underground river. Fortunately for us, a quick reconnaissance revealed the passage ahead to be flooded for only a few yards, that there was spare breathing room again on the other side of a brief underwater journey. We proceeded in single file, one at a time, holding onto a rope, each taking a deep breath before vanishing beneath rock and water. When it came my turn I felt for some reason a vague urge to linger beneath the water a little longer than I had to, letting go the rope, drifting along the cold hard bottom, eyes wide open, seeing nothing—only the chill of liquid black, sound of my heart, and the nearness of rock pressed close: the weight of the mountains above me.

It is said that in Endless Caverns someone once found the tooth of a woolly mammoth, an animal believed by some to have been hunted to extinction by spear-hurling packs of humans in ages past. The mammoth recollection directs me again to the perhaps altogether unavoidable specter of conflict, with other beings of the world and among ourselves, both in the now and in times now distant. When I pass through a place known as Tenth Legion, south of which, in an area called Lacey Spring, there once stood a popular inn called Lincoln's Tenth, my thoughts are narrowed further, inevitably it seems, toward human conflict of the military variety. *Athowominee*, after all, the trail in whose ghostly shadow I continue to follow, means "path of the armed ones," and the warriors of various eastern North American tribes had long used it for raids against each other, these small campaigns—sometimes covering hundreds of miles and requiring many days of travel, though few men were involved—undertaken during favorable periods of weather, usually the dry time of late summer and early fall. Ironic to me that from this martial tradition comes the rather mellow seasonal term "Indian Summer."

Few current expressions that reference North America's early inhabitants are as peaceful or kind, and old histories generally depict Indians, almost without fail, as marauding barbarians, devoid of strategic thought or European morality, rightfully vanquished. Yet their repeated military successes against settlers, militiamen, and the British army suggest they thoroughly understood the concepts of both campaign and diplomacy. For instance, the great Shawnee chief Cornstalk, known among his people as *Wynepuechsika* or *Keigh-taugh-quah-qua,* whose wisdom was said to equal his prodigious physical strength, skillfully conducted a series of retreat-and-maneuver engagements culminating in the bloody battle of Point Pleasant in October 1777, after which he wisely sued for peace in the face of overwhelmingly superior numbers and resources. However, when Cornstalk later approached the English on a peaceful visit, he was imprisoned in their garrison at Point Pleasant and later murdered in his cell, along with his son and a young chief named Red Hawk, by a mob of vigilante rabble—an incident that supposedly outraged colonial officials, who nevertheless ultimately found no one at fault.

The nature of Indian strategies and tactics, their impact on settlers, and lack of influence on the British army would have consequences throughout the second half of the eighteenth century. In 1755, near Fort Duquesne, along the Monongahela River, General Edward Braddock's British Regulars were routed by an ambushing force of Frenchmen and Indians, an event stemming mostly from Braddock's overly rigid conceptions of strategic maneuver and supply, and his complete indifference to Colonel Washington's counsel that his assumptions would have to be altered to accommodate the nature of warfare on the North American frontier. As the effete British officer confided to Benjamin Franklin prior to the campaign, "These savages may indeed be a formidable enemy to your raw American militia, but upon the King's regular and disciplined troops, Sir, it is impossible they should make any impression." The price for this haughty shortsightedness was the lives of many of Braddock's men, as well as his own, his purported dying words, "Who would have thought it possible?" ringing in the ears of the survivors on their long march back to Winchester. Yet we should be reluctant to assign Braddock undue ridicule, since the British army and its many officers generally would retain the same strategies and tactics up through the American Revolution, an unbending, prideful assurance of military theory, successful on so many other battlefields, that would condemn their better-organized, superior forces to defeat. It is not difficult to imagine the spectacle in the abstract even now: Englishmen and foreign mercenaries in red, marching forward across an open meadow to the clean strike of drum and fife, bayonets fixed and flaring white when the cloud passes and the sunlight strikes them, while before them, in a dark grove, crouched behind the trunks of great shady trees, colonial militiamen await the order to fire.

Resting along the roadside, amid the shade grass of a fine white oak, fingering an arrowhead, wondering idly when the last war party of the Shawnee may have passed this way. The vague thought slowly gives way to a compulsion, capricious urge, to bury here the arrowheads that have come into my possession. Having carried them with me for a time, I have come to be of a mind—as I say, a compulsion rather than a reasoned position—that it is wrong to bear them with me any longer: better that they become the Valley's once more. Opening my pack, I draw out the Kabar knife, with which I gouge a shallow hole in the ground. Kneeling, I commend the ancient implements to the earth from which they came, were honed, used, lost, and discovered again. Having crumbled the soil upon them, I rise and step firmly, twice, with my left foot.

Whether a gesture of sentimentality or grim resignation, a kind of farewell to the many conflicts the Valley has known and those yet to address us, I remain uncertain. And only later do I recall those strange legends of vanishing road wanderers: curious drifters who pass on or disappear but leave behind some manner of token, something curiously substantive and material in the wake of their dissolution. But I do not believe that phenomenon describes me. Always departing, I feel myself nonetheless ever present in the place through which I am passing—the living domain that is the visceral continuum of the traveler, experienced and remembered. It is fanciful in any event and perhaps ultimately irresponsible to wish to disappear entirely, dissolve ourselves utterly, from the inevitable conflicts that afflict the human who lives among other humans—the cruelties we collectively visit upon animals, each other, and the world itself—as well as the more harmless manifestations and vestiges: abstract cultural clashes, the packed professional wrestling arenas and football stadiums—those grand American coliseums, the coarse weekend battle towns of our time.

Outside forces propelling us into scenarios and identities we could never have imagined, ours remain lives that drift indefinitely so long as they are. And sorrowful is the soul swept on a strong current, rudderless, until at last it finds that stagnant pool, where still waters offer up the morbid image of what it truly is—this dying thing it never intended to be. Yet so long as there is intention there is hope, for intention is a window that opens upon the heart. Being can never be dead so long as we mean to become something. And one can do worse than mean well. Therein, lies a meaning. . . .

II

What I am becoming, what this journey is making me, may give rise to the question of how I came to the journey, or perhaps rather how it came to claim me, awakening me to my surroundings, both of the now and the bygone—the wedding of history and experience conspiring to create for me an amalgamation of a world long hidden and the one before me, resonating across time. It is a realization sprung singly from a camping trip made years ago, an excursion of the then-present undertaken with a knowledge of the past, not far from where I now find myself—experience long passed into history, joining that which it already knew, the echoes of which reverberate still. . . .

The end of a September, camped on the southern fork of the Shenandoah River in the eastern part of its valley, on the other side of long Massanutten mountain. Had spent the dry afternoon wandering aimlessly, a span of hours when summer seemed to float just on the brink of autumn, only a few of the maples beginning to blaze bright scarlet, while just a premonition of dull brown lurked behind the green leaves of their neighbors: towering chestnut oaks and beech for the most part, with wiry sour- and dogwoods beneath. In the late afternoon sun hawks had assembled on air above a long mountain to the east, just another part of the Blue Ridge to my eyes but something more to theirs, possessed as they are of the intensity of telescopes—a gaze that may track diminutive prey hundreds of feet below, even through wisps of cloud cover and glare. Assembling with instinctual, ritualistic purpose on felicitous air currents, an unseen physics of wind and gravity pushing them upward without so much as a dip of a wing. Preparing yet again, the Blue Ridge their guide and reference point, another uncounted year of another uncounted century, in the comfort of their numbers, for the long journey south for winter. Or so it seems to this blind, ground-bound observer, having wandered aimlessly this afternoon among others in the finite numbered time of human reckoning—of a still-new century: ours.

The gay, brightly clad party of cavaliers had ridden forth from Williamsburg in August of 1716, crossing the York River just a few miles to the north and proceeding as far as the Rappahanock before turning their course upstream and westward along the banks of that river. This merry group had been zealously mustered by Alexander Spotswood, governor of Virginia. His object in sallying forth amid the intense heat of late tidewater summer was not only adventure or war, but the enduring, albeit superficial, bedfellows of these phenomena: fame, glory, vanity, and greed. From his prosperous post in Williamsburg, Spotswood had heard tales of the vague, bountiful lands to the west, claimed by the crown but only marginally explored. In the hopes of promoting public awareness of this indistinct territory, populating it, and fattening his purse through its dispensation, Spotswood had resolved to venture into the region himself with as much pomp and fanfare as he could muster. The artful governor would be joined in his self-appointed quest by a number of gentlemen on horseback; he himself would travel comfortably in a fine horse-drawn carriage. All would be attended by their servants. However, it is altogether likely that these gallant men never would have found their way far beyond the Rappahanock had it not been for the presence of several Indian guides and rangers. The Indians, of course, would know all the loping ancestral paths of the region, most of which strayed along rivers and took into account the gentle vagaries of geology and elevation. The rangers would know many of these paths as well and a few that would be less familiar to the Indians. Wandering explorers of the western wilderness, rangers often made paths of their own as they laboriously climbed trailless hills and ceaselessly recorded in their minds what rested just over the next rise. It was from these rangers that Spotswood had learned of the West's extensive bounty and the discovery of a pass through the easternmost mountains. At a price, these same rangers had agreed to lead Spotswood on his journey. Yet one wonders at what they must have thought of the nature of the venture, its method and unfolding being so drastically different from any of their own. Likely they grew impatient as Spotswood's servants laboriously cut rough, wide roads through the underbrush and sulked beneath the curses that rang out from his jolting, perfumed carriage. But the rangers were being paid handsomely and such reward usually extends the patience of most men while just as often serving to perpetuate even the most flagrant foolishness.

As they moved west along the Rappahanock and on to the Rapidan, Spotswood and his companions likely would have noticed that the land was beginning to roll with gentle slopes, like so many geological ripples emanating from the ever-closer mountains. Yet they seem to have marveled little at the terrain's beauty. In fact, their daytime humors began to sour noticeably as the hills became steeper, the trees and undergrowth thicker and more unyielding, and the streams deeper and more difficult to ford. Hornets and yellow jackets plagued man and horse alike, and many a gentleman's silken sleeve and velvet hat were ripped and torn by the tips of branches and rocks. Servants were berated and the rangers questioned about the validity of their route. Far from Williamsburg, these gentlemen found themselves worn-down and frustrated, out of their element in an environment that made no allowance for breeding or rank.

Yet their spirits would be uplifted at the beginning of September when they passed through the Blue Ridge at Swift Run Gap and into Virginia's Great Valley. Admiring the vast richness of the area—opulent wild pea vines, grapes, currants, and cucumbers—Spotswood immediately comprehended its value to future settlers. Coming upon a beautiful river in the valley, Spotswood learned from one of the rangers that the Indians called it Shenandoah. Believing this to be an insufficient, savage word, he rechristened it "the Euphrates," perhaps hoping that this valley, this very river, might come to constitute a new cradle of civilization, which would remember him as its father. The gentlemen forded the waters with great ceremony and proceeded to bury a bottle in the ground on the other side which claimed all territory beyond the river for King George I. They then ordered their servants to prepare a great feast, after which they drank to the king's health and fired a volley. Then they drank to the prince's health and fired again. Finally, they toasted their leader Spotswood and delivered a final volley, a resounding exclamation point on the self-proclaimed consequence of their achievement.

Back in Williamsburg, Spotswood wasted little time writing up a much-publicized report of his journey to "World's End," as he called it. The composition of the document was accompanied by his establishment of the fraternal order of the Knights of the Golden Horseshoe. Each of the gentlemen who had made the trip was initiated into the fellowship and presented with a small golden horseshoe bearing the inscription *Sic Juvat Transcendere Montes:* What a Pleasure It Is to Cross the Mountains. Of course, Spotswood's trip across the Blue Ridge had not been pleasurable at all, but he hoped that it would appear so to land-hungry Virginians and Englishmen. The adventurer John Smith had done the same thing for the same reason exactly one hundred years earlier, and travel and real estate agents of our own time employ identical methods. Spotswood was not especially evil or greedy—at least no more so than the cavalier gentlemen of his era or the real estate people of our own. He was merely a notable agent of English expansionism in his time, hoping to advance commerce and dissuade French aggression. Had not Spotswood made his journey and romantically memorialized it, the Valley would have filled all the same. It is difficult then to resent him entirely, to wish for him to eat humbly the ashes of the civilization he helped father. In the grand scheme of this history, Spotswood appears as only a gaudy minor figure, but nonetheless an essential, recurring, and familiar one.

Later, sun of September gone, a clear night beside a fire with a clay tavern pipe, camped along the river Spotswood named, only a few miles from where he crossed it, sky and water wedded in the reflected stars on its calm surface. The hawks are as gone as the sun, asleep, perched in the dark somewhere among their kin, miles to the south. Spotswood and his cavaliers are departed as well, though they might have taken their leave just this afternoon rather than three hundred years ago, their visions of ownership and development as real today and undeniably triumphant as they were then, though their individual greed, presumption, and humanity—the bright burdens of existence which are also our own— have faded and dissolved like the gay colors of their clothing, long since rotted on their forgotten bones. Recognizing this we may begin to perceive that, even into her more enduring tales of despair, those that are still with us and unfolding, history playfully weaves her ironies: Spotswood's name for the river is as forgotten as his own. Not only this, but the hawks still follow it southward today, as did the first humans on the continent for centuries, and the Europeans who succeeded them. So, distant history, the events and trends of even the remote human past, are not so far from us as we would care to imagine. Like stars on water, they are with us and discernible though not really there—only an echo of experience to each of us, including this one lone man, camped on this riverbank, imagining it all. But caught up in that unavoidable pride of existence, he must grasp for the humility to remind himself of his own imminent death, his inevitable capitulation to history, who will see to it that his own life and works are forgotten soon enough, taking their rightful place of ignoble distinction in the empty vacuum of innumerable spent lives. He must remind himself too not to miss the river for the stars, or, more precisely, not to forget the innate relationship between them. He wonders then at the value of his own suspect knowledge since the first humans on the continent knew this intuitively and brought it to us, in another of history's seductive ironies, through the name of this very river, retained and perpetuated by their successors on account of its lyrical beauty rather than its meaning. The word is Shenandoah, which in the tongue of the people who named it means "Daughter of the Stars."

On the road once more, in my own time, in the midst of this journey of the now, I enter the town of Harrisonburg, founded as Rocktown during the hard winter year of 1779, resting on land originally owned by Thomas Harrison, a successful local innkeeper along *Athowominee*. In Harrisonburg I am struck most notably by the startlingly new, slick visage of James Madison University, a place I have visited before but hardly recognize, many of the buildings possessing the bright appearance of having recently risen, scrubbed and shining, out of the Valley floor. Though the campus seems mostly abandoned, I spot a cell phone here and there, pressed against the dreamy young, blank face of a student, globally connected but appearing more or less oblivious to the immediate surroundings—a slow-walking, unconscious, preoccupied catalyst of the future. Often I have noted that places where the young are massed, irrespective of environment and structures, generally bear the peculiar atmosphere of the generation at hand, though the nature of that hazy ambience varies slightly from place to place and significantly from culture to culture. I recall, for instance, walking only a few years ago with the woman I had just married through the narrow streets of the Latin Quarter, south of the Seine, in Paris on a May day that felt like the middle of summer, and being struck not only by the youth of the faces around me but the light they bore in looking at each other, the numerous art galleries that dotted the avenues, or perhaps something else I could not quite see, being perhaps too much in love, or a little too American, or generally overenamored with French champagne and the intoxication of my own youth. Try as I might, and memory is always uncertain, I cannot remember anyone trudging along, eyes fixed on the ground, with a piece of plastic pressed to their head.

In this era of apparent telenecessity I do not own a cellular phone, generally viewing them as yet another new and needless way to be distracted, bothered, kept from more valuable things. But I realize too that this kind of opinion may very well relegate me to the ever-changing category of cultural relic, like the people who still insist on using typewriters, the once-new mechanical innovations of decades past, for their writing. Technological advances, the ever more speedy forerunners of historical change, have always favored the young, regardless of education or anything else. The pale boy who can't or won't pass algebra or pen a clear sentence "writes" the ingenious computer virus that crashes his high school's Web site and enables him to place a funny-looking digital cigarette in his principal's mouth on the school Web page. Like the evasive learning of the late Roman thinker Boethius, the root of his abilities and the process of his education remain a mystery. Just as Hypatia and her Alexandrian students held their secrets close since they believed they would only be misunderstood by the lower classes, so the accomplished young technos of the computer age masterfully ride the fluid tide of information technology, conversant with each other but concealing from the larger population the peculiar underpinnings of what many of them consider an elite art.

The area south of Harrisonburg's downtown constitutes a continuous strip mall—a kind of small-scale urban sprawl of horns, stop lights, and concrete—

punctuated, just outside the city limits, by a labyrinthine Sysco building—a massive structure both of and outside of Harrisonburg, seeming to exist, at once, in as well as against the nature of this place. That the region of Virginia once known as its breadbasket should house a branch of North America's largest processed-food corporation, based somewhere in Texas, strikes me as a development both logical and ironic. Perhaps the Valley's distinguished agricultural history and ongoing productivity partially explain the company's presence, though the fresh crops of the area, long delightful to the Valley's people and animals, are now treated, frozen, and packaged—sent to other parts of the globe, or perhaps returned, in the wake of their processing, to the very homes of the people who grew them: locals purchasing food—now old, vitamin-deficient, preserved with chemicals—harvested from the very fields that surround them.

Dwelling upon this state of things does not lead me to lament the departure of a more locally based agriculture, for Harrisonburg's farmer's market thrives and the pervasive demand for natural foods across North America has led increasing numbers of growers in the Valley to sever ties with national food corporations and the chemical-laced practices of industrial farming. Better, in general, not to mourn vanishing phenomena since it is always possible they may return again, history come full circle, its tenets new in guise and terminology only. Recognizing this intermittent process, it is easier to forgive and embrace whatever it is the things and places around us are becoming—what they are—for better or for worse; helpful too in reminding ourselves from time to time that even where we live we are never really at home, but rather, as Montaigne said, "Always beyond. Fear, desire, hope, project us toward the future and steal from us the feeling and consideration of what is, to busy us with what will be, even when we shall no longer be."

These musings, as all eventually do, give way to the moment, the life and event at hand: the crossing of North River, which wells up out of the mountains to the west, not far from the West Virginia border. Unable to see either mountain chain, east or west, I feel the land lowered, pressed against me, a condensing of feeling and vision. Having left the Burketown area, I reach Naked Creek, where, hot and tired yet again, sweat-drenched shirt chafing me about the back and shoulders, I take the waters' name for a sign and resolve to change clothes. Up the stream, away from the road—solitary among trees, water, and bird-song—I lie nude in a place where the current runs shallow over sand and flat stones, sky a hazy blue above me, framed unevenly by green on either side, the creekside treetops creating a wavy boundary to the canvas of the heavens. Once, while walking along the Isar River on a warm spring afternoon in Munich, I unexpectedly encountered a party of nude sunbathers, stretched out silent, apparently oblivious to me, eyes fixed on the firmament, trancelike. Alone here, tired and cool, water curving around me in the shape of my body, sky and stream are enough, holding my vision: in this moment, all I need.

Drying myself on the sandy bank, my eyes are drawn down from the heavens to the waters, attracted by the peculiar hypnosis of liquid movement: of liquid itself. When light hits it right, it is hard not to gaze at water, much in the way the camper stares into the fire or the farmer dwells upon his hearth, each drowsy and reflective in the wake of his labors. It may have been my overheated condition and the confusion of fatigue, but to me the current of Naked Creek had felt as though it bore strange waters, flowing as it does from Seawright Springs and Wise Hill—peculiarly named local places glimpsed on a map, unseen by me: water-giving mysteries of the Valley. Fixated on the enigma of water, Rome's second king, Numa, was said to have gazed for hours into a favorite fountain, from which he claimed to acquire the measure of wisdom necessary to bring about successful reform in his fledgling nation. Later, people whispered that it was with the water nymph Egeria that he held council and from whom he received his groundbreaking knowledge and innovations. It is a pursuit of idle wonder to imagine if, after a long afternoon or morning of watery watching, an instant finally arrived when the king truly believed some godlike murmur had issued forth, somewhere beyond his reflection, from the quiet lapping of the pool. Or did he merely claim to hear such utterance in a calculated effort to deflect the risk-laden decision-making for his growing nation away from himself—radical policy softened and made gentle through the customary invocation of religious legend? In my own experience, most people will think you brilliant or wise only if you tell them what they already know or intuitively feel—something that may be somewhat new to them, but also vaguely and comfortably familiar. Real innovation usually succeeds only in invoking fear and hostility. As the scientist Albert Einstein famously observed, "Great spirits have always encountered violent opposition from mediocre minds." Here, looking over the waters of Naked Creek, now fully clothed, I like to think of Numa emerging from his chambers after long hours of water gazing—of searching for a nymph, the unlikeliest of answers, in a watery image of himself.

The idea of abstract reflection, image and identity shared and offered back to one another, exists in more tangible terms throughout this part of the Valley. Rockingham County, for example, is home to more than one Naked Creek, the other lying away to the northeast, emptying into the Shenandoah at Verbena, on the other side of Massanutten Mountain, where the peak closely resembles Gibraltar. And names here, as in other parts of the Valley, echo both locally and globally, two nearby hills carrying the unlikely designations of Betsey Bell and Mary, dedicated for mounds of like appearance in Ireland's County Tyrone. This particular case of transplanted naming is significant for its insinuation of an early Irish influence in this section of the Valley, here at Verona, where I cross Middlecreek and the signs of development pick up amid the outskirts of what was originally called Fort Staunton, an outpost and village named for the wife of Virginia governor William Gooch. It was to a site nearby that John Lewis, father of Andrew Lewis, the noted surveyor and French-Indian War officer, led a group of families sometime in the early 1730s after fleeing Ireland in the wake of having killed his landlord, Lord Clonmithgairn, in a property dispute. Here, Lewis's company began laying the groundwork for the town that eventually would come to be known as Staunton.

The Indian presence in the Valley was much stronger in the 1730s than it would be just a decade later and the Lewis settlers found themselves in frequent amiable and, as yet, unsoured contact with the Shawnee, which, among other things, gave rise to a unique romance of sorts between the daughter of John Lewis, Alice, and Omayah, the son of a Shawnee chief. The pair were fond of walking together and it pleased him to make her crowns of laurel and flowers, which she collected as keepsakes and wore whenever they were together. Alice, whom Omayah called White Dove, was especially delighted when he presented her with a fawn he had tamed. White Dove's family viewed her friendship with Omayah as harmless and a positive factor in their favorable relations with the Shawnee; however, when Omayah publicly asked for her hand in marriage, both her family and the settlers were shocked, and John Lewis forbade the union, shortly after which Omayah and a party of his tribesmen spirited Alice away into the countryside. Recovered through peaceful means a few weeks later in a limestone cave, White Dove was reunited with her family, and though she was still forbidden to marry Omayah, it is said that they continued to see each other frequently and remained close friends for many years—a small anecdote of hope, an island or mirage, amid the dominant themes of hate and violence that would come to define the tragic epic of settlers and Indians over the course of the next two centuries.

Leaving Staunton, having just glimpsed my journey's first mall—its bland heaped concrete and meandering traffic aligning it closely with most any other mall—I am cheered, just above Shenandoah Valley Cooperative Electric, by an open and unique view of the Blue Ridge, a prospect from which one may take in its directional shift from a relatively straight north-south bearing to one that curves southeast. Traveling in Virginia in the late 1780s, an Italian naturalist from Milan named Count Luigi Castiglioni described Staunton as "situated in the middle of the pretty plain that . . . lies between the Blue Mountains and the Alleghenies," an observation that causes me to wonder if this particular vantage point, along this road—already ancient in Castiglioni's time—may have aided in formulating the Count's positive impression of the Valley floor.

It goes without saying that our view of the mountains is shaped by the position, real and temporal, from which we contemplate them. Count Castiglioni had come upon Staunton having journeyed slowly from Charlottesville, some forty miles to the southeast, where the valley-mountain network is much smaller, more intimate, the hills gradual, less abrupt, the land more rolling. By contrast, the views from Staunton are grand, vast stretches of the miles-distant Blue Ridge and westerly Appalachian ranges glimpsed from the center of the great low-lying Valley. Yet, the smaller natural places to the east are not without their legacies of magic and mystery. Departing Charlottesville, Count Castiglioni would have glimpsed, to the south, a small chain of wild and dreary hills, an eastern offshoot of the Blue Ridge, known as the Ragged Mountains, the hollows and ridges of which remain home to many strange stories. It is among these coves and rises that day-hiking students from the University of Virginia occasionally have been known to lose their bearings amid the curious mist of the Blue Ridge in summer; and it is in these same hills that a weird nineteenth-century tale unfolds: of a poor deluded apothecary who mistook a venomous vermicular sangsue for a leech, prescribing the creature in his art with fatal results.

Even now there are cryptic species that remain hidden from taxonomists because of their close similarities to known ones, chameleons without intention. Such phenomena remind us that it is not difficult to mistake what we see. Peering too closely at some things only serves to push us farther away, especially when our points of reference become mixed up, sometimes to the point of vanishing altogether. The poet Randall Jarrell wrote, "I hold in my own hands, in happiness, Nothing: the nothing for which there's no reward." On a whim, I had once followed a jeep trail over Newcomb Mountain, a humble peak of the Ragged Mountains, but no strange mist encompassed me, and though I frequently wandered from the path, half hoping, I never lost myself—the hills left no impression, I emerged as I had entered. There are many such places I feel that way about, nowhere places—to be in them is to be anywhere—present evasive and history blurring herself to the gaze, teasing us to move on and look upon other things, as if to say, "Since forever, there is nothing of interest here." Of course, all such places have their stories, though some speak to us less readily than others, wrapping themselves in a shroud, partially obscuring what Edgar Allan Poe might call their brief "epoch in the night of time," unfolding beneath the dark of the moon.

South of the Greenville area, Ragged Mountains receding far to the northeast, is the old Providence church built around 1750, resting place of Cyrus McCormick, inventor of the reaper; and, three quarters of an uneventful day's march beyond, one proceeds up a long hill and into the old part of the village of Fairfield, on the other side of which rests the grave of John McDowell, killed along with ten other colonial militiamen during a needless confrontation with a southward-bound party of Iroquois warriors at a place called Balcony Falls, miles to the southeast, in December 1742—considered by some the first significant military battle between settlers and Indians in the Valley. Weighing vaguely all the tragic European-Indian conflicts that would follow in its wake, I find it difficult here not to dwell upon the nature of McDowell's ambivalent inaugural run-in with the Iroquois. As the writer H. P. Lovecraft noted, "The oldest and strongest emotion of mankind is fear, and the oldest and strongest kind of fear is fear of the unknown." Though Europeans and North American Indians had been interacting periodically for over a century, they continued to understand or know each other very little. Even today, not much is known about the various Indian cultures that existed on the continent around the time of European arrival, for they were oral societies whose original tales and languages are now somewhat merged and tangled with one another. As much as early settlers feared what they considered savage about the Indians, they were also bothered and occasionally seduced by the free and comparatively untroubled manner in which they led their lives and embraced their surroundings. Accompanying John Lederer on his last expedition into the Valley in 1670 was the Englishman Colonel Catlet, who left Lederer after a time to live among a tribe along the Rappahannock River; and, far to the north, Puritan settlers evinced a manically religious fear of turning savage, going Indian, or succumbing to the ways of the "dark man of the forest," as the devil was sometimes called—he who played inaudibly the strange siren tune that lured young Puritans to the intimate confines of dense bracken or the more open frolics of the maypole.

    This general lack of understanding among the European groups who would eventually become Americans persists even in the modern era. As late as 1972, Valley historian Alvin Dohme summed up the Indian reaction to European encroachment as follows: "In the classic reaction of all original inhabitants, since time immemorial, who were threatened with eviction or total extinction, the savages began to turn aloof and sullen." For Dohme the Indians in their resistance seemed somehow to have constituted something less than human, yet what human would not turn defensive at the prospect of personal and societal annihilation? Questions remain too regarding the nature of the 1742 engagement between the traveling party of Iroquois and McDowell's men, little having been offered as to its cause beyond the fact that the southward-bound Indians may have overstayed their welcome in the area and possibly slaughtered a settler's hog or two. In any case, at some point county lieutenant James Patton ordered McDowell to raise a militia for the purpose of expelling the Indians from the neighborhood. When the contingent of settlers overtook the Iroquois, the ambiguous skirmish ensued which cost McDowell his life, as well as the lives of ten other settlers and several Iroquois—the first of many such corpse-ridden conflicts, the particular causes of which are now long forgotten.

I find it ever more difficult to remember, to reason, as my journey continues, thoughts as indistinct, yet familiar, as the shades of my ancestors, hovering somewhere ahead of me, on the horizon to the south, while the body's communications remain clear, direct—sharpness of joint pain, dull throb of swelling, the persistent sweat of late summer. The road is deserted, white and scorching, motionless in heat. John Smith, an adventurer who traveled great distances and orchestrated problems of his own, albeit on a much smaller scale than McDowell, with the Indians of his acquaintance—the Pamunkey tribe in the eastern portion of the Virginia colony—said of the region's weather, "The sommer is hot as Spain, the winter colde as in France or England. The heat of sommer is in June, Julie, and August, but commonly the coole Breeses asswage the vehemencie of the heat." Though Smith's perceptive international weather comparison remains largely accurate, it is not entirely true on this particular windless day, the heat that pummels my head and rises from the road conspiring to dull and blur my thoughts, turning them as hazy and as still as the air, motionless amid the motion of the body.

Before descending into a bottom several miles north of Lexington, I am greeted by a memorable view of mountains, slightly below and to the east of which once stood a log cabin in which Sam Houston was born in 1793. He would have been but a boy, perhaps playing in the yard, when my own ancestors wandered through, one more family of settlers moving southwest along the road he would one day follow to the lands of the Cherokee, whom he would live among extensively before destiny summoned him farther west. It is also in this vicinity that the Shenandoah Valley, my companion for so many miles and days, finally gives way to hills, the great fertile trough taken at last by mountains. It is difficult, perhaps impossible, to say precisely where this transition occurs, the topography shifting so gradually, a slow narrowing of the Valley, fields and pastures now swelling atop rises, whereas before the land they rested upon had been flat or rolling—a shift so slow that it exists suddenly behind me, already past, ridges and hollows before me, the Valley now but a memory.

This dissipation of the Valley into hills is shortly followed by my arrival at the mountain town of Lexington. In 1789 André Michaux had described the place as "a little town which maintains rather sustained trading with the settlements along the western Rivers." At that time, the diminutive mountain village, so different in its rocky topography from the Valley towns through which I have traveled, had been known as Lexington only for a year, the new designation derived from an important colonial military victory far to the north more than a decade earlier. The area had taken a strong interest in the American Revolution, sending over a hundred barrels of flour to Boston after the city's port was closed and going to severe lengths to preserve local order while the war continued: in the wake of the frigid winter of 1780 one man and two women received multiple lashes at the whipping post for various acts of theft. Before the village was renamed Lexington it had been known as Gilbert Campbell's Ford, a small gathering of cabins near a body of water we now call the Maury River. The humble school that would one day come to be known as Washington and Lee University was west of the town at the time and, passing along the outskirts of its modern campus now, flanked on the other side of Route 11 by Virginia Military Institute, I determine that the former institution is the only one I have passed thus far that would have been in existence when my ancestors made their journey. It was called Washington Academy then, a tribute to George Washington's support of the institution—his desire to "promote the Literature in this rising Empire"—and had already been in existence for almost half a century, though it would be razed by fire in 1803. Once rebuilt, Professor Farnum would gaze out toward the mountains from an upper window of the main campus building in 1805 and exclaim in admiration, "If this scene were set down in the middle of Europe, the whole continent would flock to see it."

Today, with many of its undergraduates drawn from fine preparatory institutions and affluent families, Washington and Lee is a prosperous private college, the eighteenth-century circumstances of which likely would horrify and ultimately break all but a few of its current students. Breakfast back then consisted solely of bread and coffee, supper of bread and milk—only at lunch did the student receive meat. As local historian Henry Boley explained, "High living in a literary institution was considered highly undesirable; it was costly, it injured the health, it obfuscated the intellect and induced habits of sensual indulgence." So the stoic undergraduate student, not unlike the initiate of some monastic order, imbibed his bread and water, read his Greek, and contemplated the surrounding mountains, crowned in their haze of blue light.

Living a vastly different existence from the sternly administered, though ultimately advantaged, students of Washington Academy, was an unusual group of people who dwelt in the hills near Lexington: an ambiguous collection of European-, Indian-, and African-descended individuals, many of them fugitives and interlopers, known as "the brown people." This loose community constituted one of a number of remote, culturally mixed societies called "maroon colonies"—small, sometimes nomadic, coteries that presented a dimension of vague uneasiness to the beneficiaries of the rigid slave-based economy of old eastern Virginia. In the summer of 1721 Governor Spotswood had worried that if escaped slaves reached the Blue Ridge "it may be hard to apprehd 'em, & if they shou'd encrease there, it might prove of ill consequence to ye Peace of this Colony." Spotswood's concerns eventually would be realized on a small scale, though such villages proved little threat to the colony as a whole, their primary objective being to escape notice and shun the risks of death, jail, or (re)enslavement. While the students of Washington Academy, many of them members of the owner class from whom several of the mountain refugees had fled, contemplated the liberal arts, groups like the brown people scraped out their mountainside existence as best they could—evading detection, squatters on land they did not own, yet masters of themselves.

As one travels through the narrow shady passes among the hills south of Lexington, it is easy to perceive how deep hollows make for ideal places to hide, the topography severely limiting the perceptions of unfriendly seekers, so long as one remains mostly silent and builds fires with smokeless wood. At the bottom of one such cove, an ideal place to make oneself scarce, I cool my feet in Buffalo Creek, absorbing the deep quiet of the wooded bottom, where one may listen long to stream and leaf, the gradual oncoming whoosh of the occasional automobile muffled considerably by a conspiracy of dense foliage and abrupt landscape. The writer Julian Green noted what many of us have felt intuitively in such places: "What Nature says is unintelligible to those who are not fond of silence. Be it ever so loud, Nature's voice cannot be heard unless you listen close." When one is genuinely watchful and silent, not so much concentrating as forgetting about concentration, the vagaries of life fall away and the mind dissolves without a sound. Coming to such a place and listening for a time, you may well discover that something inaudible has been waiting for you, revealing itself only on the other side of a long stretch of voiceless quiet. Poe wrote that "there is a twofold Silence—sea and shore—body and soul," the one a natural companion to the lone soul, the other a strange empty shadow "that haunteth the lone regions where hath trod no foot of man." As I walked alone amid these hollows, the forlorn hiding places of others, following physically in the footsteps of millions, my path, the journey of a single soul, shares in this two-fold silence: the isolated human shell presses on, while the stowaway being within, mindful of where it is being led, treads its own unpeopled void, both of this world and not.

I make a gradual ascent toward Fancy Hill, where the ground breaks open into clover and orchard grass, rolling beneath the hooves of the glossy-maned horses that frequent the area, the top boards of the long wooden fences square and un-gnawed, a sign of the animals' contentment within the bounds of their pastures: rich, fertilized fields with fine barns and stables where the bountiful grain pours forth for them, morning and evening. Somewhere between Fancy Hill and the minor tourist destination of Natural Bridge, such pastoral scenes of groomed animals and nature begin to give way to man's made-over artificial images of them, the initial manifestation of this shift taking the form of the Holy Cow, a large, lifeless bovine figure which stands as a kind of ridiculous sentinel before a long-defunct amusement park, another failed venue from the heyday of Route 11. This forlorn divine cow, guardian of nothing, is complemented, closer to Natural Bridge, by an imitation Stonehenge, constructed on a hillside overlook-ing a cow pasture and the highway, mutely suggesting that one wonder of the world is not enough for the area. But then Americans are constantly turning their uniquely beautiful natural sites, impressive enough if left alone, into some-thing perceived to be better, the stunning seashore or lakeside complemented with theme parks, condos, malls, and movie theaters until nature, the original basis for the arrival of all these things, becomes itself a minor sideshow, and we find ourselves unfortunate travelers or vacationers in one more unremarkable, sprawled, developed area: the once-pastoral weekend getaway having become something many of us would prefer to get away from.

The area of Natural Bridge does not appear overly built up, but it does guard assiduously its renowned natural feature, the local economic boon, for which it is named. Although Route 11 passes over Natural Bridge, or rather is built onto and into it, a network of roadside vision-blocking barricades—strate-gically placed signs, fences, and walls—make it nearly impossible to know that you are actually passing over the geological oddity, channeling those interested in viewing the feature to a gaudy carnivalesque fee area. Having looked upon Natural Bridge before and being vaguely irritated by the censorship of the tourist industry, I am very nearly compelled to move on without taking it in. Upon further reflection, however, having paused in the shade to remove my pack and drink some water, I begin to believe that viewing Natural Bridge is somehow essential to this journey, since it constitutes a memorable perspective beheld by so many who followed *Athowominee,* perhaps even my ancestors. After additional water and shade, mind cooled and made pliable, I decide at last it is something I must see.

At the busy information desk a female employee wearing heavy makeup eyes me uncertainly, put off probably by my filthy appearance and strong body odor, before asking me whether I have learned of Natural Bridge from a brochure, roadside sign, computer, television, or other propagandist medium. I inform her that I had wanted to see it ever since reading about it in a highly entertaining book called *Notes on the State of Virginia,* a title she'd not heard of but that delighted her since she seemed to believe it constituted a recent book and thus a new marketing medium for the area. Still somewhat vexed by the tactics of the local tourist industry, I choose not to correct her erroneous assumption. Any vague ill feeling, however, falls away when I follow a paved crowded path down to Cedar Creek and am finally able to look upon the natural wonder itself: the great arch of rock, a massive grooved accident of architecture, over two hundred feet tall and nearly one hundred wide, surrounded by the tired green of late summer—trees that tower below it and small weeds and bushes clinging precariously to its sheer face. All around me, I overhear adults reciting to each other the blandly familiar tourist lines of admiration or disappointment, whereas the children, often the truest appraisers of something's intrinsic value, voice a genuine enthusiasm, shouting and pointing at particular rocks and features. Yet, however much modern tourists, and there are a lot of them here today, may gape at the feature's startling appearance, its historical importance to humans was always practical rather than aesthetic. As Thomas Jefferson observed, the bridge "affords a public and commodious passage over a valley, which cannot be crossed elsewhere for a considerable distance." Animals and early North American humans recognized the bridge's geographical value and utilized it, making it part of the *Athowominee* route long before Europeans came to admire the formation in the abstract and bestow upon it the title "wonder of the world." Unlike the more leisurely travelers who would follow in their wake, early colonial settlers crossing the bridge, bound for indistinct destinations in the far southwest, viewed the passage more in the manner of the Indians. Mindful of the trials and dangers of muddy, eroded thoroughfares, travelers constantly prayed for dry weather and good roads. A stream easily fordable at the end of a rainless August week could easily swell to become treacherous after a day or two of steady rain. High and dry, constructed of hard rock, Natural Bridge most notably constituted a firm, dependable stretch of road.

Rain is approaching on this August day of my own time, announced by the steady arrival of thickening clouds from the southwest and an oppressive humidity—a heavy, expectant stillness. There is something out of the ordinary, something peculiarly elemental, in watching such clouds roll slowly over a unique manifestation of nature like Natural Bridge—an archetypal human awareness of symmetry between earth and the heavens, hidden and unfelt in most places, that is strangely powerful here. Glancing away from the bridge, down toward my upper right arm, I watch the first stains of rain appear on my sleeve before I can feel any drops on my skin or see them in the air. This brief overture of precipitation is followed, in a manner of seconds, by a hard downpour that sends my fellow sightseers scurrying, children and more cumbersome companions in tow, for the nearby café or, beyond, their family vans and sport-utility vehicles. In the midst of the stampede, a balding, obese middle-aged man in a bright orange and purple bermuda shirt stumbles to his knees before me, fumbling his camera, as if he had just hurried a little too quickly out of some particularly ill-considered travel brochure. He retrieves his wet camera, rises stiffly, and hurries on, flashing at me the false grin of the uncomfortable good-natured American tourist who finds himself standing reluctantly, face to face, camera in hand, before a weird naked figure carved into the wall of some foreign cave or tomb.

I stand where I am, getting wet, happy to have Natural Bridge to myself, trying to ignore the asphalt footpath and green benches, visualizing it, as best I can, as an unpeopled place. When I weary of peering at the bridge, my gaze falls to the stream flowing beneath it, Cedar Creek, ancient maker of the arch. I have always enjoyed dark warm days with steady rain, if for no other reason than to watch where the water goes or tries to: the how and why of drainage, which, in a sense, is water's way of telling an ongoing story. It is interesting to imagine this tale, if in fact we can, on a grand epic scale as well, as if poring over a vast topographical map or looking down upon the earth from the window of an airplane. The roads we can see are ignored in favor of the contours of terrain, for water is the great shaper, hydraulics cutting into rock or, in the process of freezing and thawing, cracking it. What is displaced is carried downstream toward the ocean, an ongoing process that seems to us the slow laborious work of shaping or reshaping continents, yet one that was in progress long before we arrived and will continue beyond our departure, mountains gradually reduced to hills and plains, awaiting the tectonic disturbances that will raise them again.

Natural Bridge is yet another character—labeled special by the collective, symmetrical geometric preferences of humans—in water's long tale of erosion and formation, the destructive and creative chance and irrationality of which speaks to a place, though we may be loath to admit it, in each of us. It is akin to the same impulse that directs me to have a poncho but not put it on, or to take it off when it begins to rain harder—to get wet anyway, without logic or reason—a gesture that nonetheless usually leads to something new: assumption without inference. And it seems right, fortunate, devoid of logic, to have water as my single companion in the presence of Natural Bridge: to stand here wet, gazing upon this monument of water, in the lone company of its creator.

As I cross a man-made bridge over the James River, misty in the early hours of an August morning, entering the town of Buchanan, my mind brims with thoughts of home, the memory of having lived for a time on a small mountain not two miles south of this river, albeit more than half a hundred miles to the east. Gazing off in that direction here my eyes are met by several sheer rocky faces of the Blue Ridge, the horizon concealed beyond them amid neighboring mountains. Traveling east by land would be a difficult proposition, but it cheers me to have encountered this familiar river, reassuring to know that I could follow it east to within a few miles of my home if I wanted or needed to. In colonial times, considerations of cross-country travel were not of a leisurely nature for settlers who found themselves lost in a wilderness devoid of roads or stores. In 1761 a woman named Hannah Dennis living on Purgatory Creek, not far from the modern site of Buchanan, was abducted by a Shawnee war party commanded by the great warrior Cornstalk after they had killed her husband, son, and several neighbors. What ensued for her was a long, arduous journey over the Alleghenies to the Shawnee homelands in present-day Ohio. Upon arriving, she quickly adapted to the arduous work performed by a typical Shawnee woman, while also distinguishing herself in the tribe through her knowledge of woodland herbs. Eventually, she was trusted enough to be afforded long trips into the forest for the purpose of gathering plants. On one such excursion, Dennis slipped away entirely, making her way into the Alleghenies while managing to evade her former captors—no small feat considering the extraordinary woodcraft of the Shawnee. Surviving chiefly on roots and herbs, which she could readily identify, she walked east alone for nearly a month before encountering a party of hunters who escorted her to the Greenbrier area, where she would rest for a time before finally making her way home.

Buchanan is one of the more recently established towns I have encountered along *Athowominee,* not founded officially until 1811, years after my ancestors had passed beyond it southward. It is named for the local surveyor and ferry operator John Buchanan, a figure aligned with older historical sites south of the town: Looney's Ferry, which began operation in 1742, and Fort Fauquier, part of the network of colonial frontier defenses along *Athowominee*. Nearly all traces of these places are now vanished but I content myself with the general absence of things—fields that are open, few cars upon the road, homes that are sporadic—knowing that just a few miles to the south one of Appalachia's largest cities, its spaces filled and occupied, lies in wait. Aware that my milieu soon will be turning urban, I find myself taking special note of curious natural things like the curve of a distant tree line to the northwest or cows grazing on a singularly odd, cone-shaped hill, looming above an old country store.

Passing through Troutville, the last small town before Roanoke, I cross Buffalo Creek twice and, just a mile or so south of the town, am greeted by the Appalachian Trail, which I had last encountered near Harpers Ferry, now two hundred miles to the north. This road-flanked section of the AT is one I am familiar with: where it passes across Route 11 and Interstate 81, and proceeds south along the latter road, bypassing Roanoke, making use of the rough natural pass between Tinker Mountain and the more easterly Blue Ridge. It is ironic to me that this trail, so beloved by conservationists, oddly empty for this period of late summer, should inadvertently mark the beginning of Roanoke Valley sprawl, for beyond it the business of compacted industry and commerce commence, broken only by my arrival in the proximity of Carvins Creek, perhaps five miles down the road, where a women's college called Hollins, formerly the Valley Union Seminary, rests among willows in the shadow of the Blue Ridge, home to the last real expanse of fields before the city or what becomes it begins.

Despite its seemingly ill-planned and haphazard urban and industrial expansion, the bane of so many other previously charming places, Roanoke remains a stunningly situated city. If you wish to glimpse beauty here, all you have to do is look up to find mountains rising around you on every side. In certain places, housing developments have ascended the hillsides to distracting elevations, though by and large the summits seem to have been protected thus far. Of greater concern is the bad air quality, a byproduct of a hundred thousand people and their automobiles occupying a river valley with mountains all around them. When the wind and weather fronts are sluggish, carbon monoxide and other industrial gasses simply have nowhere to go, conspiring to create dangerous ozone levels and a special variety of Roanoke Valley smog. An irony to know that people are suffering from asthma and slow asphyxiation amid such natural beauty; one coughs or reaches for an inhaler even as the evening sun, creeping along the Valley from the west, casts its long crimson glow upon Green Ridge, Tinker Mountain, and Read Mountain, blinding the traveler who drives or walks into it.

The long story of Roanoke now finds itself choking in mid-chapter, a tale of the troubling present, but it once breathed long and deep, its habitat a unique natural flourishing place for animals and other living things. The site of a geographical crossroads since the first migratory mammals and humans arrived thousands of years ago, the area consists largely of a wide flat valley along the Roanoke River surrounded by a number of passes through the mountains, making it an ideal access point for travel in various directions and, due to its numerous salt licks—which attracted elk, deer, and buffalo—a fine hunting ground. On account of its geographical accessibility, it is hardly surprising that the Roanoke Valley was stumbled upon during one of the earliest European inland exploits. In September 1671 Captain Thomas Batts, Robert Fallam, and Thomas Wood, guided by a well-traveled member of the Appomattox tribe name Penecut, entered the Valley in search of "the ebbing and flowing of the Waters on the other side of the Mountains in order to the discovery of the South Sea." They would find no ocean, but in the Roanoke Valley they came upon a village of Tutelo Indians, peaceful and living comfortably, who freely offered their hospitality.

In the mid-eighteenth century a small community called Big Lick developed near a series of salt springs. Traveling through the area in the early spring of 1750, Dr. Thomas Walker, a physician educated at the College of William and Mary, discovered that the vast herds of game originally reported in the vicinity already had dwindled greatly, slaughtered by settlers for their fur or for amusement, depending on the circumstances—carcasses, stripped of their coats or wholly intact, lay piled and rotting near salt licks where the animals had once wallowed and watered. By the early 1790s the woods buffalo, significantly smaller than its plains cousin, was hunted to extinction in Virginia.

Roanoke owes its contemporary distinction of being one of Appalachia's largest cities to the fact that early settlers and then the railroad made use of its accommodating geography as a means of reaching the areas of Kentucky, Tennessee, and the West in general. The salt licks are all long since covered up by pavement and concrete, but the streams that fed them still run beneath the city, the buried briny hope of those who secretly suspect Big Lick will come again, subtly or suddenly, myself envisioning the latter: on a warm spring night after days of rain, the river running high, Victory Stadium mired and then swept away at last by the high current, water both pooling from the downpours and welling up from the saturated subterranean salt deposits, arriving, converging together from above and below, each enriching the other, until tree roots and long-dormant seeds in the warm fecund earth begin to swell and grow upward at prodigious intervals, splitting the pavement and sidewalks of streets, caving in concrete foundations and bursting through basement walls, unlooked-for hemlocks and impossible American chestnuts sprouting out of storm drains and upward through power lines, rising to unbelievable heights, until all electricity fails, the neon star atop Mill Mountain dark, silent, vines grown round it, while below the roads too lie tangled, broken and impassable, the locals rubbing their eyes at dim first light, their alarm clocks and refrigerators silent, gazing out into the strange misty forest risen about them overnight.

An idle dream, summoned as I tread Roanoke's curbs and sidewalks, inhaling bad air, vaguely heading west amid a confusing urban puzzle—not a particularly unpleasant one but large and loud enough. In the late afternoon the houses I pass emit the odors of cooking and the forgettable banter of televisions and frolicking children. To walk in a city is to experience a wall of sensory input, perceived phenomena overlapped and inclined together, fogging collective distinctions. One of my favorite things to do while wandering in urban areas is to try to file away all the different sounds, smells, and so on that surround me, one by one or in pairs, like putting away socks in a drawer. Walking along, performing this exercise here, I sense eventually a kind of shadow on the mind that slowly gives way to a constant variable: one that does not recede or modulate. I discover, in due course, the constant to be a figure, following perhaps thirty or forty feet behind me, pausing and changing his course as I do, trailing behind in my wake regardless of the streets I cross, the convenience store I enter, or the city block I needlessly circle before resuming my route. Strange companion still in tow, I begin to walk faster, taking long strides. After a few moments, I sense him falling back and, in the span of a quarter of an hour, I can no longer perceive him at all, though I take care to change my course, trading one west-bearing street for another.

Somewhere along Melrose Avenue, streetlights popping on in the dusk, the follower materializes again, this time perhaps twenty feet behind me. I pick up my pace once more, assuming he has used some alternate form of transportation to find and catch up to me, believing I can probably lose him again. On the other side of a street I have just crossed, I turn to view my pursuer hurrying down the far sidewalk, grinning at me even as he pants, a small balding dumpy man in an army-green waistcoat. We make eye contact and, against all reason, I feel my face forming into a wide grin that matches his own, before I turn and take up my long stride once more. And so it continues for perhaps two hours, all through Roanoke, and into Salem, where I am planning to spend the night. Eventually, I would pull away from my winded fellow traveler only to encounter him again after an interval, falling in behind me from a storefront or parking lot, his short legs moving quickly, propelled by some purpose I cannot fathom. Not wishing to lead him to the door of my host, I lose him at last on successive ill-lit streets, from which I am able to alternately jog and walk to the neighborhood where I am to spend the night. Once indoors, pressed to notify the police of my experience—feet resting in a bowl of ice, cold packs on my knees, frigid beer in hand—I am content to let it all pass, though I discover later that the recesses of my mind do not let loose so easily. That night I dream, as I often do, of foot travel—underground, beneath strange dark seas, on hazy other worlds—but wherever I roamed, whatever strange land sprang forth from the mind's deep murky pools, an indistinguishable presence accompanied it, trailing somewhere near. Having lost my follower, resting from my waking journey, some shadow trace of his presence, a kind of residue of being, nonetheless remained with me amid the chartless wanderings of slumber. Vanished from the world we share with others, that some call "real," my image of him sought me still—the echo of recent experience drawn and translated into those shifting and interlocking rat mazes of dream, from which none of us may escape.

Next morning, stiff and bleary, no sign of the follower, I continue my journey through Salem, founded originally by Lutherans, now a slightly less-developed suburb of Roanoke, though it was once its own town. When, in 1806, it became the seat of Roanoke County, Salem was home to probably less than forty families and Big Lick lay several miles to the southeast; now the two are nearly indistinguishable from each other where they touch and overlap. On the western outskirts of Salem, Route 11 runs close to the banks of the Roanoke River, the proximity of which calls to mind the colonial Renaissance man William Byrd II, who at one time owned more than thirty-three thousand acres along the river before selling it all in 1736. Byrd produced easily the most interesting and entertaining diaries of colonial North America and, along with Jefferson, probably was the most versatile and gifted of the colonial Virginians: writer, naturalist, surveyor, government official, planter, and ribald lady's man. Glad to be leaving the Roanoke metropolitan area behind me, I recall too that city life had been largely unlucky for Byrd. After the death of his first wife, who succumbed to the debilitating smallpox virus that infested early-eighteenth-century London, Byrd had sought, for some time and at great pains and adversity, another wife in the capital of the Empire, all the while luring common women to his chambers on Beaufort Street, west of the Savoy, or the grasses of St. James's Park—a practice that rewarded him with a prolonged and very troublesome case of gonorrhea. Jefferson could have been lecturing Byrd when he wrote that cities are "pestilential to the morals, the health and the liberties of men," which leads me to think of my follower of the night before, wondering whether formulated inclination or some curious urban malady had directed him to take up his bizarre pursuit—noteworthy, in any case, that it had taken place in the only real city through which I have passed. For whatever reason, perhaps for the simple fact that I grew up on a farm, I have always been more comfortable and at peace in remote places. As the Roman poet Martial rhetorically explained in one of his witty epigrams, "You wonder if my farm pays me its share? It pays me this: I do not see you there."

Passing through the area of Glenvar, bound for the Blue Ridge and remoter climes once more, history propels me, temporally and geographically, backward and westward, for it was from somewhere near here that the local surveyor and military officer Andrew Lewis embarked in the winter of 1756 on the debacle that would come to be known as the Big Sandy Expedition, leading an ill-fated party of frontier militiamen, joined later by mercenary Cherokee warriors, against the Shawnee. The Cherokee had been coerced into service by Governor Dinwiddie, who had followed Colonel Washington's sound advice that "without Indians to oppose Indians, we may expect but small success." Hoping to exact vengeance upon the Shawnee for their numerous successful raids against western Virginia settlers, Lewis's force was plagued by harsh icy weather in the Allegheny Mountains, which encouraged desertion, and the group never made it to the Ohio River, beyond which the main body of Shawnee lay. Ascertaining the hopelessness of the undertaking, the Cherokee, under the guidance of Chiefs Outacite, Round O, and Yellow Bird, melted away to the south, in the direction of the Smoky Mountains and their Overhill towns. On the return trip—supplies exhausted, feasting upon the flesh of their horses in the midst of a particularly bleak Appalachian winter—the remaining members of Lewis's war party came upon an area along a river where they had hung Buffalo carcasses from large oak limbs during the march westward. Desperate for nourishment, they feverishly tugged and ripped at the dried flesh, only half-broiling it before wolfing it down. It is in light of this gristly event that the nearby river came to be called the Tug.

Today the river's name has a different kind of resonance which plays powerfully upon the imagination, a number of the mountains surrounding it, whose springs and creeks feed into it, having been relentlessly blasted down to the size of small, flat, barren hills—bizarre, horrifically unnatural wastelands reminiscent of moonscapes. As mining companies, both the pride and bane of eastern Kentucky and southern West Virginia, grope and tear at the mountains—the dynamite, backhoes, dozers, and endloaders delving deep enough to disrupt and befoul water tables while creating massive flooding on the mountainsides through the sudden and severe annihilation of elaborate, centuries-old, natural drain fields, at the bottom of which the Tug River now flows muddy and swollen—the people living along the river watch for the next devastating local natural disaster, its inevitable arrival only a question of time.

Here, in the Blue Ridge, in my own time, departing the Roanoke Valley, perhaps having left it already, these things are far to the west, distant clouds on the horizon of the mind. As for Lewis's unfortunate men, many of them never would see the Roanoke Valley again. Shortly after their lurid feast near the then-pristine banks of the Tug, the dispirited force haphazardly disbanded altogether, the men attempting to make their way back across the mountains either on their own or in small groups. Several dozen froze to death, succumbed to starvation, or were dispatched by Shawnee scouts, who had been aware of Lewis's movements for some time and followed the ragged band, perhaps out of idle curiosity or amusement, as it haplessly staggered eastward through the unforgiving winter mountains, haggard freezing men leaving scattered shuffling footprints in the snow, melting into invisibility.

It is strange to recall Lewis's doomed men here on the fringes of the valley to which they so desperately wished to return, that they likely dreamed of in death, as I follow the route that bore them west, away from their families, across the Blue Ridge, to the New River and, finally, the Alleghenies, from whence they would never return. Though they perished far from home, amid unpeopled ridges and vales, they do not lie buried in obscurity, their tale and their fate—inglorious as both may be—recorded for perpetuity: experience merged with our memory and telling of it. History, then, has claimed them, just as, in a different sense, history continues to claim me—as it takes anyone who journeys, bearing along with his pack an invisible burden: the past tales of his future destinations. In this way history ever navigates and directs us: to *past* places now hidden that are, at once, the *same* places beckoning us in the present. Bound for habited places, home also to netherworlds, our journeys commence and continue. History claims us all.

VIRGINIA

New River and Southern Valleys

I have learnt from experience that the established
Authority of any government in America, and the
policy of Government at home, are both insufficient
to restrain the Americans; and that they do and will
remove as their avidity and restlessness incite them.
They acquire no attachment to Place: But wandering
about Seems engrafted in their Nature; and it is a
weakness incident to it, that they should for ever
imagine the Lands further off. . . .

—Lord (John Murray) Dunmore,
last royal governor of Virginia, 1773

As silent as a mirror is believed
Realities plunge in silence by. . . .

—Hart Crane, "Legend"

I

Southwest of Roanoke the Blue Ridge becomes both taller and wider, a kind of high plateau, the degree of its ascension and expanse echoed by the dark, hollow, interstitial places beneath, implied on the surface by the occasional yawning subterranean entrance, of which Dixie Caverns, resting in a narrow hollow between Highway 11 and Interstate 81, is but one. Walking alongside 11—built alternately atop or near the ancient Indian footpath *Athowominee,* tracing it, as I have for these past two hundred miles, bound for Tennessee in the footsteps of my frontier ancestors, separated from their journey by a span of more than two hundred years—I cross a bridge over the Roanoke River into Montgomery County, named—like the counties in fifteen other states—for the Irish-born officer Richard Montgomery, killed in a swirling snowstorm while attempting to wrench Quebec from the French on New Year's Eve 1775.

Follower of this ancient route, already a wagon road for settlers at the time of Montgomery's death, I am ever met, encountered on the road ahead, by history, yet a church billboard I pass announces, "Whose little footsteps are following your own," the question mark forgotten or perhaps purposefully left off, as if the expression were part of an enlightening phrase: the tale end of some vanished explanation. Given my strange recent episode of having been trailed by a peculiar diminutive man through the evening streets of Roanoke, the sign has a curious resonance, as, admittedly, believer or no, such passages often do. However, a glance over my shoulder reveals a highway empty of pedestrians, only the intervaled coming and going of automobiles, and the heat and haze of the summer road, above which, to the south, Poor Mountain rises high, jutting eastward into the Roanoke Valley, melting away to the west, another collective peak of the Blue Ridge.

As I walk along this quiet stretch of road, glad to have quit Roanoke, history in silence curves back upon itself, curious visages of the present echoing stages of the past: the Norfolk and Western railroad, innovation of eras gone, rusty and mute, flanking me on the left; and, in the Elliston area, the curious sign for Southland Log Homes, harkening back to a time when such habitations, smaller and more roughly constructed, were the only ones that stood here in the hills along the Roanoke River and its forks. And containing a deeper degree of resonance, possessed of vast implications far beyond this region, somewhere between Elliston and Shawsville, along the foot of Poor Mountain and Pedlar Hills, one of American history's most familiar personalities came precariously close to meeting his end, George Washington and two companions narrowly avoiding an ambush by a Shawnee war party. It was October 10, 1756, a day of steady rain on which the leaves of the uppermost boughs were just beginning to show their autumn colors, bright fragments of foliage peaking here and there through a heavy green canopy. Traveling southwest, as I am, along *Athowominee,* Washington was determined to perform an inspection of frontier defenses, even though he had been informed that Indians were active in the area. Indeed, as it turned out, the Shawnee were monitoring this route from a position high above the trail amid the rainy mist of a dark forest when they glimpsed Washington and his associates approaching. Yet, unaware that one of these oblivious colonials was in fact Washington and being on the lookout for a particular militia group that would be moving northeast, they allowed their unidentified nemesis to pass in peace.

Looking up at these ridges now, I find it strange to dwell upon how differently American history might have unfolded had Washington and his companions been bushwhacked here, descended upon, slaughtered and scalped swiftly and ignobly by the Shawnee, stripped of their purses and buttons, their hacked corpses dragged away into some nearby hollow, to be covered slowly by the falling leaves of autumn. Would the dynamics and even the outcomes of the French-Indian and Revolutionary struggles have been any different, minus the man who understood Indian warfare, who uncompromisingly demanded discipline, who could crack open walnuts with his bare hands? Or would that be ascribing to one man, however gifted, too much weight and influence amid the vague forces of history? Would events merely have proceeded similarly or the same, fed by vast mindless forces, their intersections and near misses having conspired to raise up another, his face gazing out at us today—distinguished, green, speculative, enigmatic—every time we open our wallets and purses to buy something with American dollars?

The ground rises beyond Shawsville as I ascend, ears popping on occasion, toward the site of one of Washington's frontier destinations: Fort Vause (or Vaux), yet another link in the chain of western defenses along *Athowominee,* fortified in early 1756 by Captain Ephraim Vause, aided by a Captain John Smith—of no relation to the seventeenth-century Jamestown enforcer—and his small detachment of rangers. Though the compound remained manned, Fort Vause's occupants consistently were of a wayward and undisciplined disposition. Unfortunately for them, their frivolous conduct was not lost upon the watchful Shawnee, who would fall upon the undermanned fort on June 25, 1756, accompanied by a few Canadians and the French captain Picot de Belestre, who, when the outcome of the contest was clear, pledged his protection to the English if they ceased hostilities. During the battle, however, de Belestre had received gunshot wounds to the shoulder and kidney that forced him to retire from the field shortly after the fort's surrender, which left the Shawnee to strip and abuse the prisoners at their leisure (Captain Smith's son would be burned to death before his eyes), and divide the spoils of victory, including a number of women and nearly one hundred horses. Even had de Belestre evaded injury, it is debatable whether he could have prevented the accumulated vengeance of the Shawnee, which they considered their honorable right as victorious warriors. Far to the north, in August of 1757, Englishmen who surrendered at Fort William Henry would be slaughtered despite the passionate pleas on their behalf by the commanding French officer, Marquis de Montcalm—imperative victory achieved at the cost of European codes of morality.

I descend westward out of the Blue Ridge into the outskirts of Christiansburg, named for William Christian and located on a plateau overlooking a further descent into the New River Valley—the northern section of Virginia's southern

valley system. Christian, whose parents had come to North America from Ireland, had been appointed by Governor Dunmore as one of the first justices of
the area and chairman of the Committee of Safety, a post from which he duti-
fully sought to protect settlers from the Indian menace to the west. Born on
Christian's Creek near Staunton in 1742, he studied law under Patrick Henry
before courting and later marrying Henry's sister, Ann, in 1768, when he was
but sixteen years old. Christian never practiced law but became instead a highly
successful merchant and trader, to the point that he began to take on eastern airs
and hired a dancing teacher for his daughters. Later, he would move into soldiering and politics, leading a campaign against the Cherokee in autumn 1776 during which he oversaw the burning of villages and crops, and then serving as a
senator—successful forays against Indians often led frontier men into political seats
of power. Christian was extraordinarily wealthy and successful for a western Virginian, a social and economic anomaly among his humble peers, which afforded
him the luxury of owning slaves, many of whom he would send to Kentucky in
the mid-1770s for the purpose of building him a home at the edge of the new
frontier. Once they had accomplished that task, Christian and his family joined
them on the "Dark Bloody Ground," as eastern Kentucky was known among the
Indians—an epithet that would appear prophetic when Christian was shot from
his horse while pursuing a party of raiding Wabash in the spring of 1786, the
mortal wound darkening the pale, newly risen grass beneath his fallen body.

Settlers who had arrived earlier to the Christiansburg area were of much
more modest means than Christian, though Indian strife and violent death would
have similar roles in their lives. One of the region's earliest families, the Irish-
born Drapers, lived to the northwest near a long horseshoe bend in the New
River called Draper's Meadows—not far from the modern campus of Virginia
Tech—which consisted of little more than a loose conglomeration of log cabins. Aided by the good offices of the Irish surveyor Colonel James Patton, a
retired seaman and friend to the late George Draper (who had disappeared
in the Virginia wilderness during a hunting expedition), Eleanor Draper had
brought her two sons to the area in the late 1740s. Although life in general
was peaceful and the family's crops prospered, their proximity to the frontier would exact tragedy in the summer of 1755 when Eleanor, her grandson,
the visiting Colonel Patton—incidentally, the same Patton who had fatefully
ordered John McDowell to confront a body of Iroquois warriors in 1742—and
a neighbor named Casper Barrier were all killed in the Draper home, which
was then burned to the ground with their bodies in it, by a small war party of
less than twenty Shawnee, stirred to violence by French insinuations of Eng-

lish expansionism and encouraged by the annihilation of Braddock's British Regulars near Fort Duquesne earlier that summer. The Shawnee had descended upon the isolated site of Draper's Meadows from the northwest, hoping that a swift, vicious attack on the far outpost would discourage further English-sponsored settlement of the frontier. In fact, their actions during the raid—like those they would later employ at Woodstock and elsewhere, and unlike the assault on Fort Vause—suggest that their aims were bent more toward psychological intimidation than systematic military destruction. Although the Draper homestead was razed and several of its occupants slaughtered, a few locals—including John Draper's wife—were borne away and later returned via ransom. Furthermore, in an incident at the end of the raid, apparently intended to destroy the settlers' morale, the Shawnee beheaded a snowy-haired elderly local man named Philip Barger and placed the appendage in a sack. When they passed the Lybrook cabin while returning northward, they gifted the bag to Mrs. Lybrook, mischievously promising her that its hidden contents constituted something she would recognize. Rather than frightening off the colonists, however, the raid only served to fuel their vehement hatred of all Indians, particularly the Shawnee, and strengthen their resolve to linger. Soon after the Draper's Meadows incident, the system of primitive forts was speedily put in motion along the frontier, and male residents hurried to join newly formed local militias.

These events appear far away, to the point of possessing an almost alien hue, as I continue what feels like a long descent toward downtown Christiansburg, passing a seemingly endless procession of car dealerships. But then perhaps industry that promotes and allows for modern travel is as appropriate a pursuit as any for a town along *Athowominee,* the first great highway of North America. Indeed, the ever travel-minded explorer Daniel Boone had lived in what would become Christiansburg for a time, the records in the local courthouse including a warrant issued for his arrest on account of unpaid debts. Boone departed the town headed southwest with his contingent of axe men, destined to hack out the route that would come to be known as the Wilderness Trail or Boone's Trace, an offshoot of *Athowminee* that would dramatically open the West to settlers. During Boone's time and afterwards, the Christiansburg area was a notable stopping place for travelers, based partially on the number of taverns to which it was home, and I find its present accommodations serviceable enough, filling my hollow stomach with hotdogs at Dude's Drive-in before piling on weight to my backpack with supplies from Wade's Supermarket. Just west of Wade's, one encounters G and G Guns, its appearance jarring in my mind a recollection of the Lewis-McHenry Duel, the first duel in Virginia fought with rifles. The particulars were Thomas Lewis, a twenty-two-year-old lawyer and grandson of General Andrew Lewis, and John McHenry, a middle-aged resident of the western part of the county. Having offended each other irreparably over the course of a heated political discussion, the men squared off at first light on May 9, 1808, near Montgomery County Courthouse, in the vicinity of Sunset Cemetery. The macabre setting would turn out to be an altogether appropriate one, for the contest claimed the lives of both men, a tragedy that would lead to the passage of the Barbour Bill in 1810, which finally outlawed dueling in Virginia—its proud and colorful tradition at last deemed overly bloody in light of progressive firearms technology.

Looking back from the perspective of our own conflicted era, one may now discern that as civilization passed like a wave over western Virginia and eastern North America, swelling toward the interior, violence among humans did not dissipate but rather took on different forms. For all the topical barbarity of an Indian attack or gun duel, they remained open and honest manifestations of brutality and incompatibility. Such visceral conflicts linger now in this country only in certain places and under special circumstances, open battle having generally given way to the more coercive, bureaucratic, and ultimately useless forms of engagement we know today: endless litigation, media manipulation, administrative denial of all wrongdoing, and so on. As a malcontented character called the "underground man," a creation of the Russian writer Fyodor Dostoyevsky, observed in the mid-nineteenth century, "Civilization has made mankind if not more bloodthirsty, at least more vilely, more loathsomely bloodthirsty." Closer to this region and nearly three quarters of a century later, a disillusioned western Virginian in a novel called *Vein of Iron* by Virginia writer Ellen Glasgow would echo the sentiment: "What we call civilization is only a different and perhaps a higher level of barbarism."

Despite the pervasively bland, soul-killing, administrative, cubicle-without-windows violence to which many Americans are subjected on a daily basis, the potential for fully possessing our lives remains wholly ours, though the decision to ignore or abjure the larger salary and big promotion is one most Americans do not appear willing to make. Cultural prestige, for the most part, continues to lie in the arena of those who possess the most powerful professional position, the largest house, the most stuff: the abstract illusions of modern human success. And the person who seeks to remain himself must carefully appreciate his own place in the current charade before he may seek to successfully quit, evade, or manipulate the game. One must humanely come to realize too that it is those whose lives are given over completely to the contest—who fixatedly fight their daily white-collar duels armed with odious memos and budgets—who are the true tragic figures, the people most deserving of our pity: for only a handful of them will ever experience the soul-shaping pain and ecstasy of genuine archetypal human existence—those traceless variables that deepen and enrich one's life even in the process of risking and scarring it.

Beyond Christiansburg I am greeted by a series of slopes and rises which carry me in the direction of the Allegheny Mountains, off in the distance some twenty miles to the west, before the road falls away and becomes tangled in curves just before entering the vicinity of the old fort town of Radford. On the outskirts, early evening, I stop in at Final Score for a beer and a few innings of a baseball game. The air that greets me tastes of thick, stale cigarette smoke, and the beer I receive is watery but the building is air-conditioned and I am glad to have a cool place to lean back and rest. In colonial times, tavern fare along this route rarely was found to be very palatable. When the late-eighteenth-century Virginia congressman John Randolph had discovered the refreshment of one tavern wanting, he addressed himself loudly to the innkeeper, proclaiming, "Sir, if this be tea, bring me coffee. And if this be coffee, bring me tea!" However, Randolph—the eccentric and immensely gifted Black Jack of Bizarre, who had been kicked out of William and Mary for dueling over the pronunciation of a word and would bring his dogs and poetry books to sessions while serving in Congress so as to improve himself and not be idle—was used to high living and leisurely travel, the demands of the road assuaged considerably by his attendants and steady opium habit. My own more visceral road experiences have led to a decidedly generous attitude toward local refreshment. Whereas normally I might liken it to old stumpwater, the tapped Budweiser before me flows like the nectar of the gods over my parched, tired tongue. In the wake of my wanderings bad beer has come to be more than good enough for me; the calorie-packed plate of prefrozen fried appetizers I order not bad either. And it is, after all, my plate. In Randolph's time, when travelers sat down at table, they were not served individual dishes but rather brought great portions to which each was expected to help himself. Etiquette generally was ignored, the men reaching across each other, grabbing and lunging for the bowl at hand, scooping its contents hurriedly with a deft spoon or hand. If someone came up short, it was not uncommon for curses to be exchanged and perhaps even blows. If a bottle or two had been emptied while awaiting the evening meal, violence of course became all the more likely. Not feeling up to a food scuffle just now, I am indeed thankful for the small plate before me, though once it is emptied I nearly fall asleep in it before pushing on to a nearby motel.

Next morning, foggy and cool, I walk out of the Tyler Motor Inn to discover myself next to the campus of Radford University, passed obliviously in
the night, notable in my mind for its dedication to the study of the Appalachian
region and the peculiar rounded architecture of many of its buildings. Ascending
a long hill takes me away from the lined shops of the university area, after which
I bear northwest, pausing where a high bridge spans the New River. Though it
possesses no towers and the river here is not so wide, the winds not so wrathful,
this bridge reminds me, perhaps chiefly because of its height, of Scotland's Firth
of Forth Bridge, a revolutionary cantilever rail bridge completed in 1890 near
Edinburgh. The Scottish bridge was the first in the world constructed primarily
of steel, its unprecedented price tag in raw materials accompanied by the lives of
fifty-six construction workers, killed while working on it, more than a hundred
others injured.

As the story of the Firth of Forth Bridge reveals, a crossing's history may
sometimes come to overshadow the infinitely longer tale of the river it spans, the
very reason for its being. However, the New is a special river, one of the oldest
in the world, and I am reluctant to pass far above it without peering more closely
at its waters. As I leave the bridge, descending into the flood plain and across a
railroad track, I recall that the early exploration party of Captain Thomas Batts,
Robert Fallam, and Thomas Wood, led by their Appomattoc guide Penecut,
had come upon the New River not far from here in September 1671 during their
extraordinary quest for a hypothetical ocean, which they believed lay somewhere
beyond the mountains. Fording the river and following it south along *Athowominee,* they noted a number of great fields, the result of repeated Indian burnings and cultivation. Bent on their mythical sea and likely distracted by the signs
they saw of Indian culture, Batts and the others seem to have afforded little
attention to the river habitat, the uniqueness of which likely would have staggered them had they considered it in any detail. One of the oldest bodies of
water in the world—over 250 million years in age, more ancient than the Atlantic Ocean, which did not exist before 180 million years ago—the New runs in
an odd direction, west and north, from the Blue Ridge in North Carolina to the
Mississippi. The river even predates Appalachia itself, its waters already flowing when Africa collided with North America, the great rippling continental
cataclysm that birthed the eastern mountains. While glaciers spread and receded
around it over the course of several centuries, animals congregated on its banks,
safe from the freezing wastelands and privy to abundant plant and animal life.
Because of this insulated quality, immensely old species of insects live along the
New even now, attracting scientists and enthusiasts from around the world. And

despite the fact that the nearby Claytor Dam has swollen a section of the river to vastly unnatural proportions and its body is infrequently bridged by steel girders and bound by banks of concrete, the water remains relatively unmolested by heavy industry, although its quality suffers, like nearly every other North American river, from various runoff-related chemical issues.

Its venerable longevity and ability to endure dramatic geological shifts notwithstanding, the New's general status today is of yours, mine, everyone's, everything's. As the philosopher Kierkegaard would say, it is "in the process of becoming," moving "into an uncertain future." This while kneeling at the water's edge, distorting the shadow of my image in the current with an immersed right hand. Though the palm and fingers hold their place in the river for as long as I keep them there, there remains in this ancient river valley, as hard and as visible as naked outcroppings of stone, the sure eventuality that all that these waters touch will pass and be borne away by them in time. Likely, the river's destiny and the crumbling of the things it meets troubles some people, but as the English poet Alexander Pope remarked, it is partly on man's "ignorance of future events, and partly upon the hope of a future state, that all his happiness in the present depends." Though my optimism is fed by benightedness, I am one of those who hopes for the New.

In the early part of the twentieth century locals had yearned for a future that would include a modern bridge across the river, though they would lose something ineffable, yet irreplaceable, when the innovation arrived. Up until the past half-century or so, residents in the area, devoid of the great bridge, would have possessed a necessary intuitive understanding of the New's power and disposition. Just as Scotland's Forth Road Bridge, finished in 1964 and standing not far from its more distinguished brother, replaced a ferry service that had lasted for eight centuries, so the old *Athowominee* route, called Rock Road here, would have led pre-bridge travelers farther south toward the old site of Ingle's Ferry—long the primary means of crossing the New. The ferry, maneuvered initially by pole and later by pulley, provided a critical service to local as well as far-bound settlers and their livestock, the New being a difficult river to ford. Flat-bottomed and generally in the range of twenty to thirty feet in length, early ferries had high gunwales in order to keep curious children and frightened animals from plunging overboard, the unsettling uniqueness of the watery journey infrequently driving them to unpredictable behavior.

The local ferry and nearby tavern were named for the person who had devised them, William Ingles, an Irish-born man who had brought his family to the area in the late 1740s, only to have his wife kidnapped, like John Draper's, during the Shawnee raid of 1755. The captivity, escape, and eventual return of Mary Ingles, following rivers for several hundred miles from what is currently Boone County, Kentucky, all the way back to Giles County, Virginia, where she encountered friendly settlers, still stands today—even more so than the ordeal of Hannah Dennis—as one of the more remarkable recorded feats of cross-country endurance and determination in North American history by anyone. Mary was joined in her escape from the Shawnee along the banks of the Ohio River by an elderly German woman who had been captured at Fort Duquesne. Armed with tomahawks, the pair evaded a Shawnee search party and made their way to the Kanawha River which runs into the New, living mostly on roots and sleeping in hollow logs or under fur trees beneath heaped piles of dry leaves. After several days, the deprivations of the journey began to wear greatly upon the mind of the older woman. Crazed with hunger and blaming Ingles for their plight, she tried to murder the younger woman in her sleep, probably with the aim of devouring her afterward. Awakening in time to effect a hasty escape, Mary crossed the river and continued her journey, following the New until at last she was discovered and, after two days of rest and nourishment, taken to Fort Frederick, where she was reunited with her husband. Against all odds, her elderly former companion and would-be assassin survived as well, having experienced the good fortune of chancing upon an abandoned settler cabin stocked with dried meat, and later encountering a stray horse which she bridled with grape vines and proceeded to ride along the New until she was discovered. When the women were reunited at Fort Frederick, the abundant joy of their traumatic, unlikely survival outweighed all ill-feeling, though Mary would remain a silent and melancholy person until the end of her days.

It is good to remind myself of the cross-country ordeals of Mary Ingles and Hannah Dennis—memorably fictionalized by West Virginia writer Mary Lee Settle in her historical novel *O Beulah Land*—from time to time as my own journey continues to unfold, a harsh trial to the body, yet laid out along a road now home to convenience stores, supermarkets, and millions of other people, travelers as well as denizens. Unless one has performed solitary deep wilderness expeditions—those remote rustications that unfold devoid of resupply points and require weeks of utter solitude—it is very difficult to even begin to imagine the ordeals of Ingles and Dennis, their bodies wracked by malnutrition and exposure, almost completely without food or equipment, sleeping in thickets, the nearest human probably hundreds of miles from where they lay shivering. Moreover, their journeys were not chosen by them, were not carefully planned, but rather came upon them as imperative matters of survival, unavoidable trials of nearly inconceivable suffering. Awesome exemplars of that almost supernatural will that bridges animal endurance and the abstract resolve of higher consciousness, Ingles and Dennis ever accompany me, possessed of my very highest respect, as humans and women.

On the other side of the New River bridge, my musings upon these two notable North American figures are interrupted and struck down suddenly by two large billboards making use of women in the present: successive advertisements for the Exotic Adult Bookstore and Caring Pregnancy Center—female identity presented and victimized against the seemingly disparate backdrops of pornography and unwanted pregnancies. Walking on amid the thick morning heat, I ponder, without much success, the cultural relevance of these signs—what they say about my own time. Though no definite answers rise to me with the heat from the road, I am nonetheless reminded of yet another troubling aspect of contemporary American culture: its inherent cheapening of the genuine superhuman achievements of figures like Dennis and Ingles in light of the present superficial ways in which women are variously manipulated, exploited, and celebrated, their images—like all other images—aligned with numerous, often conflicting—though usually equally irrational—media agendas. That these strange billboards should be paired here probably also says something about the specific culture of this area, which, on occasion, has been home to decidedly alternative worldviews. Crossing Ingles Ferry in 1750, for instance, Thomas Walker came upon the Mahanaim settlement of Dunkards, a curious and especially mystical branch of Pennsylvania Ephrata Brethren, whom he described as "an odd set of people, who make it a matter of Religion not to Shave their Beards, ly on beds, or eat Flesh. . . . The unmarried have no private Property, but live on a common Stock." Dunkard's Bottom, as it was called, constituted both rich farmland and an important strategic position, but it was ill suited to the strange sect of German settlers who chose to make their homes there. Though they were well versed in numerous trades, built the first mill west of the New, and distinguished themselves as farmers, the theological pacifism of the Dunkards made for a poor match with the necessity for self-defense against the periodically marauding Shawnee. Eventually, the settlement disintegrated with the majority of Dunkards returning to Pennsylvania or joining the Moravians of western North Carolina. And in 1756 Dunkard's Bottom would become the site of the first military fort west of the New River (now submerged beneath Claytor Lake), a development that no doubt troubled the few remaining Dunkards in the area. Fort Frederick, as it came to be called, would be occupied briefly that same year by Andrew Lewis's doomed would-be Indian killers, who paused there to gather supplies before lucklessly pressing on into the Alleghenies.

On this day I relinquish my hiking early, smitten by a prospect that arrests me: one that affords memorable views of the Alleghenies—most notably, Walker Mountain and Cloyds Mountain—as well as the Blue Ridge, stretched across the horizon back behind me to the east. Built upon this fine rise is Dogwood Lodge, a beautifully situated motel, far from Interstate 81 yet apparently enjoying a comfortable measure of business: a splendid location to rest and simply gaze east and west—to fall into a slumber of a dozen hours while watching the far skies—a site from which one might search in vain for the curve of the earth and where the dreams that come just before dawn may almost be seen lingering on the horizon, just as those who have lived in dreams glimpse when they wake a glimmer of the glory they abandoned. For me it has always been amid such high places, in the dark before first light, where the best dreams come; not the close recognizable faces of joy drawn near but distant images—visions from a far country where shadows weep.

In the midst of resting here, enjoying that rare leisure to gaze and dream, I recall how years ago I had kept for a time a dream journal, undergoing the familiar progression from remembering only fragments to summoning multiple dreams in their entirety. I have always been one who dreams vividly, in colors, shapes, and sounds. On occasions when I write heavily without respite, I occasionally dream of letters or words, glowing in different colors, covered sometimes in vines, and bearing with them various odors. Awakened from an unfolding dream, I can sometimes resume it in sequence upon my return that night to the regions of slumber, as if taking up a book again after having been interrupted in mid-chapter. At such times the waking mind and the unthinking one seem close together, perhaps even overlapping. So the task of transcribing my dreams into the conscious world came to me easily enough. After a while, though, I honed my watchful consciousness to the point that I began affecting the flow and action of my dreams, willing them into certain shapes and outcomes. At first, this was an exhilarating discovery, although my sleep was less restful. But eventually my dreams began to diminish, their color, sound, and variety failing. What was yet to dawn on me was the fact that he who comes to control his dreams is no longer really dreaming, the thinking mind having come to inhabit unnaturally the brain's more nether regions. This, however, did not occur to me until at last I dreamed of a blank cell, in which I sat surrounded by imprisoning whiteness, the close boundaries felt rather than seen. There, I was struck by a profound sorrow, not for myself but because I believed the world had run out of words. The next day I destroyed my dream journal and began the slow work of attempting to forget my dreams at the hour of waking. Having powerfully conditioned my mind to the opposite purpose, the process went slowly, but in time my dreams became again shadowy and indistinct, smoke on the horizon, only occasionally vivid, safe in their twilight unreality from the waking mind.

The respite at Dogwood Lodge—of vistas, dreams, and slumber—refreshes me and makes inviting once more the hard realities of the highway, which, as it turns out, are not so toilsome here: where the relatively level, smooth road passes into Dublin—a prosperous town today but a quiet, sparsely populated place in the last years of the eighteenth century. One resident of that time who would come to make an impact on events beyond the immediate area was the German-born Henry Trolinger, a powder master who settled near a saltpeter cave northeast of the modern town for the purpose of having easy access to an unlimited mineralogical resource for gunpowder. He prospered during the Revolution, his trade in great demand, his son doing most of the mining while he steadily refined it above ground. Nearly a century later, his descendant James Trolinger would perform the same function on a larger scale when Virginia seceded.

In Dublin I purchase supplies at Wade's Supermarket, morning business slow, parking lot and road quiet. The miles unfold beneath me outside of town, but the heat blooms also, heavy light cast upon me, bright late-morning sun glaring and glancing off the road, exacting its toll upon those creatures who choose to stir beneath it. Somewhere between Dublin and Pulaski, sweat in my eyes, on the verge of overheating, I encounter a hill where huge shady oaks line the road, natural towers unleaning, seedlings of the 1800s, probably old enough to have witnessed Civil War cavalry rushing up and down the road. I stagger up to rest beneath one, brain cooked to the point that it nearly fancies a ghostly ring of nymphs and fairies dancing about the immense trunk. Tumbling down upon the cool grass between enormous roots, pack slipped off, I lean back against the trunk, gazing up into the tree, noting that though the air is still around me, the uppermost leaves flutter slightly, hands waving slow gentle goodbyes to something already far off and indiscernible. The top branches bear the marks of severe periodic pruning, and I wonder at the reason why these gigantic trees have been spared at all, granted reprieve, while nearly all others of comparable age are long since dispatched by saws, blights, insects, droughts, lightning, and whatever else over the course of decades. Perhaps it is because there is the highway on one side of them and a narrow drive on the other, the small piece of ground on which they stand lying fallow in between. Or perhaps this was a popular place for

travelers to take their rest, sitting in the shade as I am, admiring the surrounding fields. But most certainly there were other central reasons, those I can never
know, long since forgotten or shrouded in legend even among the locals.

As I cool down, having poured water upon my head as well as down my
throat, my mind conjures up the Greek tale of Erisichthon—the story of a pro-
fane man who resolved to chop down a gigantic aged oak, one upon which
locals were fond of carving loving inscriptions and about which they hung hand-
wrought wreaths and garlands. It was rumored too that the Dryads, or oak
spirits, were fond of dancing about it. Yet, despite all this or perhaps because of it,
Erisichthon was bent on the tree's destruction, to the point that he struck down
a pious man who tried to stop him, before swinging his axe into the mighty
bough, which emitted an almost human groan, the wound gushing forth blood
of deepest crimson, indistinguishable from our own. Undeterred, Erisichthon
and his servants kept up the gruesome work, hacking at the trunk in strong jagged strokes until the upper branches swayed and thick ropes were set about it.
When the servants of Erisichthon pulled the tree to the ground, it crashed and
shook the earth with a sound resembling thunder, destroying many of the grove's
delicate shrubs and smaller trees beneath its immense sprawled bulk.

Nymphs of the forests, Dryads were so closely attached to their environment that each inseparably bonded with an individual tree of her choice. When
a Dryad's tree died, she perished as well—a metaphor for the close relationship,
the interdependency, between the human spirit and the natural. So it was that
when Erisichthon destroyed the Dryads' beloved tree they too were devastated,
and in great sorrow, wearing garments of mourning, traveled to Ceres, goddess
of the harvest and all growing things. Hearing their tragic account of the tree's
barbarous death, Ceres, outraged, resolved to send upon Erisichthon the terrible
spirit called Famine from her wasteland domain: that gaunt being who wracks
the human bodies she encounters with incessant, unquenchable hunger. Plagued
by Famine, Erisichthon quickly consumed the crops on his extensive lands, before selling off all his property and using the profits to purchase more food, none
of which could sate him. As his hunger grew and his means of procuring sustenance diminished, he took to ingesting his own appendages, his mad starvation-
wracked hunger outweighing the excruciating pain of self-dismemberment,
until at last death consumed and fulfilled him.

In addition to constituting a fable of needless natural consumption and its
greed-begat consequences—one to which we of this age might all give more
heed—the tale of the doomed tree and its executioner tells us much about the
special adoration the ancient Greeks bestowed upon oaks. For them, the trees

were majestic conveyers of portents and prophecy, and they meticulously maintained groves of oracular oaks. In Dodona the will of the gods was said to be heard in the soft rustling of oak leaves, and the Dryads were thought to be the keepers of the rain. The Akadian Greeks even referred to themselves as *Eggenoi Dryos,* "the sons of Oak." Much later, in Rome, the vestal virgins tended perpetual oak fires, and Jupiter was honored in the form of an old oak tree. Other cultures held the tree in high esteem as well, the Germanic tribes of northern Europe burning the wood in honor of the deities they believed dwelt within the bark. Mistletoe, a frequent resident of the uppermost branches, was thought to carry the soul of the tree through the frigid months of winter, and it was this attractive clinging plant, beneath which it is the custom of modern Americans to kiss, that took the life of Balder, most beautiful and beloved among the Norse gods.

These thoughts lead to an idealized image of the immense red oak, *Quercus rubra,* behind the place where I live in Appomattox, Virginia, standing in a small circular grove between fields with young dogwoods and cedars growing beneath it—a sapling when Longstreet's men strung out their last line on the high ground just above it, a sloping hayfield now, and set about digging the last shallow breastworks of the Army of Northern Virginia. I have built beneath this elder tree a fire pit of stone, constructed of heavy, gray river rock, roughly square or rectangular—once the foundation blocks of some dwelling or barn, piled and forgotten, heaped in a nearby wood for me to discover. When nocturnal fires burn, the branches of the great red oak span over all that is visible, a far-reaching single-tree canopy, the fringes of which are indistinct, concluding somewhere in the night beyond the ring and range of firelight. Light and shadow waver on leaf and bark, the river rocks absorb the heat, far from the stream that formed them.

As I sit here, stiff and reluctant to take up the road again, the image of the Red Oak dissolves back into the fancy from which it has ushered forth, though its appearance may have possessed some semblance of literal grounding, the sap of the tree having once been employed as a salve to relieve joint ailments. If I could, I would apply it now to the knees and ankles of my own body, but I rise instead, knowing I will only be troubling myself more if I allow them to cool any longer. Withering roadside grass receives them, I am in motion, line of senescent oaks behind me, thrall to the road once more.

Clouds gradually arriving from the southwest, moving and massing slowly, a light drizzle begins to fall as I tread through the streets of Pulaski, a railroad town come into its own long after my ancestors passed this way. The roads are quiet and misty here in the light rain, automobiles gliding slowly, headlights on, the place bleary, foggy—almost dreamlike. On the southern outskirts of town there begins a long curvy ascent up Draper Mountain, a peak from which iron ore once was mined, the road badly eroded in places—a result of mining or the grade of the slope, the cut of the road, I cannot tell. I lean into the climb as best I can, the steepest and longest I have yet encountered, wishing for hiking poles but thankful for the misty weather, the comfortable temperature and absence of sun. Before the journey began I had considered bringing with me, more out of fondness than need, my favorite old walking staff: a sycamore limb gnawed at both ends by beavers—creek dwellers on the horse farm where I grew up. Over the course of a couple of years, the creatures had erected a dam, initiated their own logging efforts, and watched as it was raised and widened by collected organic refuse from upstream, backing up water and notably altering the appearance of the creek banks, where saplings lay timbered by teeth, a few standing half-gnawed, crowned by brittle dead branches. I recall walking along the creek after a week of spring rain, muddy water gushing, and finding the dam recently collapsed, the water newly shallow, rushing over black slimy rocks, shiny in the windswept sunlight of March after lying submerged and invisible, dark bottom dwellers, for months on end. The rocks' appearance marked the fading of the beavers, upstream, downstream, or somewhere else I will never know. Walking on I discovered, not far from the fringes of the ruined dam, resting against a decaying stump, a gnawed stick of sycamore, perfectly smooth and sturdy—a hard, tough wood, extraordinarily difficult to cut, saw, or break when dry. It leaned so casually against the stump as to appear that someone had set it there, leading me to wonder if flood water, through some natural coincidence of physics, had washed it into that position; or had the beavers placed it there, dragging and flipping it toward their doomed home, hoping somehow to reinforce their dwelling against the successive tons of water backing up behind—a pressure and danger felt without knowledge? Ever after, the smooth sycamore has been my staff of choice whenever whimsy or need directs me to take up a hiking stick, for the beavers made it, there along the creek on the land where I was raised, not long before nature claimed their home, saw to their vanishing.

Weather clearing, temperature still comfortable, shafts of sun on the mountainside, I rest in the grass and shade near a National Guard armory which sits upon a graded slope, piled and carved out of Draper Mountain. Still wishing irrationally for my walking stick or a pair of poles, knees swollen, I rise, time and encroaching stiffness directing me to continue the ascent. Later, when the summit is finally attained, I am well rewarded, overlooks on either side of the road, east and west, providing wide panoramas of the Blue Ridge and Allegheny ranges—sky sparklingly clear, sunlight as of autumn, horizon rinsed clean by the morning rain.

As many hikers have divined, there is nothing much better, little that cheers the heart more, than a fine prospect of space and far hills after a long ascent during which your face is more or less continually pressed close to the mountain before you, towering summer foliage altogether obstructing the occasional grand views of winter. It is luxurious, having negotiated such places, to dwell upon the labor in the wake of its completion, brow swept by mountain breezes, clothes now drying, becoming light again, the moisture of drifting, misty mountain clouds having passed on, evaporated. And before, ahead and below, the happy thought of a long descending slope, clear weather to the south, from which a light wind swirls and blows. Surveying here the open leagues of landscape, this tiny sliver of eastern Appalachia, immense in the small framing orbs of human eyes, one may perceive that for all the abuses it has endured, for all the changes it has undergone, there remains much, even in this settled landscape of our own time, to be admired—much too to imagine in the lands farther off, toward and into which we shall soon be traveling. Atop such farseeing precipices of perspective, destinations become lamentable, conclusions things to be avoided—the fleeting enigmatic revelations of the journey and the places through which it passes stretched below, waiting to unfold with myth and majesty so long as we continue to approach and embrace them: an endeavor worthy of a thousand lifetimes. "This is still a beautiful country," proclaimed the Mississippi writer Elizabeth Spencer. "We only need to find the blue highways and travel down them forever." Worn and a little beat up, I am nonetheless glad, thankful, my journey does not conclude here, that the road stretches on, beyond the horizon. For even having followed *Athowominee* this far—across three states, closing in on three hundred miles—I know I have yet to truly discover it, indeed may never come to know it, its nature spanning ages beyond the counting of its distance: an ancient pathway, an almost infinite course, along which unfold not only the lives and places of our own time, but others as well. Deeper than any distance, as old as North American man, it remains, like the human heart, a mystery laid out upon eternity.

II

Here, in southwest Virginia, having departed the scenic overlooks atop Draper Mountain—the long, memorable prospects of the Blue Ridge and Allegheny ranges, east and west, respectively—I descend the south face, following Highway 11, into a small valley of the same name, both natural features memorializing

John Draper, an early frontiersman who had survived unscathed the Shawnee incursion to the north in the summer of 1755 and later came to settle in this area. Cornered in a cabin while her husband toiled in the fields, Draper's wife, Bettie, and their infant son were not so fortunate when the Shawnee swept through, the woman sustaining a bullet wound to the arm before witnessing the agonizing death of her baby at the blunt end of a rock-hewn tomahawk. Yet, like Mary Ingles, Bettie's life ultimately was spared and she was spirited west across the Allegheny mountains to the Shawnee villages, though, unlike Ingles, she would not be so fortunate as to effect a quick escape. Enduring an initial period of torture and abuse, Bettie eventually distinguished herself as a tribeswoman of some importance among the Shawnee, a result of her skill with the needle and in preparing food. Though her husband constantly inquired after her and sought out friendly Indians for information, she would not be reunited with him for six years, at which time he finally located her and purchased her freedom.

It seems the farther I follow this highway built along and upon the ancient Indian footpath *Athowominee,* the more bloody and lamentable episodes of the North American colonial frontier I find myself recounting—an apparent natural outgrowth of the fact that it was on this route that the first frontier settlers, including my own German ancestors, sought new lives and lands, though the places they sometimes settled upon had been home to other lives for generations: a fact from which great suffering often arose. Indians protected their places for they feared losing them, so much lost already, wrested away through the lies and treachery of colonial officials. Western settlers moved on because it was all they could do, walking or riding away from death, their goods in a wagon and their hopes on the horizon, the cultures into which many of them had been born severed now by an ocean, the so-called civilized lands to the east beyond their means to purchase.

When, a mile or so from the foot of Draper Mountain, Route 11 merges into Interstate 81, the point is brought home that people are still moving, wandering on a grand scale, today—cars and trucks, coinciding caravans of them, hurtling and roaring, commanded at extraordinary speeds, toward the sundry destinations of their operators. The American interstate system represents the federal government's mid-twentieth-century attempt to channel and funnel that wanderlust into a flowing, efficient, closely monitored grid. As its government creators pointed out, the interstate system was as much a philosophical construction as a practical one:

> Construction of this modern road network . . . involves
> many problems and radical changes in thought . . . . The

benefits of controlled-access construction are numerous. A
modern, controlled-access road transforms, in many ways,
the area through which it passes. . . . This type of road promotes safety, saves travel time, reduces the strain on drivers
and aids the economic development of the area.

Built upon these abstract assumptions, the interstate system has turned out to
be much different in actual application than any of its builders likely imagined.
Controlled access often means driving on unnecessarily, sometimes for many
miles, if a desired exit is missed; economic development at access points can be
problematic or even undesirable; and safety amid these corridors of large speeding trucks, inattentive drivers, and seedy rest stops often is wanting—an irony
that many people now eschew the interstates for the old secondary roads they
were designed to bypass, trading the speed and anxiety of the big road for considerations of safety and slower, more relaxed traffic.

The quiet service road carries me, vehement traffic flanking me all the
way, to Fort Chiswell, the proximity of an outpost built under the direction of
William Byrd III in 1759, largely on account of its position in a natural pass between Lick Mountain to the south and, to the north, Ramsay Mountain, the northwest tip of which pushes up against the village of Max Meadows, the location of
one of the earliest frontier academies, founded in 1792. Here, *Athowominee* met

Most all systems are arbitrary or become so in time, arising as they do out
of incomplete, finite philosophies. The German thinker Johann Fichte pointed
out that system makers "proceed from some concept or other. Without caring in
the least where they got it from or whence they have concocted it, they analyze
it, combine it with others to whose origin they are equally indifferent, and in
reasonings such as these their philosophy itself is composed." Amid such variously drawn hodgepodges of thought, much inevitably is either misinterpreted,
misapplied, or altogether overlooked. Here, standing before Interstate 81, I constitute one such wayward variable: an agent not allowed for in the creation of
the system, for 81 is banned to all foot travel and those typically glimpsed ille-
gally walking along such thoroughfares usually are labeled immediately as bums
or pariahs—destitute, aimless people lacking the means to drive, rather than
purposeful travelers exercising a rational preference for hiking. Fortunately, a
service road running parallel to the interstate allows me to trace the congested
corridor without literally being on it—a prospect ultimately more dangerous for
me than the system's fearful drivers, disturbed and perhaps a little inquisitive,
at the strange figure passed: fading in the rearview mirror, walking alongside,
moving in slow motion amid, the furious velocity of heavy modern traffic.

with another old, albeit less-traveled, path running north and south. The fort was named for Byrd's friend John Chiswell, who would discover lead mines several miles to the south along the New River, near present-day Austinville, in the 1760s that would later supply colonial forces during the American Revolution. He also was responsible for widening *Athowominee* south of Wytheville, all the way to Long Island (now Kingsport, Tennessee), so that it would better accommodate wagon traffic, the great tide of western development. On January 30, 1775, Fort Chiswell was the meeting place of the "Freeholders of Fincastle County," who established a number of local resolutions in concert with the wishes of the First Continental Congress. The agenda of that meeting also reflects the history and concerns of the area's people at that time: their simultaneous, proud, hard-won independence and united willingness to serve the other colonies, as well as their joyful relief that the Indians were "now happily terminated."

Progress has its price, an inevitability ever relegated, pushed, to the fringes of collective human consciousness. The Virginia frontier was gradually becoming settled but with it came machinations that would alter, deprive, and scar the land forever. Closing in on Wytheville, walking by turns along service roads and upon grassy fields, tracing the course of the interstate, which—incredibly—is also *Athowominee*'s, I encounter a blasted quarry area, glimpsed off to the left, south of 81: gray barren rock jutting out from a clawed hillside, bereft of foliage, sur-rounded by loose and eroded brownish-red soil. It is but a small suggestion of the long practice of mining—that mad industry that gripped, dug its human fingers deeply into, southwestern Virginia, West Virginia, and many other places—and continues to do so. Mining—its appearance, science, techniques, everything about it—has always suggested to me an ecological form of rape. Even the indus-try's terminology, words like "strip mining" and "mountaintop removal," im-plies wanton destruction, total acquisition. For the land that is mined, there is no recompense, advantage, or silver lining—it is irrevocably maimed and torn, though the wounds may be so deep as to appear all but invisible, save for the brackish, acidic ground water and befouled wells, the inexplicable sink holes in the terrain, the uprooted trees, the suddenly eroded slopes.

Most of this peculiar destruction lies west of here, the regions that truly may be called coal country, crumbling landscapes with mountains toppling evermore, from which the centuries will burn rich loads under which the people of those places have groaned. They are surreal areas, remote wastelands of the industrial era, twisted nightmarish episodes of rural Appalachia briefly turned modern and then abandoned: small dilapidated company houses pressed against rusty railroads, centered by a slightly less decomposed company store; all—the homes, the railroad, the store, even the roads that lead to them—now partially sunken in and defunct, the rare figure or vehicle that moves among them suggestive of an unlikely survivor from some twentieth-century apocalypse.

I once spent some time in McDowell County, West Virginia—the poorest district in the state, its county line less than fifty miles northwest of Wytheville—passing most of my days in the coal villages of Caretta and War, or between them, drinking beer at Cecil Johnson's roadside Rock View Inn. Once flourishing towns, home to every modern convenience, they are now ghostly places, hollows where steel cankers and vines wrap about the broken sidewalks and abandoned railroad tracks—trees grown up through roofless houses and schools, among the best that could be built when their foundations were laid in the 1920s and 1930s. The population is aged, the youth having fled in search of work, a different kind of life, propelled by an indefinite need to escape—many of those remaining indigent and unemployed, drugged out and uneducated, subjected to conditions worse than many Third World countries in a county that lies three hundred miles from the capital of the United States.

The people who settled McDowell County were similar to my own frontier ancestors: independent, stoic, poor folk arrived to a place where they could finally afford land, carve a living, however humble, out of the close-pressed ridges and hollows of the Appalachian mountains. And so they got by, enduring rather than prospering, but doing so on their own terms, decade after decade. The arrival of modern coal operations dramatically altered the traditional local economy from one of hardscrabble agricultural subsistence to an even more tenuous, crude, industrial one. The land and/or what lay beneath it was steadily acquired—covertly as well as forcibly—by absentee coal barons, the people herded into coal camps, they or their children eventually compelled to mine, the terraced hillside rows abandoned for dark subterranean passages, cribbed with lumber, water dripping amid the creaking of timbers.

People often were paid for their underground labor in script, which allowed them to buy goods only from the company store. The company provided everything, ensuring that all or most of the real money it paid and spent upon miners and their families eventually made its way back into the coffers of the company one way or another: if not the company store, then the company doctor, the company church, and so on. The psychological impact of such a society was much worse than its nefarious practical exploitation, for over time it encouraged and produced an unhealthy culture of paternalism, miners expecting the company to provide everything, stripped of the formidable initiative and independence of their forefathers. When industry failed and the companies pulled out of the region, few knew where even to begin, the lucky ones moving away, those who remained struggling with poverty and unemployment, the slow disintegration of their communities—many of them yearning in despair for the return of the very system that exploited them.

Today, in McDowell County—rated one of the top ten poorest counties in the United States, eight-tenths of its land owned by people who don't live there, home to staggering rates of illness and illiteracy—there exists, to some degree, a troubling marketing of victimization, an advertised human deprivation that openly attracts and recruits philanthropic groups and tolerates their various ideologies for the purpose of attaining whatever material benefits may be involved. Sometimes, a measure of genuine good is accomplished. Overall though, one can't help but feel troubled that those who arrive with aid are, in some sense, not all that different in their paternalistic material capacities from the coal companies of old: a new benevolent crutch to replace the old malignant one, though a crutch remains a crutch, as the saying goes.

Despite the excruciating toll exacted by the mining industry on both the land and the psyches of the people who continue to live upon it, there exist many individuals who maintain enviable reservoirs of resilience, independence, and self-sufficiency. Cecil Johnson—ageless barkeep of the Rock View, who, well into his nineties, grew his own tobacco and vegetables—is one, or the Muncy sisters, leaders in their local church and dedicated ATV enthusiasts, who have constructed a family compound in the hills above War and spent an entire afternoon riding a friend and me around the summits and gas fields of all the local ridges, telling us about the people who once lived there, showing us the rusty ruins of an old still. "Virginia is way over there on the other side of them hills," one of the sisters told me, pointing into the evening sun from the mountaintop where we stood. "We can take four-wheeler trails anywhere you want to go. Point and we'll go there. . . . I could ride you all the way to Grundy." There are still such people in McDowell County, those capable of gazing beyond a long history of suffering, oracles who scan the horizon, for whom there are still possibilities.

Mining operations persist in many regions of Appalachia today, the black specter of coal omnipresent though often shy, the smaller, modern operations tucked back among the hills, grinding and clanking, loaded-down Mack trucks hustling along, brakes burning—the odor of roasting rubber and hydraulics—as the heavy vehicles rumble down the mountain, going in slow, bursting out of, switchback curves. The universe holds a different reality or menagerie for each human being, viewed as it is by the separate, imperfect minds that behold it. My notion of coal country remains an ill-defined, incomplete one, for it is an Appalachia I still struggle to know, one generally removed from where I now tread, to which I remain a foreigner: a stranger with another past, for whom the people of these areas are, by turns, familiar and alien. Appalachian coal country is a different kind of Appalachia, from what people eat and think about all the way down to the traditional means of heating one's home, the smell of coal smoke on the evening autumn air having long ago replaced the sharp sweet odor of kindling aflame or the slow, smoky simmering of wet wood, set for the night at the back of the woodstove. Though it remains a mystery to me, it is a region that plays upon my mind whenever I encounter denuded terrain or venture very far into southwest Virginia. Here, the hills are intact, but not far to the west, at days end, the waning sun sinks behind hollowed mounds—tragic, riddled peaks: the wounded heights West Virginia writer William Hoffman once called "the dark mountains."

It is breezy and cooler in Wytheville, the town's elevation of nearly twenty-three hundred feet the highest of any municipality through which I have passed. Downtown, I eat at Skeeter's World Famous Hot Dogs, the reputation well earned, and load up later on water and nuts at the ACME Market. South of town, Route 11 emerges again from the interstate, its own road once more, defined by languid, infrequent traffic and the welcome provincial quality of the roadside: the delightful fresh fruit I buy from the Wythe Produce fruit stand. The recently ripened goods are inexpensive, probably due to the fact that the fruit stand rests a considerable distance from the interstate. In fact, a similar local situation existed on a much grander scale at the end of the eighteenth century, when the immense distance to large markets and the problems of traveling with goods made the overall price of vegetables and livestock in the region very low: a bushel of corn or wheat bringing as little as twenty-five cents, a healthy steer only five dollars.

Later, eating strawberries as I cool my feet in the cold water of Reed Creek's north fork, my thoughts turn to something that has occupied me periodically over the course of my journey: the idea of what I am experiencing as opposed to what is experiencing me—my presence in these places, however unobtrusive, ever as insidious and as palpable as the displacement created by my feet in the waters of Reed Creek. The philosopher Edmund Husserl claimed that in order "to distinguish within experience that which experiences from that which is experienced, one must suspend natural beliefs; this suspension of belief is made possible by a method of bracketing by which we talk not about trees and selves as items external to experience but of the 'trees' and the 'perceptions' of experience." Such thoughts serve, on the one hand, as healthy and humble reminders of the finite human ability to comprehend our most basic surroundings, and, on the other, as formulas for despair, for to what limited degree may we really overcome ourselves, our unconscious beliefs, our human limitations, and their manifold relations to the puny, incomplete degrees to which we experience the images of reality? What shaky value lies in our respective surface recognitions of a thing in its being and our erratic and divergent human perceptions of it?

Back on the road, these questions give way to a belated literal perception: the prominence, here—valley to the south, long Pine Ridge off to my right— of occasional German-style barns, standing in fields or on hillsides, painted or weathered, in various stages of use and decay. The builders of such structures often took advantage of slopes and direction in choosing construction sites, frequently including a long overhang or forebay on one side, often the warm south face, in order to protect livestock from bad weather—the wood hammered with wrought-iron nails, the roof dry and tight, perhaps significantly better than the one atop the house, its functionality essential to protecting the valuable hay, livestock, and other goods beneath.

As I pass these barns amid the heavy haze of late summer, they all appear motionless, no creaking doors or cattle swishing their tales in the shade—not so much as the slightest swirl of tall grass, the flutter of a leaf. Of course, all the while, beyond my perceptions, there exists the reminder of constant, furious activity—energy unfolding: a barely perceptible breeze, the breaking down of cow manure, termites gnawing at the lower boards. Yet, these events may only be surmised. To my limited eyes the barns appear as frozen images, possessed of the stillness of objects unchanging. The Deist philosopher Gotthold Lessing maintained, "Since painting, because its signs or means of imitation can be combined only in space, must relinquish all representations of time, therefore progressive actions, as such, cannot come within its range. It must content itself with actions in space; in other words, with mere bodies, whose attitude lets us infer their action." Sometimes vision can be the same in the quality of images it paints upon the canvas of the mind, the limited gaze of human eyes met with the illusion of motionlessness, the actions it cannot see left to the devices of the imagination, summoned like ghosts from the hollow depths of perished experience.

In the evening, I am greeted by the literal human arrangement of images when, several miles down the road, I walk into the Hiland Drive-in: an outdoor cinema, its screen a consistent source of entertainment since 1952, improvements to it over the years having conspired to make it the largest viewing surface in the state of Virginia. Though I do not have a vehicle to sit in, the ticket man permits my entry, after which I walk about in the cool, deepening dusk, trying to find the best unoccupied piece of ground to sit on before the lights go down. In the midst of this search I am invited to climb into the long bed of a large pick-up truck, its three friendly occupants kindly motioning me to an empty lawn chair. They are local folks from nearby Rural Retreat, the man a garage owner, one of the women a waitress. Settling in comfortably, sipping something fruity and strong from an offered thermos, I think of the last chair I had sat in at the Dogwood Lodge, now half a hundred miles to the north. This night, I fancy I am probably the most grateful lawn chair occupant in the entire state of Virginia.

Drowsing through the film previews, I try to focus as best I can on the evening's main draw, *Alien vs. Predator,* remaining conscious enough at least to establish the plot: how the vast, super-wealthy, yet somehow bumbling, Weyland Corporation—an obvious amalgamation of any number of familiar big American businesses—detects a large, ancient pyramid buried beneath the arctic wastes, which turns out to be a spawning ground for a species of aliens bred for the sole purpose of being hunted once every century or so by another, more militant race of advanced anthropomorphic beings. The ill-fated Weyland employees—stock, clichéd, and boring (in other words, startlingly realistic corporate administrators)—get generous screen time early in the film—sharing photos of family members, exchanging bad dialogue, and so on—as the director makes a few half-hearted attempts at generating empathy for the cast before having them systematically impregnated and/or maimed and slaughtered by the warring extraterrestrials.

I fall asleep perhaps a little over halfway into the film, though I am nudged back into consciousness with time enough to light my pipe and witness the irrelevant conclusion. As the epigraph reads on the movie poster outside the drive-in, "Whoever wins . . . we lose," which was chosen I suppose to draw the viewer in and make human existence seem tenuous and suspenseful, but speaks to me instead as a kind of unintended warning, a guarantee, that this film will let you down regardless of the outcome. Infinitely more interesting explorations of the movie's themes appear in little-known, cinematic science-fiction hiccups of decades past, such as 1965's *Frankenstein Meets the Space Monster,* the script of which—composed, incidentally, in the Virginia foothills of the Blue Ridge Mountains—insinuates violence and impregnation rather than graphically conveying them, the desperate band of aliens from a war-ravaged sterile planet having landed in Puerto Rico for the purpose of abducting bikini-clad earth women as breeding stock to the tune of a British Invasion soundtrack. Forty years before *Alien vs. Predator* a particularly grim, autocratic character from *Frankenstein Meets the Space Monster* named General Fred Bowers bluntly summed up the role of the beleaguered earth dwellers in both films: "It's time to fish or cut bait."

It is fun to consider aliens, our ideas and images of them—the mirror we can never seem to escape even in the most outlandish of our creations—sitting here among my own kind. How often—even now, with access to a staggering array of visual technology—the villainous, eldritch creatures of science fiction and horror continue to appear as human-like bipeds rather than truly alien, perhaps wholly unrecognizable, forms of life. Or perhaps this is altogether appropriate, since, more often than not, the creatures end up coming across as not so foreign after all, having traveled not from another galaxy, but rather from the looking glass at the bottom of the archetypal abyss that attracts our darker rumina-tions—the distorted images, foreignness made literal, of that which exists inside us. It reminds me too that, even were this drive-in empty, in viewing this outra-geous film I would still somehow be in the company of humanity—something I have trouble remembering from time to time out there along the open lonely stretches of road. As the German philosopher Martin Heidegger put it, "Man is a being-in-the world, in that by participation and involvement the world becomes constitutive of man's being." As the credits begin to roll, the woman sitting next to me passes the plaid thermos of vodka-laced jungle juice. "Kill it!" she says. The liquid, warm in my mouth and stomach, emanates throughout my body, a heady reminder of all my parts as well as the bodies of those who surround me— an ill-defined feeling of human fellowship among strangers: the people in the truck, the drive-in, even the imagined denizens of the region, of our world, lonely in its circuitous journey through the frigid void of space. However super-ficial or finite our interactions may be, the world that we live in remains a world shared with others.

Next morning I enter Smyth County, which did not exist in 1800, much of the land from which it eventually would be formed having belonged to the inglori-ously slain James Patton during the decades of the mid-eighteenth century. Shortly beyond the boundary I glimpse a diminutive low-flying aircraft making a landing approach, watching as it disappears below the horizon. A brief distance ahead I discover its destination: the Mountain Empire Airport, a small landing field used mostly by private, single-engine planes. From a vantage point just off

Route 11, I can watch planes coming in and taking off with interstate traffic behind them, 81 lying parallel only a couple of hundred feet north of the second
runway: a deep, visionary field of motion and transportation, planes lifting and
landing, automotive traffic rushing behind them, northeast and southwest, the
plane that takes off catching up to the car beyond it, before passing it, lifting up
above it—an overlapped image of modern travel that feels to me like some curious recitation of a dream.

Just past the Mountain Empire Airport, not far from the red door of Pleasant Hill Lutheran Church, the Appalachian Trail crosses Route 11, a brief stretch
of perhaps eight miles where the modern continuous footpath strays from Glade
Mountain and the Blue Ridge toward Little Brushy Mountain, Walker Mountain, and on down into Brushy Valley, where it skirts along Possum Jaw Creek
in the shadow of Bryant's Knob. On the lookout for a nearby strip mine, I had
forgotten all about the Appalachian Trail—at least this particular section of it,
where it temporarily forsakes one range of mountains for another. I hike in a
short distance both ways to see what I can see, failing to encounter anyone,
though the late-summer trail nevertheless appears worn, packed and dusty in
the middle, grooved boot and shoe prints, mud molds dry now and hard, along
its outer edges. Heading back toward Highway 11, however, from the section of
path that strays along Dry Run and Davis Valley, I am met by a hiker journeying
from the south who identifies himself by the trail name Glass. Each of us happy
to have encountered someone else, we swap trail mix and destinations while
drinking water. A former marine, Glass had left Springer Mountain slightly
before the summer solstice, a determined single-season through-hiker traveling
light, fast, and alone. Our divergent directions and purposes have conspired to
lay out separate roads before us, but Glass, low on supplies and plagued by the
through-hiker's periodic craving for heavy civilized food, decides to accompany
me south to the nearby village of Atkins, the last reliable supply point before
Pearisburg, a town along the New River near the West Virginia border.

As our various conversations eventually would reveal, Glass, like many
hikers of the Appalachian Trail, was not so much motivated by the physical
odyssey before him, but rather by the search for a number of abstract things,
including the nature of himself. He carried with him a small cache of hardcover
self-help books, perhaps six or seven, which surprised me on account of the
extra weight they added to his pack. Although he would follow my suggestion
of cutting off the front and back flaps, he remained doggedly determined not
to leave a book behind until it was read—the mastery of the pages motivated by
the prospect of a lighter pack, a more enlightened mind. With a palpable sense

of accomplishment, he told me he had already mailed two to his home address, somewhere in the Northeast.

We eat at the Atkins Grocery and Deli, a place that likely enjoys a healthy measure of trail business, before resolving to spend the afternoon consuming calories and resting: that is, drinking beer and watching television, numbing our tired bodies and brains—hanging out, you might say—at the aptly named Relax Inn. Possessing on its grounds an old covered bridge, the inn strikes me as yet another encountered intersection point for the past and present: its qualities oddly at odds yet somehow shared, divergent styles and means jumbled across time. For Glass, it is a place where the skies are clouded and the storms of the past threaten to overcast darkly the present. In his late twenties, haggard and a little wild-eyed—which, after all, is an appearance shared by many through-hikers—Glass radiates a distinctive sense of displacement, maladjustment, and even fragility, odd for a youngish ex-serviceman, that makes his unusual trail name seem somehow appropriate, though I remain unsure if the connection has occurred to him—his blurry, wavering person of the present forged by the fire, sand, and trace elements of a place far away, on the other side of the world. Yet, for all this, for all our own separate experiences and beliefs, or perhaps the collective lack thereof, we are not all that different, bibulously lounging here, drinking Yuengling, myself headed south following in the wake of ghosts and ancestors two centuries distant, and Glass, northbound, trying to determine who he was and is, and, perhaps a little presumptuously, who he might come to be for the rest of his life. Only a couple of years older than he and fraught with many doubts, I have no opinions or suggestions I feel good about when he asks for some after crushing an empty beer can against his forehead. All I have to offer is a mangled, partially remembered paraphrase of something very general by the French philosopher Merleau-Ponty which sounds not unlike New Age self-help: "Man is not determined by his past, his temperament, his situation; but neither is he radically free in relation to these motivations." I elaborate half-seriously that I don't believe one should seek to resolve his life too much since, for me, order is the natural enemy of the individual mind. To this Glass only replies that he hates the French, but I write down the philosopher's name on a piece of hotel stationery anyway and slip it inside his backpack the next morning after breakfast, just in case he finishes all the self-help books and needs something else to read.

Several miles down the road, entering Marion, which in the 1770s was known as Royal Oak, I cross the middle fork of the Holston River, a body of water I hope to trace in earnest if I can make it into Tennessee. In Marion I pause briefly to pick up fresh produce from the Pioneer Restaurant before pressing on, the balls of my feet exuding a spring they have lacked for some time, my pace recently having been more leisurely, a conspiracy of circumstance and general fatigue. But now I feel wonderful, almost as if I am the recipient of a new body, though I am reminded that my appearance is less than desirable when I glimpse myself in a large gym mirror while stopping in for water at Mike's Health and Fitness. Beneath the moderately aged beard, my face is thinner, my body lithe, though it projects a subtle gaunt quality rather than an athletic musculature— the appearance of something forced from time to time to call upon more fuel than it has: to, in effect, feed upon itself. I have shed pounds while eating poorly, consuming fatty foods and beer at odd hours, at long intervals or before going to sleep, gorging myself whenever a store or restaurant materializes into being from the far-glimpsed mirage I initially take it to be. Of course, grease-laden frontier food contained large amounts of fat as well, and its availability often was sporadic: subject to the impact of weather patterns on crops, the migrations of animals. Fat stores, however, were useful then, often drawn upon: for walking great distances, working from dark to dark, or enabling the body to negotiate periods of famine. In our own time, this chair-bound byproduct era of industrialization, few of us work our bodies to their physical potentials, though many of us still eat as though deprivation were imminent.

Below a hill that affords a fine view of the Appalachian Mountains, I cross the middle fork of the Holston again at Seven Mile Ford, carved out of land that once belonged to William Campbell, the hero of King's Mountain, who also established an infamous reputation by executing several Tories without trials or due process. Once a significant crossing point, the area is quiet now, sleepy, indistinguishable from many another southwestern Virginia hamlet. As the German philosopher Johan Gottfried von Herder would say, "The time of flourishing is gone," but then who is to say what the nature of flourishing truly is or what the future may have in store for this place or any other—or even, in that present of long ago, what destiny was to hold for Herder himself? I remember distinctly standing in the Herderplatz in Weimar, the town where he had died nearly two centuries earlier, in the last hours of a late spring afternoon, having walked from the Bauhaus Museum, debating whether or not to wander along the river for a while or head back to my quarters at Beethovenplatz, perhaps stopping by the market on the way. The thought of Herder was present with me there, for I had read and then spoken his name—an appropriate occurrence since chief among his many aims was a desire to clarify the process of thought arriving from language. My own mind shudders at that undertaking, its contents far too jumbled for any such task, its state frequently murky: a limbo inside which what is now, gone, and to come collectively play notes that are by turns dissonant and overlapping, creating a music of existence in which everything and nothing, substance and emptiness, vie for the definition of the object(s) at hand. Though my vision remains unsteady, its confusion does manage to lend a peculiar perspective to my view of the places I encounter, the terrain and man-made structures before me alternately blurred, tempered, filled by an incomplete knowledge, an image, of what once was.

Here, along this narrow middle stretch of the Holston River, is no exception: watching the water as I walk, studying or erasing the man-made features along it, contemplating the manner in which it would have been followed, skirted, viewed, in a time before roads. Although this region was still considered Indian country, Colonel James Patton, the same gentleman who would abdicate both his scalp and his life to the Shawnee at Draper's Meadows in 1755, had begun surveying and selling areas of the Holston River region of southwestern Virginia in the 1740s. Stephen Holston (anglicized from Holstein), the German for whom the river is named, settled on its middle fork in the 1740s, raising corn for a time before selling his land and moving on. Though Holston would not retain his property and Patton was hacked to death, each met his doom, embraced his destiny, having taken the chance of achieving something new and different in a place far from others. And chance—or in their cases, desperate gambles, high-odds castings of the bones—strikes me as the main justification—the most appropriate thought arriving from the apprehension of their names—for recalling their lives now. However unfounded he may have been in his myopic overvaluing of humanity, the philosopher F. C. S. Schiller was right when he maintained, "Real freedom involves indeterminism."

Of course, freedom gives rise to many eccentricities: the preferences and actions we cannot explain, the unreasoned directives we are allowed to follow in performing the deeds that define us. And though we may share identical perspectives and courses of action, the outcomes they bear back to us often are very different. At a discount tobacco outlet I purchase a quantity of the organic dark leaf for my clay pipe, altogether aware that the habit is deemed unhealthy, yet knowing that my body's individual response to the chemical composition of the plant is different from the reactions of others. Though ultimate outcomes often may appear similar, we all respond variously to identical things, bodily and in the abstract. The poetic thinker Stanley Burnshaw noted that lysergic acid diethylamide (LSD), when ingested, competes with serotonin for a specific enzyme. Yet, as Burnshaw explained, "No two organisms have the identical constitution or identical ways of responding, hence nobody can predict the outcome . . . whether the thought processes will be mildly or severely affected, whether the taker's brain will be temporarily or permanently altered." Thus, some people are intensely altered, even driven mad, by various stimuli and narcotics while others remain largely unaffected, body and brain chemistry creating in each of us different limitations and possibilities, the reactions that are ourselves.

An immediacy, a kind of case in point, is lent to this train of thought when I nearly meet my end—as violent, sudden, and senseless a potential demise as any I have yet recounted—obliviously crossing a dangerously narrow, shoulder-less bridge, the road that had been utterly empty occupied suddenly by vehicles speeding toward one another from opposite directions, myself between them with nowhere to go save over the bridge. Even as a pale blue car sweeps into view from around a curve in the oncoming left lane before me, I hear the rumble of a larger-engined vehicle approaching directly from behind, having time enough only to turn and greet the considerable bulk of a dump truck and its piercing overlapped cries of brakes and sliding rubber, as it awkwardly skids to a stop per-haps five feet from me, the car sweeping past in the other lane, vague music blar-ing, seemingly unaware, speed unchanged. Heart fluttering, pins and needles in my legs, goose bumps everywhere, I turn and jog to the end of the bridge as the dump truck clumsily changes gears and begins rumbling forward. Trotting off the highway and onto the roadside grass where the bridge terminates, I turn to watch the large dingy red vehicle, which slows as it nears me, its driver, a bearded man in a yellow baseball cap, leaning toward the open passenger window, eyes hard. "Stay off the fucking road, dumb ass!" are the words hollered at me, before the truck engine revs and I am left alone, shaky but unharmed.

Momentarily heeding the driver's advice, I move farther from the highway and slip off my pack, removing my water bottle before unsteadily sitting down, adrenaline pumping, hands shaking slightly, forearm hair still at attention—my body's chemical responses to the imminence of death. Rather than replaying my obliviousness, the inattention to my surroundings that had nearly been my undoing, I do my best to breathe deep and focus on where I am, the grounding quality of my surroundings. In the process of clearing my mind, an enormous weeping willow on the other side of the road attracts my attention. Like many other people, I have always considered willows beautiful and mysterious, mostly on account of their long drooping branches which hide their trunks, the true centers of their beings, not unlike long-haired humans concealing their eyes and faces behind wavy locks. There is something calming about willows, something sleepy and secret, and I am glad to have this one here to invite my consideration, subdue my pulse. It has always struck me that on some primitive level long hair continues to suggest a nameless fascination for humans in the same mysterious manner that willows do. In fact, in most cultures the transition from long to short hair among males occurred along with a shift in overall perspective from the magical to the worldly, a cutting away of nature's perceived excess, a shearing of the animal. For a man to have long hair after this cultural change was to be considered quaint, needlessly whimsical, feeble-minded. As the old Russian proverb goes, "Hair long, mind short." Of course, it was acceptable for women to cultivate their locks since in most cultures they were expected and encouraged to remain ignorant and capricious, defined by their animal bodies. Yet, for all this negativity of connotation, hair in abundance, especially for artists, remains an indeterminate symbol and guardian of that original human magic, of the unshorn body and mind—a curtain of wavy strands, behind which glint a pair of indefinite orbs.

All this is not to say that, as much as any other physical characteristic, hair does not remain an incidental ornament, a superficiality, of our literal lives. Against the prospect of death—of meeting our ends on roads, hills, rivers; of my own long blonde hair, lying bloody with the rest of me, not unlike one of the many mangled animal corpses I have encountered, on some narrow southwestern Virginia bridge—the patterns of our lives exist, draw, and repeat themselves on much deeper levels. The German writer Ernst Jünger, who lived to the age of 102 after fighting in both world wars (receiving wounds on fourteen different occasions), experimenting with powerful psychoactive drugs, and traveling extensively, concluded at the age of 90, "If a man's life shows an overall unity, this is due to his character. You can be thrown into the most diverse situations. Yet what we might call the 'melody of life' has been there from the very outset. And until the ship goes down, we keep playing the very same tune, as they did on the Titanic." Though our vessels be ever sinking, we hum our individual refrains even as the waters of nonexistence rise about our ankles. And except for those of us who resolve to throw themselves overboard, to dictate the nature and hour of their drowning, we have no real alternative but to continue on our sinking ships, or, if our bodies make landfall, to keep our pace, our tune and time, in the midst of our journeys, though each footstep, another spent moment of life, brings us closer to death.

The word Chilhowie means "Valley of Many Deer," but I do not perceive any while passing through the village that bears that name, though I encounter and enter in succession the Tastee Freeze, Food City, and Speedwash Laundromat, each a useful stop albeit experienced in a kind of somnambulist haze. Whether or not I am still unconsciously stunned at nearly having been crushed by a dump truck or simply worn down by the constant mental toil of close observation, I cannot determine. While remarking from time to time on the trials of the body, I have considered little the effects of long journeys on the mind, especially those undertakings in which the intellect is not only expected to process its surroundings for itself, but expend additional energy attempting to conceptualize them in such a way as to achieve a coherence useful to others. In general, extensive hiking is really more a matter of the mind than the body. It is not athletic in the least. Good athletes are fast, strong, agile, and possessed of acute hand-eye coordination. None of these qualities are required in order to walk great distances, to bear the firmament as it bears you over a span of days. Provided that your body is more or less functional, the key ingredient is merely to be possessed of the will to do it. But, of course, even the firmest of wills wanders and wanes eventually, the process of which I am perhaps becoming a victim at last. ·

Along with the old bodily plagues that always accompany this kind of travel—being overly hot, cold, wet, hungry, thirsty, constantly fatigued—I have been eyed with malignant suspicion, stalked, showered in trash and fuck yous, and nearly run over—all of which conspire to wear upon the senses over time. Yet, these are not experiences to take pride in or perversely celebrate in the tradition of Dostoyevsky's underground man, that alienated self-conscious cynic who, in sneering at humanity's barbarity and inviting its rancor, only succeeded in painfully disconnecting and dehumanizing himself. They are, instead, invitations, reminders, of the tenuous nature of our being, the vividness of our interactions in the now, which, in turn, provides us with a greater appreciation and valuing of our future lives—a kind of hope—as well as those already lived: the patterned existences of the past. As the theological philosopher Franz Rosenzweig said, "To escape the power of the past, to transcend the law which constitutes causation, the moment must, at each instant, be reborn. The future is the inexhaustible well from which moments are drawn; every instant new-born moments rise and replace the moments disappearing into the past." So moments cling to us through memory even as the essence of them is abdicated forever, continually replaced by the unlimited reservoirs of that which is yet to come.

Among the spent moments, here in this place, is the now-distant measure of time expended by Dr. Thomas Walker, who in 1750 had helped Samuel Stalnaker build a log cabin nearby—the farthest western settlement of that period. Stalnaker had been one of the first Germans, along with Jost Hite and several others, to enter the Shenandoah Valley in the 1730s. However, his decision to eventually part company with other families and venture so far south would have grave consequences. In the mid-1750s he and his family would be taken prisoner during a Shawnee raid and though Stalnaker himself would escape captivity, his wife and son, Adam, were killed. Against all threat of danger and death, all sense and caution, something seemed to draw Stalnaker to the personal trials, independence, and isolation demanded by the frontier wilderness. Could it have been that in naming his son Adam he hoped to cultivate his own edenic garden here, himself its maker and master? On account of the language barrier and other cultural differences—as well as the practical collective endeavors of planting, harvesting, slaughtering livestock, and raising houses and barns—German settlers usually moved together in groups, reluctant to strike out on their own. Yet Stalnaker was a resourceful hunter, trapper, and guide who often strayed into the wilderness alone for long periods of time. He was the first European to come upon the Cumberland Gap and knew the ancestral Indian paths of eastern Kentucky long before Daniel Boone ever ventured into that area. In fact, Dr. Walker would ask him to guide an exploratory party into the Kentucky country in 1750. Although Stalnaker declined to accompany Walker, on such excursions he would have worn a cape to wrap about himself in foul weather and which also served to cover a loose-fitting shirt of deerskin or linsey. Clasped over the shirt, about his waist, would have been a belt of leather from which hung a hunting knife and possibly a tomahawk. Somewhere on his person—whether in a sling, pouch, or sack—he would have carried provisions: dried meat, meal, pemmican, salt. His breeches and leggings would have been of deerskin and possibly his shoes, though he may have had means enough to purchase boots. In cold weather Stalnaker probably would have worn a cap wrought of raccoon or beaver hide. However, his most crucial implements, both for hunting and personal safety, would have been his flintlock rifle—probably a *Jaegar,* a product of Pennsylvania-German gunsmiths—and the accompanying powder horn and shot pouch.

Like that of many frontiersmen, Stalnaker's relationship with Indians was ambivalent. He amicably treated with them during his travels, and his house was an occasional meeting place for Indian leaders and His Majesty's Commissioners. On the other hand, Stalnaker was deprived of his family by the Shawnee and later pressed for the construction of forts in the area. Over the course of his many journeys, Stalnaker likely came to understand their views and ways better than all but a handful of colonials, yet what this knowledge ultimately meant to him remains a mystery. Bloody episodes between settlers and Indians were rarer and defensive measures later to arrive in this particular southwestern portion of Virginia. In fact, south of the vicinity of Stalnaker's dwelling, I come upon the site of Fort Kilmachronan, not built until 1776 and of which there now remains no sign—its rough wooden beams and boards long since rotted, or carried away to lend heat to a fireplace or material for some other building: as invisible and forgotten as the events that once took place here, as capricious and mysterious as Stalnaker himself.

Part of our whole life is an attempt to discover when our spontaneity is whimsical and irresponsible and when it is an expression of our deepest tendencies and self. The other, of course, is the fundamental reckoning and balancing of all we touch, see, feel, and otherwise perceive. Somewhere between these two phenomena lies my own minor decision to enter the Ernie Sullins Outlet on the outskirts of Abingdon, a kind of thrift store, where I buy a shirt to replace one that has become almost threadbare, offering little cushion against the rubbing of my pack. Incidentally, much of Abingdon's early history too, including its original naming, is heavily steeped in whimsy and curious perception, those indefinite catalysts by which things come to be known. Walking through town, I encounter the site of Black's Fort, named for Joseph Black, who built the structure in 1774 for the purpose of protecting local residents from Indian attacks. Yet, it was Daniel Boone who had passed through the area much earlier, in 1760, and given it the provocative name Wolf Hills after a pack of cave-dwelling wolves attacked his dogs. Such creatures were common in the area and a nuisance to settler's livestock, but as early as the end of the eighteenth century their population had been greatly diminished. In 1785 the Virginia General Assembly raised the bounty on mature wolves to more than three hundred pounds of tobacco per head, the dark leaf preferable to American and British currency, both of which were in use at the time. Bounty hunters brought great sacks full of decapitated wolf heads to outposts like Fort Chiswell, where they would be reimbursed for their morbid labors. The sack set upon a great wooden table, the putrid heads spilled forth, dried or rotting, in various states of decomposition, a dream feast for maggots, while a government official busily recorded the number and whether or not the skulls were full-grown or merely those of pups, since the latter fetched a much lower price.

Like many other places, modern Abingdon is seemingly oblivious to the more grisly and capricious nuances of its past, offering its history instead in a shiny upbeat package, always positioning its best side toward the highway—a strategy that appears to have worked rather well, for on this sunny day of late summer slick-looking tourists abound, ambling along streets, large shopping bags in hand, full, I suspect, of local souvenirs. I buy some perishable keepsakes of my own at the farmer's market, well-shaped creations of the soil of

Washington County, its minerals and other qualities drawn from the ground by the shallow root systems of plants and fruit trees, lodging in the buds as they swell, plucked along with the fruit—brought here to be sold and, in turn, consumed by me: passed into my body and borne away.

I am glad to depart Abingdon and relieved when the town's moderately heavy tourist traffic is funneled back onto 81. Local fruit having failed to appease my hunger entirely, I undergo a greasy calorie infusion south of town at Hi-Lo Burger before pausing again, a few more miles down the road, at Red Barn Tobacco—an outlet and gift shop located inside a large converted barn built originally in the German style. Soon thereafter begins the outlying sprawl of Bristol, land and businesses in transition, physical features and man-made monikers cropping up or vanishing into oblivion forever. Among them the heaped ruins of the Robert E. Lee Motel, while close by a relatively new-looking Christ the King Apartments appears to enjoy a healthy collection of tenants, though it too, like all these local human phenomena, myself included, remains in my peculiar mind's eye only dust on a dragonfly's wing, matter riding the flutter of time.

Inside these outward constructions, those still inhabited, are the people and lives that dwell and unfold within, the worried faces entering and emerging from doorways, bodies hustling to and from their motorized vehicles, eyes and expressions bent upon something other than what is before them—the abstract anxieties of civilization. Rosenzweig warned, "Man should remain human; he should not be converted into a thing, a part of the world, prey to its organization." Yet freedom from man's system usually involves some kind of successful preliminary negotiation of it—an intervaled capitulation to the rules, a planned deferral, until one has the means to defy or ignore it. This is an opportunity those crushed by the system at the beginning are never afforded, while the rest of us play along, or pretend to, with the banalities of society, paying lip service to that lesser, crude beauty which constitutes human culture.

The ground begins to fall away toward Bristol, which was surveyed in 1749 under the name Sapling Grove Tract. A few decades later, in 1771, a Welsh-descended Marylander named Evan Shelby, a veteran of Lord Dunmore's War destined to become Kentucky's first governor, would build a substantial fort and store on the banks of Beaver Creek which would collectively come to be known as Shelby's Station. Tract or station, then and now, Bristol has always been a popular stopping spot—a place between places—for travelers drawn elsewhere. Today, the city is split into neat halves by the Virginia-Tennessee state line, home to a kind of limbo of identity, hemmed in geologically by a series of knobs to the south and east, and the foothills of Walker Mountain to the north. Feeling

the press of terrain, the dimming of daylight, knowing the Tennessee line to be
near, I stop to pass the night among a specific group of modern through-travelers:
the motor-home contingent at the RV-laden Lee Highway Campground. Massive vessels, drawn side by side, their rope-like power cords plugged into nearby
outlets, these recreation vehicles resemble so many anchored boats come in to
port, tethered for some indeterminate span of time, resting in this inland harbor—a respite from the great storm and tide of the interstate. And just as sailors
and fishermen may socialize and interact at a dockside inn, so the various RV
operators swap food or discuss vehicle maintenance while the evening grills are
fired and children run about—an adult, here or there, embarking on or returning from a walk to alleviate a long day of stiff chair-bound travel; myself, by
contrast, sprawled in the dampening grass, savoring the body's stillness, absorbing the rewards of motionlessness.

Sitting beside my tent, pipe lit, drowsy in the midst of the motion surrounding me, the flutter in twilight before night, I glimpse an enormously obese man
climbing laboriously out of his recreation vehicle. From his features and hue
it is easy to discern that he is of Indian ancestry—the only such person I have
encountered over the course of my entire journey. For all his ponderous bulk,
he walks softly with a slight limp, attracting no one's attention, disappearing in
the direction of the main office. Painted on the side of his RV in large purple
cursive are the words *Tenaco's Ride.*

I empty my pipe bowl in the grass beside my tent and lean back to watch for
the arrival of the stars, the heavens dimming above the last of a pink horizon,
waiting for the mosquitoes to set in on me in earnest. Despite everything that
has passed, the skies are all but the same in this still new century, the signs and
objects we ponder now in the heavens nearly identical to those gazed upon by
the North American travelers of the distant past, Indian or settler, bound in the
same direction along a path, a wagon road, a highway, an interstate—*Athowominee,* which is becoming to me more and more an idea, a direction, a bearing,
than an actual road: as instinctual and indefinite, as unknowable, as the senses of
the animals who first established it, migrating vaguely, joined in time, followed,
by the bipeds who sought their flesh, their fur. Since that time in which it was
established by the pounding of hooves, the soft pad of feet, *Athowominee* ever
has welcomed and borne new travelers: animals, Indians, settlers, and modern
wayfarers, propelled in their chariots of fiberglass and steel on an all but invisible
route of antiquity clad now in concrete and asphalt.

Athowominee, whatever it once was, is gone, along with all those beings
who suffered and died, the tears and blood of millions, along it. Yet an idea
of it, a roughly translated spirit, remains, palpable even among these modern

travelers—their possessions, their lives, packed into RVs, as once they would have been into horse-drawn wagons. And despite our divergent means of travel, among them I feel a kinship, for the road beckons to us all—our immediate hopes, lives, drawn out upon it. Though it is likely that none of us will ever see each other again, tonight we sleep close together, and on the morrow the road that lies before shall be the one that each of us embarks upon. All of that, however, remains woven, for now, into the as-yet-unrealized unfolding of a day still to come; in the twinkling of the present, sleep arrives with the stars and takes us: the slumber of the weary traveler bears us our separate ways.

TENNESSEE

Holston River Valley

The land bears the scars
of minds whose history
was imprinted by no example
of a forebearing mind, corrected,
beloved. A mind cast loose
in whim and greed makes
nature its mirror, and the garden
falls with the man. . . .

—Wendell Berry, "Where"

The philosophy of history is an interpretation of
man's past in the light of his ideal development.

—George Santayana

As Bristol is divided by the Virginia-Tennessee state line, creating two cities possessed of the appearance of one, so its main thoroughfare, Route 11, the Lee Highway of Virginia, is made twain, severed within the limits of a split city: 11 East actually strays south of Bristol along a natural pass between Beaver Creek Knobs and Whitetop Knobs, while 11 West skirts along the Virginia-Tennessee border in the general direction it announces. Still following on foot, as I have for nearly four hundred miles now, the Indian path *Athowominee* in the ghostly tracks of my frontier ancestors, who passed through this region over two centuries ago—bound, as I am now, for the ever-nearer Smoky Mountains—I trace my course along the more venerable western branch of 11, steps drawing me closer to the geological confines of the Holston River Valley.

Home as it is to split cities, divided roads, hilly terrain, it comes as little surprise that this portion of eastern Tennessee, once a western section of the North Carolina colony, was a region of contention and limbo during the last decades of the eighteenth century. The mid-1780s saw the arrival of the Franklin

controversy—a clumsy, messy attempt by certain regional leaders to establish a
new state independent of North Carolina. What ensued was a violent, corruption-
laced struggle for power between John Sevier, a man made famous for his vengeful hatred of Indians—most notably, his brutal burning campaigns against the
Cherokee—and one of only a handful of slaveholders in the region, and John
Tipton, a veteran of Lord Dunmore's War who lived on a farm near Sinking
Creek, just two miles south of present-day Johnson City. Maintaining a closer
allegiance to North Carolina while Sevier sided with the doomed Franklin
government, Tipton is said to have come off the better, at least in the short
term, although the attacks the two men heaped upon one another with the aid
of their goons largely negated any political gain for either party, while also needlessly inhibiting the peace and progress of what eventually would become East
Tennessee. Such behavior on the frontier, however, was more or less the norm.
Writing in 1782, the Frenchman Crévecoeur characterized western North American leaders as "often in a perfect state of war; that of man against man, sometimes decided by blows, sometimes by means of the law; that of man against
every wild inhabitant of these venerable woods, of which they are come to dis-
possess them." For the Englishman of letters Samuel Johnson, Americans of the
same period collectively constituted "a race of convicts." More than two centuries later, the Mississippi writer Eudora Welty would trace the same essential
spirit of these descriptions to the people in her state she liked to call rednecks:
"Scare everybody, outwit everybody, beat everybody, kill everybody—that's
the frontiersman's mentality."

    In the midst of these mordant reflections, walking alongside the highway,
sticky heat of late summer pressed about me, saturating hair and clothes, I am
brought back to the immediacy of the present by a vague dizziness and peculiar
weakness of the limbs. Attributing the sensations to overheating, I pause beneath
the sparse shade of a roadside loblolly pine, retrieving water from my pack and
drinking as well as pouring it upon my head. When the symptoms fail to dissipate after several moments of rest I know the problem lies elsewhere—a reaction,
possibly, to something I have consumed, a virus: something against which my
body feels it must fight. For now, however, here, along the road, there is nothing
for it but to keep going, albeit at a more measured pace. In fact, as bad as I am
beginning to feel, I manage to summon a perspectived degree of thankfulness
for the measure of good health I have enjoyed thus far, over the course of the
journey's first four hundred miles. And, still dwelling on the bright side, I reflect
that there are, after all, treatments for whatever malady I may have that simply
would not have existed in the time of my traveling frontier ancestors. To be sure,

remedies, panaceas, and anodynes existed back then if you happened to be feeling poorly, though their degrees of effectiveness could be quite varied. A laceration, for example, might have been sucked and then filled with salt or gunpowder, or perhaps merely spat upon with tobacco juice. And injuries and illnesses of greater severity often were treated with techniques most modern people would consider crude, dangerous, and gruesome. For instance, scalped settlers left for dead sometimes managed to pull through, in which cases holes would be bored into their skulls for the purpose of facilitating skin growth. James Robertson, having learned the primitive procedure from a Dr. Vance in 1776, reported, "I have found that a flat pointed, straight awl is the best instrument to bore with as the skull is thick and somewhat difficult to penetrate. When the awl is nearly through the instrument should be borne more lightly upon. The time to quit boring is when a reddish fluid appears on the point of the awl . . . The scalped head cures slowly. It skins remarkably slow, generally taking two years." All of this would have been performed outside, next to a camp fire probably, perhaps with the anesthetic benefit of whiskey, perhaps not.

The more minor aches and pains of the time usually were treated with animal grease, the rubbing probably affording more therapeutic benefit than the substance itself. I have my football career to thank for a six-inch steel plate in my left leg (the aching presence of which often notifies me of weather changes and for which I have a special airplane pass), a formerly dislocated shoulder that sometimes throbs, and Achilles tendonitis that periodically flairs up. And each of these things, regardless of the amounts of lotion or grease I apply, will only wear and worsen with age. As Tibullus said, "Youth goes by us too swiftly, nor returns, nor stays at rest." Miraculously, however, the body usually learns to manage and compensate for its damages over time; worse, in the present, is the unaccounted-for mystery of this newly arrived virus or pathogen, the real root of my discomfort. The nature of my malady leads me to recall darkly too that as much as nine-tenths of the North American Indian population was destroyed by European-carried pathogens: everything from chicken pox to African yellow fever—an event many Europeans took to be the rightful supernatural anni-hilation of the heathen by an accommodating Christian god. The sickly writer Kafka proclaimed, "I like the Americans because they are healthy and optimis-tic"; I wonder whom exactly he was talking about.

I had hoped to enter the land of my more immediate ancestors under a shroud of ideal circumstances, but chance and destiny have ruled otherwise. As Herder might have tried to remind me, "The sense of the world must lie outside the world. In the world everything is as it is, and everything happens as it does

◇◇

happen: *in* it no value exists." It is an unfortunate welcome to Tennessee but carry on I must, continuing to note my surroundings as best I can, for what they are, beyond the shortcomings, the tenuous being, of the plagued animal body.

It is through Sullivan County I am slowly journeying, founded in 1779 and named for John Sullivan, the son of a highly educated Irish exile who distinguished himself in the American Revolution and afterward received favorable posts in George Washington's administration. Whether a result of my poor health or something more intrinsic in the area's makeup, Tennessee's 11 West feels somehow more forlorn, a loneliness that is more than solitude. There are fewer businesses and more rundown structures here than along the vast section of 11 that runs through Virginia. Against my ill condition and drab surroundings I try to cheer myself as best I can, reminding myself of Blaise Pascal's assertion: "To be miserable is to know one's self to be so, but to know one's self to be miserable is to be great." As bad as I feel, such a philosophy appears only silly and grandiose to me, and I wonder if perhaps Pascal was joking when he coined it. Schopenhauer, on the other hand, was more measured: "By his understanding man forms the world of phenomena, and by his reason he achieves harmony in a world of suffering."

Doing my best to take refuge in the realm of abstractions, of reasoning, I amble along—mixing and matching, confusing, ideas—stumbling occasionally, until the chorus of the body's agonies drowns out the quieter patterns of the mind and I take a break, or rather give out, at Waterman's Store, entering stagger-footed and probably a little crazy-looking, the man behind the counter giving me a guarded stare. Visiting the restroom and purchasing bottled water, I return to the highway as deliberately as I can. If anything, however, the water makes the dizziness and disorder of the mind worse. After perhaps a mile of slow walking I leave the road for the shade of a small wood, air cool as a result of its close proximity to Reedy Creek. On a rootless bed of dead leaves I unroll my foam pad and drop down upon it, the leafy canopy above me slightly rotating counter clockwise as the ceiling might above the bed of a drunken man. It is with a numbed, addled stare that I watch the shifting bits of sky beyond the uppermost branches until an uneasy sleep descends.

I awake at dusk a couple of feet from the sleeping pad, a rock beneath my shoulder, covered in sweat and mosquito bites, bits of leaves and dirt clinging to my damp hair and skin. I feel much better, though, even when I stand up, and resolve to walk for a time amid the cooler hours of evening. From my night spent in Bristol I know the moon is approaching its fullness, the phase when nightwalking is ideal. I have always enjoyed nocturnal wandering when the light of the moon is generous enough, pausing in the midst of my day hiking around mid-afternoon and dozing in a shady place until well after dark. It is during such late night journeys, when the road, still warm from the day's sun, is empty and open and the moon revealing more of itself, that the mind tends to wander and the eyes play games with the lunar glow, which often seems to cast a perfect coat of ghostly winter's snow upon the whole landscape, even as the humidity of late summer presses near. Time and distance become different too, not slower or longer but cast differently—the dreamlike unfolding of a moonlight mile passing under intervals of reflected paleness and the unceasing arrival of ancient starlight.

It is beneath such a veil of moonlight that I enter the city limits of Kingsport, marked too by a nearby sign for the Hillbilly Vette Shop. The bemusement I feel at the name of the business, however, is quickly erased by the noise of a vehicle decelerating behind me. Turning to perceive a pair of headlights drifting onto the shoulder I am walking along, I move over into the ditch to make way. When the car—a white four-door American-made model, a Ford perhaps—pulls up alongside me I am brought even with the open passenger window, beyond which, on the driver's side, sits a man, ball cap pulled low about his eyes, his bare right arm extended toward me, the hand of which aims in the direction of my face a semiautomatic pistol of indeterminate make and caliber.

"Gimme watcha got" are the words that come out of the car. From my right pocket I slowly withdraw a credit card, explaining as casually as I can that I have no wallet and my backpack is full of dirty clothes and camping gear. I hold out the credit card but the driver tells me to empty my pack. I swing it around slowly, undo the top and dump the filthy, foul-smelling, dirt-streaked clothes and gear onto the roadside. The odor of the heaped contents must drift into the car for the driver covers his nose and mouth with his left hand. "Nasty motherfucker" are the words that reach me before tires screech and the car jerks back onto the highway, speeding off toward downtown Kingsport.

Possibly because of my illness, my being slightly out of sorts, I am not especially shaken by the encounter, kneeling, after gazing down the road for several moments, to scrape my rank possessions back into my pack. I am, however, suddenly very tired, as if all the miles I have walked suddenly have descended upon my body, revisited it, simultaneously. Rising to one knee, I bring the pack around to my shoulders stiffly and awkwardly, the way a feeble, elderly person might. Slowly, I rise and continue down the road, feeling only half-awake, brownish-orange glow of city street lights having erased the stars from the sky, diminished the moon's light. Miles unfolding in a daze, I check into a motel at some point toward morning, finding a bed onto which I fall rather than slide into, slumber upon me almost before my body strikes the smooth top covers.

Late next morning I am awakened by a Comfort Inn cleaning woman and manage to take a shower before tardily checking out. Refreshed and clear-headed, greeted again by the busy highway, the events of the previous night cause me greater uneasiness in retrospect, though I conclude that everything had unfolded about as well as could have been expected: no shots fired, the foul stench of my possessions an unexpected ally. Anticipating just such an occurrence, I had resolved before the trip to carry little or no cash on me, only a credit card, which I could easily deactivate by phone if stolen. I had brought with me no wallet or other form of identification, meaning that if I were killed and my card taken, no one would know the name of my body if it were ever found, stumbled upon, like some old high-line pole, half-rotted along the highway. Yet, in a strange albeit selfish way, that had appealed to me too: the idea of dying anonymously— of having vanished, in a way, been taken, claimed, like so many others, by the journey itself.

I am surrounded, alive and well, among these diverging streets and loud road noises, by the unremarkable sprawl of Kingsport, once known by the frontier designation Long Island but now a small global city, its growth fueled, like more than one other section of East Tennessee, by the proximity of the federal government's military-industrial complex. In a book celebrating the modern city, historian Margaret Wolfe calls it "a glittering new industrial jewel in the green mountains," even as she notes the "plumes of smoke and vapor that routinely rise from the floor of the Holston River Valley." An industrial jewel it is perhaps, though it does not glitter in the light of midday and not all the mountains surrounding it are green, a drab, smoggy haze hanging about them.

One of Long Island's more interesting early settlers was Joseph Martin, a native of Albemarle County, Virginia, who had journeyed with the explorer Dr. Thomas Walker. Martin came to the area in the late 1760s and in the ensuing decade performed his reluctant colonial devoir as a settler, participating in various military actions against the Cherokee, including the William Christian–led campaign of 1776 which involved the incineration of crops and villages. However, unlike many of his contemporaries, Martin also admired the Cherokee, and his respect was reciprocated, even to the point that he was adopted into the tribe and took an Indian wife known among the settlers as Betsy Ward, despite the fact that he was already lawfully married. Though his children and neighbors frowned upon Martin's additional matrimonial connection, it was highly advantageous to the region in quelling hostilities and promoting peace among settlers and tribesmen. In 1790 Thomas Jefferson and Patrick Henry, citing Martin's friendship with the Cherokee, urged George Washington, president by then, to appoint him governor of the territory. Washington instead chose a North Carolina slave trader named William Blount, a mistake that would later have far-reaching consequences. Martin, however, was untroubled by the setback and would go on to work closely with President James Madison and, of more lasting importance, survey the boundary line between Virginia and Tennessee in 1800.

Other cultures and lifeways exist in the Holston River Valley now, as demonstrated by the place at which I stop to eat lunch: Fortune Dream Chinese Restaurant. The establishment's name is an appropriate one for its cookies offer destinies aplenty. Among the fanciful portents that crumble forth for me are the following three: character is built upon the rubble of dreams; furious activity is no substitute for understanding; the best prophet of the future is the past. All of these proverbs appear applicable in various degrees to my endeavor and situation, albeit no more so than a coincidental church billboard or astrological forecast. I neither discount nor embrace them while chewing my food. Reluctant to take them for a sign, their intersections with my life are duly noted, though my life remains my own (or at least I continue to believe it to be).

Moving west in Kingsport, belly full, mind bent toward the future, I approach the vicinity of the Holston River's south fork, near which once stood a small garrison built in 1760 for the purpose of protecting Long Island's strategic importance on the frontier. This locality was significant, not unlike Virginia's Fort Chiswell area, in that it rested in the midst of a natural opening marking a kind of geographical crossroads. Most settlers arriving, as I have, from Bristol would have turned north here along a path that is now roughly Highway 23, which leads into Virginia, curves east around Clinch Mountain, and then cuts west after passing through Moccasin Gap, onward to the Clinch River and, beyond, the Cumberland Gap—famous portal to the West. Fewer would have proceeded west along the Holston, though that is the route my ancestors would travel. Continuing in their footsteps along 11 West, I recall how the irascible Anne Royall, attended by her slaves, had followed the Holston toward its source in the early 1800s, describing the fertile land and abundance of crops. This entire general area, stretching from the mouth of the Clinch River to the present-day North Carolina border had been ceded in 1791 by the Cherokee to the federal government, represented by the venal North Carolinian William Blount, the administrator of the area chosen over Joseph Martin by President Washington, for the paltry annuity of one thousand dollars and various undisclosed gifts. This meeting, which unfolded atop the karst limestone of White's Fort, the aberrant current site of Knoxville, came to be known as the Treaty of Holston and was later decried by the Cherokee for the willful mistranslations and outright lies, symptoms of so many other meetings with United States representatives, employed by the conniving Blount, whom the Cherokee contemptuously labeled "the Dirt Captain" on account of his unabated lust for property.

Tennessee would not achieve statehood until 1796, when Sevier, the region's most popular figure, would be appointed governor. Blount became one of the state's first two senators, only to be disgracefully impeached soon thereafter on matters related to his clumsily aggressive, underhanded land speculations. A county south of Knoxville now bears his dubious name and its seat, Maryville, that of his reluctant frontier wife. The appointed senator to replace him, albeit briefly, was a young expansionist named Andrew Jackson. Though they had much in common politically, or perhaps because of that fact, Blount and Jackson despised each other. Sharing and partially emulating Blount's lust for land and hatred of Indians, Jackson was destined to ascend much higher in power, position, and ambivalent legacy than the Dirt Captain, who died in March 1800 at his home in Knoxville. Years later, as president, Jackson encouraged Americans to settle on Cherokee lands, despite a John Marshall–authored Supreme Court order to the contrary and outcries from such luminaries as Henry Clay, Daniel Webster, and Davy Crocket. He also sent a bogus minister among the Cherokee, J. F. Schermerhorn, who, in the European colonial tradition, deployed Christian theology as a means of deceiving the tribe into yet another exploitive agreement, the 1835 Treaty of New Echota, which guaranteed the Indians land in the western United States, assisted removal to their new home, and five million dollars. In return the United States received roughly seven million acres of land. When the Cherokee denounced the deception and refused to move, a force of more than seven thousand men under General Winfield Scott was gathered in 1838 for the purpose of rounding up the resistant Indians into a series of concentration camps stretching from Tennessee on down into Alabama. Families were seized and often prevented from carrying their goods and possessions, which fell into the hands of Scott's men or the civilian thieves and marauders who followed in their wake. Livestock was divided, homes burned, and burial mounds desecrated in the hopes of finding jewelry and other valuables. Mortality among the Cherokee was high in the camps and continued as the long journey west commenced in the winter of 1838–39. However, what came to be known as the infamous

Trail of Tears was not the conclusion of their hardships; in Oklahoma many of the ancestral ways of the tribe, already diminished, were lost or diffused among the customs of the Chickasaw or the Seminole, the Choctaw or the Creek. And as the frontier expanded west, they would all be forced to move again—prisoners of a shrunken destiny—farther still, until few could recall their distant past, which had strayed beyond them, and fewer still relished the future that lay before them, their collective cultural identity having come to border on extinction.

At the western terminus of modern Kingsport, crossing over into Hawkins County, founded in 1786 but initially settled by Joseph Kinkhead and John Long in 1769, the sprawl continues unabated, though I am greeted off to the left by the visceral presence of a national military policy lingering in East Tennessee today: the rusty chain-linked and barbed-wired perimeter fence of the Holston Army Ammunition Plant—a 465-building base positioned on a bend in the river at the foot of Bays Mountain, originally constructed in the early 1940s in conjunction with Eastman Kodak for the purpose of manufacturing Composition B, a powerful explosive mixture of RDX (cyclonite) and TNT. After going on standby status in the wake of World War II, during which it produced only fertilizer, the plant was reactivated in 1949 under the Holston Defense Corporation, a new subsidiary of Eastman Kodak. The site would enjoy major production upgrades over the next couple of decades as the army exerted itself in Korea and then Vietnam. In the early 1970s, however, production was reduced, although around that time the plant also began processing special-order explosives and propellants for specific military initiatives, including the navy's Trident program. It still performs that function today while also handling and storing material for the national defense stockpile.

Surreal images follow the appearance of the military base boundary. Among them Pal's Sudden Service, where a massive hotdog sits oblong upon the roof of the aqua-blue restaurant proper, wherein hotdogs and burgers are manufactured to feed the people, who in turn build the explosives, which in turn feed the need for . . . and so on and so on. Perhaps recognizing its strategic culinary importance to the nearby base, President George Bush awarded Pal's Sudden Service the 2002 small-business-category Malcolm Baldrige National Quality Award in recognition of its performance excellence as a locally based drive-through restaurant. Still comfortable from my meal at Fortune Dream, I do not feel compelled to verify Pal's distinguished, award-winning reputation, though I encounter an even odder dining concept a short distance farther down the road: the Mountaineer Restaurant, its large roadside sign crowned with an immense

cartoon hillbilly. I feel as though I am a considerable distance from the mountains here, yet between the Mountaineer Restaurant, Hillbilly Vette Shop, and
several other places, it is not difficult to discern an unmistakable frontier legacy
in this area—a postured Appalachian element, however strange and fanciful,
very much in evidence.

History asserts itself again, beyond the gaudy images of the present, just
below the Mountaineer Restaurant, upon the old site of Patterson's Mill, which
served as a fort around the time of the American Revolution, affording protection against the attacks of a Cherokee war chief known as the Raven, who led
his bands across the mountains from the village of Kalanu, now Ravensford. It
was the Raven who at the 1777 Treaty of Long Island eloquently asserted that
he hoped the newly agreed-upon boundary line between the settlers and the
Cherokee would be "as a wall to the skies." Although the pact specified that
the demarcation would remain "forever hereafter," it was of course soon vio-
lated and then ignored altogether, which does much to explain if not justify the
Raven's vengeance upon the invaders. It is an odd contrast: the bizarre, synthetic
modern visages of the Mountaineer Restaurant and Pal's Sudden Service against
the visceral, poignant stories of Patterson's Mill and the Raven, as well as—not
far from the mill—Carter's Store, which had been pillaged by the Shawnee in
1774, in compensation for which owners John Carter and William Parker were
later given a large portion of what would come to be known as Carter's Valley:
the old tale of new ownership and development in the wake of war and conflict,
homes and commerce built upon the blood of the earth.

I bear away from 11 on the other side of Surgoinsville, following the Old
Stage Road to the mouth of Big Creek, the appearance of which is actually small,
brown, and murky. This area, known as Dodson's Ford, marks a point where
an artery of *Athowominee* once crossed the Holston—a place I have resolved to
spend the night, here along the river, dense white clouds moving in as I set the
tent. Rain and darker clouds do not follow, however, the billowy thunderheads
content to merely follow the river, cool breeze blowing from downstream, out
of the southwest. Sitting on my level spot overlooking the water, smoking my
pipe, enjoying the wind and the clouds, I feel as peaceful as I have since my journey began. Steinbeck said, "We do not take a trip; a trip takes us," and I wonder
at the degree to which travel, the open road, the encountered elements of nature
and human civilization, and the things for which they stand and reflect—in
my case, the history of my ancestors, my kin of long ago—have conspired to
become a part of me. It is said that as people get older they revert to the accent
and terminology that surrounded them in their youth. Perhaps it is the voices

of the people from their youth, calling to them from the beginnings of their lives, even as the end approaches. There are those strange, unexpected moments when dead relatives, the essence or residue of them, seem to draw near, falling on us gentle and unnoticed like the long shadows of trees at sunset. They come calling most often in the grey time between waking and sleep, when all of us, young and old, stand a little unsteadily with one foot in one world and the other in another.

After nightfall, lying in the tent, I recall how my grandfather, having suffered a stroke, struggled to speak coherently but infrequently was still capable of carrying a harp verse or quoting scripture. Once, while family stood at bedside, he spied through the window an uncommonly large, white Charolais grazing in the pasture. Without warning Papaw exclaimed, "Behold! Yonder stands the Holy Ghost!" It follows that we evoke our memories through language even as remembrance constitutes a peculiar tongue of its own. In this way language, according to the philosopher Wittgenstein, becomes "a way of life." They move on together, the recollection and the telling, even as we do, in looping, curving patterns, propelled and extinguished by our dreams of sleep.

Perceptions of the night still with me, I awake on a hill overlooking the bright clear flow of water with the lines of a song:

> I will meet you in the morning by the bright waterside
> Where my sorrows have drifted away.

As I hum the words half-asleep a light that is love sparkles on the morning waters, the welling-up of something bright and familiar from long ago. Harp songs, the songs of my fathers, are good walking or working songs since they require no instrument or accompaniment, although they do sound better when lots of folks are singing them. In the mountain churches, where the congregations generally were too poor to afford pianos, the people set their chairs in a square pattern, facing each other. The song leader, almost always a tenor, would stand and strike up the tune, humming the notes from a shape-note tune book or, more often, since most people could not afford books, from memory, establishing the song's pattern before the others joined in. My grandfather had been one such song leader and even after his paralyzing stroke, when speech became increasingly impossible, could still hum fragments of tunes.

Although separate localities practiced the tradition differently, harp singing was not an Appalachian innovation, but rather an adopted distillation of the late-eighteenth-century sight-reading singing of the Northeast, brought south by traveling evangelicals, which in turn derived from the English folk song and Elizabethan ayre. Rich in gapped scales and pentatonic and minor modes, many of the songs possess a peculiar mournful quality, irrespective of lyrical content. Though the musical form did not originate in eastern Tennessee, it has enjoyed a healthy stewardship here, long after having passed beyond the cultural memories of other parts of the country. Even today, one does not have to travel far on a weekend in this section of the state to find an afternoon singing in progress, although it is difficult not to notice the generally advanced ages of the participants—an indication that the twenty-first century may very well be the tradition's last.

I find myself unable to remember entire songs, just melodies and fragments of verses here and there, half-sung or diddled while walking. Mostly I recall images of my father and his four brothers and five sisters, the ten of them, a simple mountain farming family, together again, singing the songs at gatherings in Gatlinburg: the expressions of joy and love on their faces as their mouths shape words and notes foreign to many of their children and nearly all of their grandchildren, while the creek rushes down the mountain behind them and laps against the worn stones, joining a much older melody to theirs, a peculiar shared sound, the voices in the river, that my mind tells me is finite but always sounds to me like forever.

> Precious memories, unseen angels,
> Sent from somewhere to my soul.
> How they linger, ever near me,
> As a sacred past unfolds.

River behind me, I follow the Burem Pike to Rogersville, founded in 1775 and home to Tennessee's first newspaper in 1791, the *Knoxville Gazette,* printed there initially because of the perceived Indian menace to the west before moving its base to Knoxville the following year. The history of this newspaper, a scion of civilization in the region, fuels my lone imagining of the pervasiveness of news in our own time, for over the course of my journeying I have enjoyed a curious respite from the omnipresent images and loud declarations of twenty-first-century media, the scanning of headlines or fragment of political conversation in a store or restaurant my dominant sources of information.

As opposed to frontier times—when word spread, quite efficiently and accurately, it turns out, from tavern to tavern and locality to locality via horseback—we enjoy, if that is the right word, the most comprehensive or invasive, depending on your tastes, journalism the world has ever seen. Someone in Delaware gazing at a television or computer screen may set down their morning coffee in order to wring their hands over a reported social injustice or massacre in some backwater of Southeast Asia or Africa without ever asking the questions: Why this story? Why now? Should I grieve for or act upon this reported adversity? What are the motives for reporting this? What other sundry evils, just as unfortunate or perhaps worse, passed either unknown or consciously unreported yesterday?

Journalism and media are disciplines of the present moment, feeding what the philosopher Kierkegaard believed to be a perverse human adoration of the ephemeral. Journalists would seek to write history except that their stories are nearly always forgotten by the following day, ever giving way to the next new headline, abdicating their value to the succeeding moment, the journalistic gaze scanning the horizon for the new exciting event or development which, though couched in terms of immediacy or even inevitable doom, is often, in the end, more or less the same thing that was reported a few days ago, last month, or a decade or two previous. The inevitable backlash to the constant hyperbole and unremitting authority of tone in contemporary journalism, which often is more a creator of news than its custodian, is the widespread and growing sense of apathy and/or disbelief among viewers and readers of it. Perhaps the situation is altogether beyond remedy, though an occasional admission of relevance, historical context, uncertainty, or even error might help. But I cannot remember the last time I heard a reporter readily admit he was wrong or did not know something. As the onetime journalist-turned-writer Stephen Crane summarized, newspapers constitute "feckless life's chronicle, a collection of loud tales, concentrating eternal stupidities." Yet, for all the fecklessness and fickleness of twenty-first-century news, we may remain certain that every day the paperboy will bring more.

On the other side of Rogersville, back on 11, along the stretch of road that runs parallel to Crockett Creek, I stop in at K.C. Country Store, where I come up two cents short for a bottle of water in a store whose name is very nearly my own. The lack of funds directs me to recall a notice I had read to "all ye whiskey drinkers" in an early issue of the *Knoxville Gazette* from a bartender who promised to "sue every person indebted" to him if they did not pay up within a month's time. However, rather than having me dig through my pack for my misplaced credit card, the man behind the counter waves me on, not unkindly.

The good fortune holds out over a day of fitful, albeit slow, hiking, all the way to the vicinity of Bean Station, where a stooped elderly woman calls to me from her yard. When I approach her she inquires how my journey is going, claiming she has been expecting me, though she admits she had believed I would be taller. She expresses these things calmly enough, without any outward sign of dementia or madness, which only serves to make our exchange all the more sur-real—weirder even than the bizarre pursuit of the wanderer who had followed me for a time through the evening streets of Roanoke: two complete strangers amicably exchanging pleasantries and carrying on a familiar conversation most people would deem completely irrational or possibly insane. In keeping with the unlikely spirit of the situation, I accept her invitation to dinner, following her around the side of a generic ranch-style brick house to a backyard of perhaps a quarter-acre, open for the most part, possessed of a small herb and vegetable garden, burnt-orange chrysanthemums about the border, corners marked by diminutive crape myrtles. I am directed to a picnic table which rests between the house and the garden while the old woman hobbles inside to finish readying the meal she claims to already have been preparing for me. Sitting alone in the yard, elbows resting on the table top, I note how the late afternoon is still now and quiet, heat diminishing, grass brushed by shadows where failing daylight falls: evening does not have long to wait.

The frail elderly woman brings out food on a tray, ramps and potatoes sprinkled with garlic and lemon balm and covered in some uncertain variety of cooking oil. She talks familiarly as we eat: of the weather and amount of rainfall, of how her garden had almost dried up but is better now. I eat and do not ask her why and how she was expecting me. Not having revealed my name or purpose for many leagues, I nonetheless accept the fact that I am sitting here, perhaps a hundred miles from anyone who has ever heard my name, eating dinner with someone who seems, or pretends, to know both who I am and what I am doing. I celebrate the mystery as best I can rather than attempting to unravel it, aban-doning all explanations for the simplicity of wonder.

A place has been prepared for me in a nondescript guest bedroom and we both retire early, though I have difficulty getting to sleep and my dreams later are troubled. Among them a long sequence in which I am carefully driving a large vehicle through an immense empty parking lot, as wide as the horizon, full of deep, crumbling pot-holes. In time the broken, eroded asphalt changes, melts, into an irregular floor of ancient stone which I recognize as a section of Dalmeny Church near Edinburgh, Scotland, a twelfth-century Norman struc-ture, engraved with the runes of masons—the wavering lines of which I once found myself staring down at several years ago, standing before a preacher, side by side with the woman I would marry.

I awake early in the morning, before dawn, and rise to depart. Having no money or goods for the kindly old woman, I leave her my words: a short note of thanks set upon the kitchen counter. Outside, having locked the front door behind me, I stand in the wet grass of the front yard, gazing to the east, watching as dawn comes slowly. When the light is strong enough for me to discern the ground I take to the highway, entering the limits of Bean Station a short distance down the road—a small locality named for William Bean II, a blacksmith and gunmaker who had built his frontier cabin nearby, along the stream that would come to be known as Bean's Creek.

I pause briefly at Holt's Food Mart before continuing, knowing, sensing, that the ground I am walking upon very nearly constitutes an island, surrounded as it is, besieged, on three sides by Cherokee Lake. Turning south on Highway 25 East, I encounter the Holston again, though it is no longer a river here but rather a part, the main middle channel, of Cherokee Lake—a swollen body of silent water with tall pines towering around it on banks that once were high slopes. Such manmade lakes never fail to appear and feel to me as strange and un-natural. The water, distended and huge, rests upon a topography not meant to bear it, coves and vague currents wrapping about hillsides that once stood cov-ered in trees and wildlife, hundreds of feet above the riverbed. Natural lakes look and feel genuine because the environment has created or come to accommodate them over thousands of years. I recall Mountain Lake, not far from the Appa-lachian Trail in western Virginia, the highest-elevation lake west of the Mis-sissippi River and one of only two natural lakes in the state, dammed by earth-quakes six thousand years ago, its cool waters, periodically rising and falling, fed continuously by cold underground springs. Such lakes are marvels of nature, whereas the manmade varieties usually appear blighted and disquieting despite their calculated surface calm—even vaguely gothic when one considers the rusted farm equipment, burial grounds, and entire Cherokee villages that dwell deep below the heavy waters, the rivers they once rested beside having come to absorb and cover them: the wide, fathomless lakes strange, bound catalysts for modern energy and recreation—expressionless and still—while beneath lie buried the murky skeletons of long-forgotten buildings and bodies.

The philosopher Thomas Hobbes believed that reasoning is the manipulation of names, while truth is the correct ordering of names. And what is a name without memory? An utterance drifted out of fog just before the waking hour, that ghostly echo that sounds new, a floating fragment of lost things: something risen into sunlight from the dark and the deep below. Speak the name *vdali*—the Cherokee word for lake—on the banks of the Holston and a shadow falls upon the mind, the chill of deep water, and we stand suddenly in the midst of a darkened region—a marred, watery landscape of buried, secret things. To the north the Clinch River, like the Holston, is bound by a dam and lake of its own, the water and hydroelectric power of which would expedite the covert atomic research at the shadowy Oak Ridge complex during the 1940s. The original portion of that facility, built in 1942 as the Clinton Engineer Works, was known as X-10 and spanned nearly three thousand acres in Melton Valley and Bethel Valley, ten miles southwest of the town of Oak Ridge. It was there that the now-historic graphite reactor was built in just eleven months, its purpose to demonstrate that plutonium could be extracted from irradiated uranium slugs. Workers began loading uranium into the reactor on the afternoon of November 3, 1943, and by five o'clock the next morning the reactor had gone critical. Four months later, Oak Ridge scientists produced the world's first few grams of plutonium.

It is not difficult to imagine this event in the abstract, here, crossing this man-made bridge over the grand, scientifically devised span of Cherokee Lake, Prophet Ridge unaltered off to the east—all part of what was once the Holston River Valley, now a peculiar valley of unrest: the waters deep, murky, swollen—blunted hills rising saturated from them—bent to the will of science, stretched and poured into some awkward, forced environment. Journeyman in a harnessed region—seized, yoked, plundered—I tread among valleys filled with water, their contours covered and invisible, or dry and fenced off, hidden away beyond chain-links and barbed wire: part of another baffling juxtaposition of our time—the strange image of the secrets of split matter unfolding, radiating, amid corn fields and mountain laurel, industry propelled by thousands of acres, millions of tons, of captive water. The sublime uneasiness I feel emanates from a vast, troubled landscape—an immense, sprawling reflection of those diminutive human minds that shaped and twisted it: an ideal equation somehow gone awry. I can never hope to explain or determine all the countless ways in which others might label these phenomena, but the utterance, the idea, that comes to me, arises, dripping and invisible, from the murky depths beneath, is *udehohisdi*—which in the tongue of the Cherokee means "disgrace."

TENNESSEE

Homecomings: Smoky Mountains

On the horizon the peaks assembled;
And as I looked,
The march of the mountains began.

—Stephen Crane, "The Black Riders"

I cannot ever pause to love my land,
Though I have love that would go in more deep
Than spade or fork or plow. Should I gaze long
There might be too much tenderness in me
For these bright acres that I turn to black,
These golden-glowing and these sky-blue places
That never again will laugh with their own laugh.

—Mark Van Doren, "Pioneer"

Below Cherokee Lake on the South Davy Crockett Parkway, the highway that bypasses Morristown, I gain the top of a ridge where a road sign reads W Croxdale, pausing on a rise more than four and a half-hundred miles from where my foot journey, also the journey of my ancestors over two centuries ago, began in western Maryland—my embarking point of a month previous and the land of my forefathers over the course of the eighteenth century. From here, gazing south, I can see, for the first time, their destination and mine: the Smoky Mountains—English Mountain and Stone Mountain, probably, in the foreground, with the larger peaks behind them, their respective outlines merged and indistinct in the distance. Among the Cherokee the Smokies were known as *Shaconage,* which means "place of blue smoke," but today, from here, the mountains appear shrouded in white—great mounds protruding out of the horizon, the mistiness about them pale and lambent, obscuring partially their great mass; prying sunlight filtered, reflected, softened by the wispy haze that cloaks them.

Glimpsing these peaks from afar—my immense motivation, imagined and envisioned over a span of hundreds of miles—I am filled with an overpowering determination to reach them with all haste, undertaking immediately what I would refer to later as "the march of the mountains," a furious burst of hiking that would propel me from the area of Morristown to the northern boundary of Sevier County over the course of a day and part of a night: skirting along the southwestern ridges of long Bays Mountain—following White Oak Church Road to the Mansfield Gap Road before crossing over into Dumplin Valley— passing through Colliers Corner and, farther along, the prospect of Shields Ridge off to my right, until at last, just beyond Dumplin, darkness and fatigue obscuring all impression, I entered Sevier County, the district of my kin and ancestors for the last two hundred years.

Arriving around midnight at the Best Western Dumplin Valley Inn—one of several motels perched close to Interstate 40, at a point where tourists file off the great thoroughfare onto Highway 66, the route that leads to Sevierville and the numerous attractions beyond—I pass the remaining hours of darkness among tourist families, cries of shrieking children in the hallways, bound for or returning from Pigeon Forge and Gatlinburg. Next morning, stiff and slug- gish, I cross the French Broad River perhaps three miles to the south on High- way 66, the tributary dammed and swollen—like the Clinch, the Holston, and the Little Tennessee—just over a mile to the east into the watery expanse of Douglas Lake. The highway parallels the Little Pigeon River, though the water- course remains all but invisible behind the nonstop ruckus of attractions lining both sides of the road. Competing "Welcome" and "Information" centers, each possessing ties to separate local businesses, beckon to travelers while contrasting images loudly vie for the area's identity: the technological appeal of Helicopter Sightseeing lying directly across the road from the nature-pedaling Ripplin' Waters Campground, the vintage Sexy Stuf Adult Store sitting opposite the much newer-looking Cherokee Trading Post.

Amid these gaudy wonders, doing all in my power to block them out, I recall a Cherokee phrase I had come upon before my journey began and admired enough to memorize: *"dv ge 'si-di 'quenv 'sv I"* ("I am going home"). Of course, the thought that this once was a very different sort of home is a difficult one to abide. In the early days of North American human history, people would not have lived on the Little Pigeon, though they certainly would have traveled along it, trading and warring, trailing game and foraging, taking what an Appalachia we can no longer imagine had to offer them. In the centuries leading up to 1000 A.D., as the tribes early European settlers would come to know began to form and farm in earnest, river valleys, already well-traveled thoroughfares, increasingly became popular regions of habitation. When the Overhill Cherokee, originally a contingent of the Iroquois Nation, arrived in the Smokies it was *Atsila* (fire) who was their chief ally in preparing river-bottom land for planting. Once the grasses and other ground cover were burned away, the loose, broken soil, rich in nitrogen and other nutrients, made an ideal growing site for the two dominant vegetables: squash and beans. Among the Cherokee, women did most of the gardening, sporadically interspersing vegetables as opposed to planting each separate type in a uniform row—a technique popular today among organic gardeners since it generally prevents insects from devastating the entire crop of one particular variety of vegetable. Cherokee women also reduced the amount of required weeding in their gardens by planting vined vegetables like squash among corn and other upward-growing plants. Moreover, they intuitively understood the symbiotic relationships among plants: a vegetable like corn, for example, which craves nitrogen, would be set in close proximity to beans, a nitrogen-fixing plant. The women farmers were also very cognizant of determining the correct planting and harvest times, trying to arrange the former to follow the last killing frost and the latter so that it would coincide with the maturing of various wild fruits and berries, which would distract and preoccupy crop-seeking grackles, crows, and insects. The men, not entirely useless, often ventured up out of the river bottoms into the mountains for the purposes of *ganohalidoda* (the hunt) and for gathering plants and herbs generally unavailable in the lower elevations, though by and large the Cherokee continued to live along the waterways, the topmost peaks treated with reverence: a guarded measure of fear and respect.

The European arrival in this particular area and its ensuing conquest would be both violent and bloody, even by colonial frontier standards. In 1775 two traders from Virginia named Boyd and Doggett were killed by a band of Cherokee, who cast their bodies into a nearby stream—the waters of which empty into the French Broad River—known ever after as Boyd's Creek. Half a decade later, in the late autumn of 1780, a battle between Cherokee and the militia of John Sevier would unfold along the same creek. In the typical pattern of frontier expansion, the settlement of what would become Sevier County began shortly thereafter, Sevier—known among the Cherokee as *Tsan-usdi*—and his men—who adoringly referred to him as "Chucky Jack"—having successfully dispatched the Indians from the area. Sevier would follow up this victory with a devastating campaign against the Cherokee middle towns, deep in the mountains. Villages such as Cowee were burned to the ground, along with all provisions for the coming winter, which would prove to be especially harsh. Many of the women and children taken prisoner during the campaign were designated slaves and later swapped and sold as such; those who escaped captivity faced the prospect of starvation over the course of the bleak mountain winter.

Though Sevier had banished the Cherokee, local settlers, like those who had settled western Virginia decades earlier, remained concerned for their safety, which led to the construction of a fort in 1783 near the mouth of Dumplin Creek. That same year Thomas Stockton built the first grist mill in the area at Christians Ford, on the French Broad River. By 1784 settlers were regularly raising cabins, barns, and crops along the Little Pigeon River and Boyd's Creek. That year also marked the declaration of the ill-fated State of Franklin, followed in March 1785 by the first meeting of the legislature, during which Greene County was divided into three parts, one of which became Sevier. At the 1785 Treaty of Dumplin the Cherokee officially ceded a portion of their lands, including Sevier County, which would result in a large influx of fresh settlers to the region. The county seat, Sevierville, was founded ten years later on a low-lying natural crossroads of travel and trade previously known as Forks of Little Pigeon. According to local history, the town's first court sessions took place in a structure that had once been a stable and was still home to great hosts of fleas and lice, which frequently plagued counsel, bench, plaintiff, and defendant alike. As the tale goes, premeditated arson, planned by the local practicing lawyers, reduced the building to rubble, forcing the county to secure new chambers. The first court of Sevier County under the flag of the new State of Tennessee took place on July 4, 1796, the dominant legal concerns for the next three decades focusing primarily on the ratification of land purchased when the region had been claimed by both Franklin and North Carolina. A jail and courthouse, both probably built of logs, followed the original stable/courthouse only to suffer an identical fate, burning to the ground in 1812. Around 1820 a new courthouse and jail were constructed, not far from the location of the current municipal building, though fire would strike the town again on occasion, as would the Little Pigeon, its swollen floodwaters periodically moving about the buildings and through the streets, mocking the ill-chosen site of the town: the foul corpses of drowned livestock—resembling bloated, decaying buoys—meandering slowly on the current, long rows of corn drooping in flat, saturated fields.

On the edge of contemporary Sevierville, the high clock tower of the modern courthouse visible to me from the road, I arrive at Highway 441, its traffic backed up on the incoming side as far as I can see, vans and SUVs mostly—hulking family entertainment systems on wheels. With hundreds upon hundreds of such gas-driven vehicles idling, the air constitutes a milky haze stemming from something more than the storied smokiness of the mountains—horizon bearing a vaguely blighted brown tinge, sky ashen and sober. Unfortunately, the very hazy quality of the Smokies that affords the mountains their name also serves to seize and retain airborne chemicals. Pollution from as far away as the sprawling industrial wastelands of Detroit frequently becomes trapped in this manner, joined on a daily basis by the exhaust gases of vehicles, together compromising both air quality and visibility. Not to be left out, the federal government contributes its share of damage as well through the offices of the Tennessee Valley Authority (TVA), whose coal-fueled plants belch thick sulfur dioxide into the air which often settles among the mountains. Summer, with its high temperatures and long columns of seasonal tourists, produces the worst of these conditions, ozone levels occasionally passing over into critical levels. As I walk south inhaling this chemical soup, I follow the progress of a particular RV that passes me a number of times in the creeping and pausing traffic, children peering and pointing at me behind a tinted rear window, before I finally leave the massive vehicle behind—stalled and motionless amid its neighbors and the heat, heavy fumes, and asphalt.

I work my way over onto Middle Creek Road before arriving, two miles south of Sevierville, onto the stretch of land first owned and occupied by my ancestors upon their arrival in the region—a patent of 126 acres on the waters of Middle Creek personally issued to John Clabough Jr. by the infamous John Sevier. Standing here along the river, Davids Knob and Shields Mountain to the south, I can see and hear planes landing and taking off at the airport, the ground around me subdivided and unremarkable, dotted with businesses, homes, and lanes of concrete, though for my ancestors it would have constituted near-virgin creek bottom soil, easy to work and rich in nutrients. Isaac Weld Jr., commenting on the German frontier people he encountered in 1796, remarked that they "keep very much together, and are never to be found but where the land is remarkably good." Weld's generalization seems to have fit my ancestors, who appeared to have understood that owning fertile ground, the key ingredient for good crops, in an agrarian society was more or less synonymous with having a chance at a decent living. More than a decade before Weld's observation, the well-traveled Frenchman Crévecoeur noted, "Men are like plants; the goodness and flavor of the fruit proceeds from the peculiar soil and exposition in which they grow." This prime bottomland would have been a site upon which one might successfully cultivate a diverse bounty, from which, in turn, a family might grow and prosper.

Though the central mystery of their coming binds me still, it is interesting that my forefathers had chosen here in Tennessee familiar, nearly identical, ground—the same sort they had worked along the Monocacy River in western Maryland: a dark loamy soil, enriched by flooding, moistened over the course of dry spells by its proximity to the flowing waters. Yet, however similar it might appear visually to the family ground near the Blue Ridge Mountains in Maryland, or even the foothill region of western Bavaria where my ancestors toiled for centuries, the character of these respective soils, despite the close likenesses in surface and topography, were and are fundamentally different, which is often true even of farms that adjoin each other geographically. As the Tennessee writer and farmer Andrew Lytle noted, "The problem on any two hundred acres is never the same: the richness of the soil, its qualities, the neighborhood, the distance from market, the climate, water, and a thousand such things make the life on every farm distinctly individual." The ground would have been familiar but it also would have concealed many new challenges: local nuances of the seasons, special growing methods to be learned, anxious trials and errors, the glum silence around the dinner table when a particular crop failed.

Kneeling on the bank of Middle Creek, I make a hole in the ground with my Kabar knife, digging down several inches, before gently gathering the brownish-black soil into a mason jar and slipping it into my backpack. Upon their arrival over two centuries ago there would have been little time for my ancestors to rest from their immense journey as they hunkered down to the familiar tasks of clearing land for planting and erecting a primitive structure of chestnut and oak. At the end of the first growing season they would have taken their corn to Clack's mill, on the right bank of the Pigeon's east fork, just above Sevierville. Hugh Blair, the village blacksmith, was closer, his forge lying south of town. Their neighbors and local tradesmen bore the blood of the British Isles, and in living among them and working this ground, my ancestors would have begun, over the years, a slow cultural transition away from their German heritage, long shared and perpetuated among like families in western Maryland, toward that of American Appalachian—a collective identity shaped by the immanence of the surrounding hills. In 1790 only one out of every twenty people in Tennessee was German, against nearly one out of every three in Virginia. The old ways died slowly over generations—a word lost here or there, a dish no longer prepared—through close association with their English-descended neighbors, the shadow of the mountains, the vagaries of the seasons—and those insistent, inexorable, minute catalysts that shape us all into the molds that best fit the places we find ourselves in, beckoning us always to become rather than merely to be.

I continue south on Middle Creek Road, avoiding the worst of the commercialism that exists on the highway between Sevierville and Pigeon Forge, though the road terminates eventually in the latter town, directing me back onto Highway 441, not far from the portal to Dollywood—that odd combination of go-carts, bungee jumping, and mountain folkways made into something buyable, shiny, and arcane: a slot machine of visions where one dreads the alignment and the payoff that comes with it. Dollywood, however, a kind of microcosm of the region's tourism industry, is not so easily dismissed as a simple crass exploitation of mountain life. Like my father and his siblings, Dolly Parton grew up poor in the Smokies, her joint development of the pre-existing amusement park in 1986—a place I had known in my childhood as Silver Dollar City—greeted by locals with enthusiasm and pride. As my uncle Frank, a lifetime resident of Gatlinburg, has pointed out to me, Dolly did not have to return to the mountains and that in loyally doing so she succeeded in boosting the economy and financial well-being of all locals. The park champions Christian values and the beauty of the Smokies, and the overwhelming majority of homegrown folks admire Dolly personally. Once, in West Virginia coal country, I encountered a woman who spoke of trips to Dollywood with the same measure of interest and anticipation an affluent recent divorcee might talk of a singles cruise. For her, Dollywood was powerful, mysterious, and compelling—a visceral dreamland that championed the mountain culture with which she associated herself. Who was I to disillusion her vision, to sour her chosen images with my own?

That once-poor Appalachians have actively benefited economically from such local attractions complicates the manner in which we perceive them. And a similar dynamic exists across the mountains, to the southeast, in Cherokee, North Carolina. Though President Andrew Jackson had done his damnedest to gather the Cherokee into concentration camps before the Trail of Tears, not all were successfully caught or kept. Evading capture, small groups clung to remote areas and the generally higher elevations in the Smokies, many of them suffering from malnutrition and exposure, their love for their ancestral lands surpassing their considerable physical privations. Eventually, decades later, the government would see fit to provide these remaining ancient locals with land and attempt to "administer" them through the Bureau of Indian Affairs—another strange story riddled with sorrow. Yet today, the Indians around Cherokee, North Carolina, enjoy, if that is the right word, a healthy tourist trade equaling or surpassing Dolly's, based predominantly on the marketing of culturally popular images of themselves—deployed in the manner Sevier County folk have traditionally sold frontier representations of their mountain ancestors—and the highly lucrative establishment of a successful gambling industry. There are, of course, cultural problems aplenty, but it is good to see money in the hands of these people. The word in Cherokee is *Nuwehnavi:* "wealth."

Beyond Pigeon Forge, following the west prong of the Little Pigeon River, entertainment venues giving way to the thick forest of the Great Smoky Mountains National Park, I am moving toward the area, the place, where this immense dynasty of mountain tourism began: Gatlinburg. Though the traffic remains heavy, it is comfortable to walk beneath the shade of hillside trees, the moist, rising cool of the nearby Little Pigeon palpable on my exposed skin. The National Park Service having shaped Gatlinburg and the entire region in an uncounted variety of ways over the decades, it seems appropriate enough that the first major structure I encounter outside of town is a National Park Service visitor center—this one known locally as the Spur, for it is only one of many. Consisting of over a half-million acres, the Great Smoky Mountains National Park is a massive expanse, engraved in my mind by the special detailed maps I pored over years ago while working as a ranger for the National Park Service in Virginia. Like most any federal agency, the Park Service as a whole is large, generally inefficient, rule-laden, and bureaucratic, which makes the various and frequently disparate missions of individual parks very difficult. Often a specific park finds itself conforming to and implementing regulations that compromise or even undermine its original purpose as a result of grand blanketing directives from the Department of the Interior in Washington, D.C. The Spur constitutes one of the better visitor centers I have encountered, though the brochure I am given appears to be based heavily on the work of Horace Kephart, a well-intentioned midwesterner whose romantic anthropological work inadvertently perpetuated and celebrated many of the region's stereotypes.

Kephart's task, however, was not easy, for the histories of places like Gatlinburg are strange and elusive ones—difficult tales to tell. Known initially as White Oak Flats, the village derived its modern name from Radford Gatlin, a shopkeeper who arrived from North Carolina in 1855 and later offered to house the area's post office, provided that folks agreed to alter the place's name to take after his own. Gatlin may have been the only person in the entire region to own slaves and, in 1861, the sole man out of 1,303 in Sevier County to vote for secession. He was driven from town under threat of violence shortly thereafter. Though not terribly far from Sevierville, which was connected by railroad to Knoxville, Gatlinburg was more or less remote and isolated well into the twentieth century. The first telephone, for instance, did not arrive until well after 1900. The primary connection to the outside world was a primitive road to

Sevierville along the Little Pigeon, an extraordinarily rough version of the one I have been following, which forded the river at several places and was prone to flooding and erosion. It usually took the better part of a day to reach the county seat, even in good weather.

When the National Park Service took over the area in the 1920s and set about the business of attracting tourists, preserving what had once existed in the mountains, as well as popular ideas of that culture, became very important. By then modest tourism already was underway in Gatlinburg, the Mountain View Hotel having been built in 1916 by former Greene County logger Andy Huff, who later campaigned successfully for the paved mountain highway that passes through Gatlinburg toward Asheville. However, it was from the National Park Service that enterprising local families learned the effective means by which to market their customs and histories, as well as those visitors expected to encounter. Local folks who had forgotten the ways of their ancestors were retrained by the Park Service and the local Phi Beta Phi school (originally a philanthropic undertaking that would later prosper under its tourism-geared Arrowcraft Shop) in traditional arts such as whittling and weaving, which they would then demonstrate for tourists who believed they were witnessing authentic mountain traditions. Increasingly, the more developed and populated Gatlinburg became, the stranger and more extravagant were the marketing tactics and entertainments it devised: each new thing outdoing the last. A defining catalyst for this transition was the 1950 cross-country tour undertaken by the town's first mayor, Dick Whaley, and a number of other locals, during which they dressed in stereotypical hillbilly garb, feigned drunkenness, danced, sang bawdy songs, and generally acted ridiculous in an effort to raise awareness of the area and draw in tourists.

These and other marketing tactics, such as the establishment of billboards in congested northeastern cities, worked to great economic advantage, for by the 1960s the area was, by any economic measure, booming. And, to the credit of the locals, it was not outside business interests that were reaping the rewards. However backward and provincial local leaders may have appeared to outsiders, they were both shrewd and farsighted in their administration and development of the town. Following tradition, Dick Whaley was reluctant to have locals sell land to outsiders, urging them instead to maintain their ownership and rent the land out while its value continued to rise. As a result, much of Gatlinburg remained under the control of a few local families well into the 1980s. Though the tenacity of the original families in running Gatlinburg is a rare and impressive achievement, and one that turned out to be lucrative both for them and their descendants, over the last twenty years the area slowly has abdicated its business interests to outside players. Just as the Overhill Cherokee gave way to the first settlers, so the lingering local descendants of those first settlers now find their once-provincial community increasingly succumbing—like so many others—to national and global forces that appear almost completely foreign to them. Of course, a primary difference is that the Cherokee suffered much and retained almost nothing save a slot-machine reservation, whereas most of the old Gatlinburg families have prospered for decades, at least economically, retaining their land and the ability to determine its destiny and dispensation.

Gatlinburg as it exists today, the visage that greets me as I tread through its streets, truly is a menagerie: part amusement park, Hollywood, frontier town, and Bavarian-Alpine village, complete with "local crafts" made by cheap labor in faraway localities—Mexico, Taiwan, China, and so on. You can stand in line in the lobby of Ripley's Believe It or Not or take a table in the Hard Rock Cafe–Gatlinburg and remove the Asian-made Cherokee action figure from your pocket to amuse yourself while you wait for the show to begin or the food to arrive. In fact, as all this demonstrates, the show has already begun and has been going on for a long time: the show is always going on in Gatlinburg.

There is no escaping all the circus neon, but I eschew it as best I can, traveling along the river road. Though billboards, jack oaks, and swales of soil-poor broomstraw abound, in Gatlinburg you tread beneath the eminence of the mountains themselves, myself a stranger below familiar slopes, where the sun blazes over different peaks at the open and close of day, above a gaudy outpost of civilization staked on the edge of over a half-million acres of wooded habitat that supports an astonishing array of life: over a hundred distinct trees, two hundred kinds of birds, fifty types of mammals, eighty varieties of reptiles, seventy classifications of fish, and a thousand different types of flowering plants. No place in North America contains as much living diversity per acre. It is more this that welcomes me, the unique conglomeration of the thing that is the Smokies, than the human culture of this particular area and era. And it is a phenomenon, a presence, easy to feel, even wading through the gaudy spectacle of town, knowing in my heart that here beneath the mountains my journey is coming to an end in an area my people have occupied for more than two centuries. . . .

. . . But there are people to welcome me as well. Among them, my uncle Frank, who, now entering his late eighties, spends much of his time contemplating Mount Le Conte through a large framed window from the comfortable prospect of his easy chair at his home on Long Branch Road. Having attended, along with my other aunts and uncles, the nearby, one-room Banner School up through the eighth grade, Frank would go on to serve in the army during World War II before returning home to run a service station and, later, dabble in the restaurant business and local government. He is a thoughtful, introspective, successful man—the anchor of the family in Gatlinburg. It is Frank who usually coordinates reunions and passes on important local information to family members living far away. He has always been fond of studying life and people: as an M.P. in rural postwar Germany, unaware of his heritage at the time, he would be struck by the baffling similarities of method and mannerism among German farmers and his own family. He is thankful for the tourism of Gatlinburg, appreciative for the benefits it has brought his family, but there is sorrow for the old, lost ways as well. He is reminded of them visiting Cades Cove in the quiet off-season, employs them in the dark soil of the creekside garden he raises behind his house, and remembers them falling asleep or awaking in his chair before the vast image of Le Conte.

Despite the tourist-driven prosperity of Gatlinburg during the mid-twentieth century, times could still be tough for folks in the off-season and agriculture maintains a foothold, albeit a small one, in the area even now. Uncle Frank, in addition to his small garden, worked a much larger plot for many years on land he owns outside of town. Overall, however, the area continued to boom and there was little want among locals. In the late 1950s a wealthy Knoxville businessman offered to build a ski lift that would carry tourists from Cherokee Orchard to the summit of Mount Le Conte. The argument, much like the more or less fanciful and ridiculous idea of making the Appalachian Trail uniformly paved and handicapped-accessible, celebrated the prospect of affording the majesty of the view without the physical expenditure previously required to earn it. Although the park rejected the offer, a lift would be built shortly thereafter, to be followed years later by a tram route that runs almost directly over Uncle Frank's house. Look out the upper portion of one window and you glimpse Le Conte, immense and unknowable in the distance, covered in deep summer green, set before the sky. Gaze upward out of another window and a sizeable tram slides by slowly on a heavy-duty suspension cable. I will never forget the first time I visited Uncle Frank's house and found myself peering through glass, as I often do anytime I am inside—at clouds, the horizon, empty space—only to have a massive gray, box-shaped object resembling a rail car suddenly and inexplicably drift into the upper left-hand corner of the window pane and slide slowly across it, tilted slightly upward, gradually beginning to ascend the steep wooded ridge behind the house. Imagine your own surprise—not having noticed the tram cable, which merely resembles a thick telephone line—as the strange object floats into view, hanging over lawns, drives, tree boughs, street lamps. Yet, whatever initial ethereal quality the experience may possess usually does not last long, broken by a tourist's face, middle finger, or bare bottom pressed against the clear glass of the window high above your own, a crisp silent slap of reality across distance to whoever might believe they are privy to a religious vision or the close proximity of a UFO.

The surreal, unknowable quality of Gatlinburg's commercial present is matched, bookended, by the vague nature of the distant past: how the first families, my own and others, came to and lived among these particular hollows. Few seem to have come the same ways or for the same manner of reasons, my grandmother's people, for example, the Huskeys, nearly all of whom had in their look and manner a strong Indian element, arriving by way of Greeneville, Newport, Fair Garden, and Pigeon Forge. Some folks came from the west, though almost no one seems to have come across the mountains from the south. It remains hard, however, to know for sure, especially since the courthouse fire of 1812 destroyed all the early records for Sevier County, the families themselves, those that were literate, retaining little information beyond what might be recorded in their Bibles. Of course, as the area began to grow and visitors desired to learn more about its quaint history, the ambiguity surrounding the roots of the old local families began to manifest itself into colorful forms of legend and myth, haphazardly drifting between family anecdotes and sporadic facts. My own family was no exception. In her 1931 book, *The Story of Gatlinburg,* Jeanette Greve describes the Claboughs as coming "from North Carolina to Blount County" and that in our "veins flows the purest stream of Anglo-Saxon blood to be found in America today." The upshot of honest errors or calculated prevarications, these impressions simply are wrong. Whether or not the late Ms. Greve or some family member perpetuated them, I cannot say. However, another seemingly romantic and fanciful passage from Greve's book has always haunted me. She records that my great-great-grandfather, Martin Clabough, was "a tall man, and his descendants are tall, sturdy men with fair hair and blue eyes." Such suspect genetic observations and forecasts often seem foolish at best, and there are many in the family to whom they do not apply. Yet, here I am, nearly two centuries removed from the birth of my great-great-grandfather, wandering only a few miles from where he lived on Roaring Fork Creek, and resembling almost exactly Greve's physical description of him. Such, I suppose, are the vagaries of history, genetics, and chance when channeled through the expectation and desire that constitute description: the difference between what we see and how we record it—how we choose to share it with others.

It is much easier to establish the lives of my more immediate relations: the families of my grandparents and the aunts and uncles who grew up in the hollows and attended Banner School. And between their generations lies an economic and cultural transformation that is nothing short of extraordinary. Uncle Frank's contemporaries witnessed and participated in the area's first lucrative explosion of tourism, but it was my grandfather's generation that laid the groundwork, literally and otherwise. When the huge logging camps appeared in the Smokies in the late nineteenth and early twentieth centuries, bringing with them their own lumberjacks, it was men like my grandfather, poor local farmers, who worked for them part-time, either cutting lumber, building the railroad from Maryville to Elkmont, or, in my grandfather's case, the mountain road from Pigeon Forge to Asheville. In time the trains and roads would carry tourists instead of timber, but not before early-twentieth-century logging of the Smokies had produced in some areas environmental conditions that bordered on total collapse. Small-scale logging had taken place around Gatlinburg as early as 1868, when Caleb Trenham erected a sawmill northeast of town on the Little Pigeon. However, such limited local operations impacted the ecosystem only negligibly. By contrast, the mechanized techniques to follow would exact a devastating toll. Machines called overhead skidders enabled loggers to work on steep mountain slopes, clearcutting immense areas. Massive timbered trees were rolled down the mountain, destroying underbrush and plowing into the ground, promoting erosion. Or the trees were deposited in a "splashdam"—a pond created by the damming of a creek on the mountainside, usually with hemlock logs dragged by oxen. When the pond was full or the cutting complete, the dam was broken, sending tons of water and lumber rushing down the mountain. The end result of this process was massive erosion to creek beds and the general annihilation of anything living in the water, as well as flooding and silt and sediment buildup in the hollows and valleys. Another problem with this kind of lumbering stemmed from the massive amount of wood and organic debris—what loggers call "slash"—left in its wake. Once it is dry, slash ignites almost as readily as kindling, and nearly all of the many forest fires that torched the Smokies over the course of the 1920s are traceable to lumbered areas rich in slash—a neglected hidden equation for additional destruction, a remainder unaccounted for in another imperfect human formula.

Despite the encroachment of industrial lumbering during my grandfather's lifetime and the early part of my father's, local folks outside town remained predominantly agricultural in their pursuits. On the mountains above Gatlinburg, perched like a hungry buzzard, the Champion Fiber Company owned vast tracts of land, but in the hollows small farmers did their best to scratch out the living of their forefathers. The work often was as exacting and tenuous as it had been in frontier times. Among the most essential crops was corn, which could hang undamaged on the stalk all winter if need be, though raccoons, squirrels, and other varmints were apt to get it if left too long. In addition to feeding the family, corn sustained horses, mules, cows, and chickens. A little might be set aside for pigs as well, though they tended to be of the free-range, meandering variety, fattened on nuts and roots. Cattle often wandered in a similar manner, sometimes covering substantial distances, accompanied by a herder, who might lead them to a fertile hollow or up the mountainside to a bald, summoning and collecting them with a resounding "Soolk!": directing them wherever the grazing promised to be good. Unfortunately, the presence of and reliance upon livestock also led directly to the general extermination of wolves and mountain lions, or painters, whose presence is just now beginning to assert itself in the region for the first time in decades. Wolves and painters were hunted to near-extinction over the second half of the nineteenth century, though sightings and rich legends surrounding the latter animal endure even now: symptoms and echoes of a vague, partially romantic desire for the return of something once terribly feared.

Livestock care usually fell among the chores of women and children, though their duties frequently went far beyond the fetching of water or wielding of a hickory scrub-broom. Among other things, they daily churned butter and helped harvest many of the crops, the women filling their aprons with smaller vegetables such as peas, emptied in turn onto a large sheet, which the men would then carry to a barn. Later, it was usually the women who threshed and cleaned the peas, snapped the beans, and shucked the corn, the stalks in the field cut and stacked by the men. Women were also important workers around planting time. When the gray mare was hitched to steel, they followed the plow, dropping seeds from their aprons. Many of them were accomplished with the hoe and the wagon as well, working alongside their brothers and husbands.

Once the crops were harvested, the men would go about gathering the winter's wood before frost moved down the mountains, felling mostly dead and dry trees that were easy to get to and preferably uphill of the homeplace. Sharp-eyed warblers and threshers would have watched them while pausing on their journeys south for winter, the autumn forest blooming in color—box elder and poplar turned yellow, maples and sourwoods red—the humidity giving way, making the work go easier. Tapping a tree with a knuckle or axe head revealed whether it was solid or doty. Some green wood would be cut as well since it would burn longer, keeping the fire going through the long, cold nights.

A crosscut saw normally was used to divide the bough into desired lengths once the branches were dispatched, after which it could be split via maul and wedge, and stacked beneath a tree or porch. Boys often were sent into the woods to find pine knots from which shards of kindling could be split with a hatchet.

Anything that couldn't be grown or gathered generally was hard to come by and highly valued. The gourd, for instance, that held the salt in a given cabin was guarded assiduously. However, numerous vittles, an astonishing array of goods, could be collected in the wild. There are ways, for example, to catch trout without hooks but they require groups of people strategically thrashing the water. Ramps, a variety of wild leek and a favorite wild food of mine, can still be abundantly found in wet areas. The plant is best when mixed with scrambled eggs after having been boiled with a fair amount of cooking oil, though the smell, not unlike garlic, can be harsh and overpowering—especially if one chooses to eat it raw. Sweeter foods include sorghum molasses, harvested from low-lying cane patches, and honey. Bees occasionally were kept but most often they were spotted and followed to their woodland hives—sometimes a highly aerobic, cross-country endeavor—after which the honey could be readily acquired, along with a few stings here and there, though the chore might involve felling the hollow tree that housed the nest.

The seasons dictated the nature of the gathering, along with everything else. One might have entered the forest in autumn in search of various nuts: acorns, hickory nuts, walnuts, and the now-extinct chestnuts. Chestnut trees in particular were cherished and constituted an important resource for a number of purposes beyond their fruit. They were the primary trees used in construction, the wood remarkably rot-resistant and easy to split, readily providing logs and beams for houses, barns, and fences. The smaller splintered and irregular pieces could be fashioned into sound shingles. Since the trees generally were very tall and the boughs as large as forty feet in circumference, one chestnut could build a decent section of fence, wall, or floor. Most fundamentally, though, they were a comfort to the belly, the nuts supplementing the diets of settlers and livestock, as well as all manner of wildlife. When the chestnut blight, originally from China, arrived in the area during the mid-1920s it destroyed, within a decade, more than three-quarters of the trees in the region: a crippling devastation that deprived animals and humans of a unique and central resource upon which they had come to rely.

On many a bright autumn day over the course of the 1920s and 1930s, my aunts and uncles, along with the other students attending the one-room Banner School, would gather chestnuts both during lunchtime and after class, before the long walk home, though each year their bounty was less and less. My uncle

Armalee, a mischievous and athletic lad in his teen years, often was able to gather more nuts than the others, with whom he might later trade or share if he happened to feel generous or kindly. On one particular fall afternoon, as the students sat at their desks working figures, a very pretty girl sitting across from Armalee asked him if she might have a chestnut. After teasing and ignoring her for a time, as was his custom, Armalee at last relented, gesturing toward his pants pocket with the instructions, "Reach in there and grab you a chestnut." Unknown to the girl, there were no chestnuts in Armalee's pocket, nor was there really even a pocket to speak of, the lined pouches of his seasoned britches having long since worn away over the course of several previous owners. Yet, her groping hand did succeed in finding something—a taut unexpected object that sent the horrified girl leaping out of her seat when she realized the true nature of the thing she had grabbed onto so eagerly.

Pockets remain empty of chestnuts in the Smokies today, though many of the other things folks were used to collecting continue to flourish. It was always the custom of children to supplement their diets with whatever happened to be growing and berries were a particular favorite: blackberries, raspberries, brown-spotted ripe persimmons, huckleberries, gooseberries. Many would be eaten on the spot, but once hunger was assuaged, enough might be gathered to make preserves or desserts later. Clever folks might also have a notion to tote their mess of berries and nuts to town to trade for candy and small manufactured goods, an enterprising solution to the widespread lack of hard currency in the region.

With commerce in mind, men sometimes ventured off into the woods for other reasons. If a man took umbrage at long hours of hoeing, he might sell a little corn whiskey on the side, or trade it for store-bought goods. Contrary to popular belief, local brewers generally drank very little of what they made and spoke of the practice seldom, even among family, though it might reveal itself in indirect ways—as in one of my grandfather's favorite sayings:

> On Vinegar's Ridge, all covered with smoke
> Smoke's so thick, fire's so hot
> I run down the hill, for fear I'd get shot.
> Rock-faldy-daldy-daemon!

As opposed to today, tobacco was a more acceptable pastime than liquor, burley being the regional variety of choice for chewing, snuffing, or smoking among men and women alike. Air-cured in a barn for a month or two rather than dried by fire—the curing method for the darker Virginia variety—burley is a leaf possessed of little sugar and a mild, vaguely nutty taste. It burns slowly, and the accompanying aftertaste is not so harsh or unpleasant as that of the darker leaf or many processed, store-bought varieties.

Most often, collecting nuts and fruits and cultivating liquor and tobacco were supplementary pursuits, either for the stomach or the wallet; however, plants gathered for medicinal purposes served a centrally valuable, intrinsic function. Among them, sassafras was considered a fine remedy for blood ailments and ragweed juice combated hives and poison oak, while ginseng, snakeroot, and pinkroot were utilized for any number of purposes. Of special note, ginseng, or sang, enjoys a new era of popularity and cultivation throughout Appalachia today on account of what the colonial Virginian William Byrd II described as its "vertues": "[I]t gives an uncommon Warmth and Vigour to the Blood, and frisks the Spirits, beyond any other Cordial. It chears the Heart, even of a Man that has a bad Wife, and makes him look down with great Composure on the crosses of the World." As far back as the early 1800s folks sought and dug sang not so much for its attributes but for the price or trade potential it would bring in town. Long a coveted item in China, the plant sold, and still sells, for a favorable market price—a dynamic that has led to its large-scale disappearance from the mountains and a number of isolated backwoods quarrels over the years that have occasionally resulted in body counts. Even today, it is not uncommon for sang "diggers" to wander onto land that is not their own—a well-weighed personal risk that invites both legal prosecution and potentially violent personal retribution from private cultivators. An herb of great reward, it remains, nevertheless, not one to be trifled with.

"Wonderful tales had our fathers of old," wrote the poet Kipling, "wonderful tales of the herbs and the stars—." The hillside forests and fields and the diverse combinations of all that lurked and grew within and upon them would impact mightily the topics and stories folks spent time discussing and exchanging: from who had grown the largest tomato or died in a logging accident to how the late-spring frost had managed to ruin the late-summer fruit crop. And from this often colorful, anecdotal subject matter would evolve a special penchant for naming and telling—an acute ear for the sheer joy and skill of creating and recollecting, yet one that often strayed into the realms of hyperbole and caprice, especially if it promised to make a story sound better. My father, for instance, always liked to say he was born in the Devil's Holler, though he actually entered the world on a farm up above Huskey's Grove. To this day, I remain uncertain of whether he really did not know his point of origin or whether he merely liked the sound of Devil's Holler better than Huskey's Grove. There are many such mysteries involving any number of events and places. Of incidental note regarding hollows, even the smallest of them had a name—usually based on its appearance or an event that had taken place there—since specifying the minutest of areas provided a way of identifying where a family was working on a given day: the place from which someone could be fetched if need be.

As is the case anywhere, some folks were better at creating certain qualities of names, tales, and sounds than others. One practice from frontier times that men continued to take pride in involved the ability to mimic animal calls for the purposes of hunting, woodcraft communication, and play—a gift that has evaded me though my father is very adept at mouthing a crow call or the braying of an ass: a facility my mother likes to say is based on the qualities he shares with those creatures, especially the latter. I have always felt that the art of animal mimicry is inherently linked to other forms of rhyming, tale-swapping, and even word invention—a phenomenon Kephart called "spang." A simile of my grandfather's like "cold as a witch's tit" seems less interested in any kind of rational conveyance and more a result of the whimsical desire to create a quar and arresting image. Likewise, one of Papaw's favorite invented exclamations— "spitchy-spy!"—appears to have had less to do with commentary than it did with evoking the essence of an undefined exaltation at the prospect of whatever happened to be occurring at that particular instant.

Many of these expressions, both within my family and in others, were devised over long intervals of work, while taking a break from that toil, in the midst of journeys to Sevierville or Knoxville, or perhaps while sitting a spell among one's more bawdy acquaintances. Often, the briefer creations would swell and lengthen into full-length stories or even literal acts of mischief, such as the time Papaw explained to me that chewing tobacco tasted a lot better than chewing gum. Being but three years old, I took him at his word and paid the price, vomiting profusely after I swallowed the offered chew, the sound of my heaving accompanied by Papaw's dry chuckling. Such pranks arose out of the inventive medium of creative jest, and my father, the youngest of ten, frequently was a victim during his boyhood years—from being forced to chew raw tobacco while holding heavy rocks in outstretched arms to being tied to a tree so as not to follow his older brothers on their journey to town. As a young child he was also the family water boy, carrying a heavy pail from the nearest spring to the field in which Papaw and the older brothers happened to be working. As he neared them, however, they would begin to hurl dirt clods in his direction. If any debris found the water he would be forced to dump the entire contents and return to the spring to draw a fresh pail—the mock-dismayed observation of a brother, "This water's got drugs in it, boy," a prelude to his long repeat journey.

Uncle Armalee, he of the empty pockets, was especially fond of weaving the comic tale and formulating the unexpected joke, even later in life. Among his favorite pastimes was teaching nephews and grandchildren the art of bee charming. In the presence of one or two children, Armalee would point at an alighted wasp or hornet with his finger and mutter a line of spang before grabbing the bee and holding it gently in his closed fist. After a few seconds of improvised conversation with the bee he would let it go, claiming that he and the bee were now friends and that his small companion hadn't stung him. Of course, he was in fact always stung quite badly but simply concealed his discomfort for the time being, waiting to spit a little tobacco juice on the swelling later. Eager to try this apparent magic for himself, the child would hurriedly speak the words, which concluded in "hokey-spokey-don't-ya-sting-me," before eagerly grabbing the next alighted bee, only to let go immediately and run to the house hollering in pain as Armalee's raspy laughter followed him. Most all my male cousins succumbed to this jest at one time or another, as did I.

Though these jokes may appear unduly cruel to some, they were always delivered in the spirit of humor and carried with them a peculiar affection and inclusion into a special vein of experience and understanding. On the other hand, punishment was a serious matter. When my father gave me his pocket knife with instructions to go into the woods to cut a green hickory branch, I was always filled with fear and remorse, dwelling upon the whipping to come and the action that led to it all the way to the hickory tree and back. There were tales, though, that sought to head off such scenarios and discourage misbehavior. Among them, the legend of a mountain creature called the Yelpinstretcher—part-wampus, part-painter, and part–everything else. It possessed the feet of an elephant, the torso of a zebra, the head of a lion, and any number of other qualities the teller chose to ascribe it. Usually Papaw would hone in on whatever aspect of the beast seemed to scare the children the most and then elaborate on it for some time, noting with pleasure his young audience's increasing fear. The tale of the Yelpinstretcher was a constant exercise in creativity, the monster appearing in a slightly different form every time it was described, though the story accomplished the literal object of keeping children close to the house and away from potentially dangerous places, which Papaw sometimes referred to as the "Yelpinstretcher's lair."

Like punishment and warning stories, a verbal pastime that was almost always serious was the art of sparking. As in any culture, a man's ability to impress women with his line of talk could prove a powerful advantage or shortcoming in attempting to secure a love interest and/or wife. Women, for their part, generally were encouraged to sort through the male prospects rather quickly, for they usually were looked upon with disappointment and pity if they had not taken a husband by the age of twenty. Farms being more or less isolated, interacting and sparking among the sexes generally unfolded in conjunction with big community gatherings: a fair, for example, or a church meeting or revival. Taking a girl home after some such function was considered the first step in the relationship, and an odd image it likely would have made: the couple walking some distance apart, attired in their Sunday best, though they likely would have been barefoot unless it was very cold, their shoes—probably made from the tanned, dried hides of cows or oxen who had outlived their usefulness—slung about their shoulders to slow the process of wear and tear. Family approval was important if the relationship happened to progress, a manifestation of which survives in my own family through the practice of nussing, in which a girl sits amicably upon the knee of her seated potential father-in-law as they converse. She might also unknowingly succumb to the more secret practice of "thumbing," which involves being sighted from a distance by the prospective father-in-law, who holds up his thumb between his eye and the possible daughter-in-law. If her figure does not fit behind the upheld appendage, she is deemed overly plump and, thus, a problematic match. Generous and good-natured, my wife was accommodating enough to tolerate and pass both these tests.

Another aspect of sparking, the pet name of the girl in question, often involved verbal invention as well and usually reflected some curious aspect of the young woman's appearance or personality. In later years Papaw was fond of recollecting a particular girl he had courted who went by the pet name Punkin, describing at great length her attributes and all the sparking they had done, including the one time she had flashed her ankle crossing a creek, or the occasion on which he had tried to impress her by running the horse-drawn wagon at top speed, only to cause the animals, fresh from grazing the wet bottom pasture, to spew runny manure all over both of them. On one particular Sunday afternoon, during which Papaw had perhaps sung the praises of Punkin for too long and in excessive detail, Gramaw, silent and impassive by nature, commented dryly at the end of his concluding anecdote, "I recollect that girl looked like a punkin, too." Though her words usually were few, Gramaw nearly always had the last ones.

To be sure, the naming and gossip surrounding a girl who was courted could easily become vengeful if there was a conflict and the relationship soured, a young woman once celebrated as a well-turned girl having suddenly become ugly as a mud fence or a crap-tailed hen. Sometimes the teasing appeared to be purely incidental or linguistic, my uncles having chosen, for example, to constantly poke fun at and make up stories about a local girl they called "Mirar," whose name in fact was Mariah. Occasionally, the sum total of such idle pastimes conspired with the often imaginative practices of storytelling to create curious sayings and half-parables: a bride, for example, should not bathe on her wedding day, for if her belly got wet her husband would become an alcoholic. Some of the sayings appear to have been developed and/or perpetuated among women, such as the motherly belief that giving her daughter a poke of wheat the night before her wedding day would ensure fertility. Given the agricultural occupations of most folks, many of the expressions were work- or farm-related—among them the beliefs that it was bad luck to carry an axe into the house and that gathering eggs after sundown would force the hen to stop laying. I cannot help but think that many such sayings, not unlike Old Testament proverbs, were designed with an eye toward supplying comfort and peace of mind against the sometimes horrible and violent events that could descend inexplicably upon a poor people all but devoid of any economic means and dependent upon a landscape and environment not always benign. Infant mortality, for instance, existed on a scale that likely would horrify most modern Americans, and it was perhaps from this fact that there arose the belief that if a baby saw itself in a mirror during the first six months of its life it would most certainly die at some point over the course of the next half-dozen—a vague, morbid expression by which to account for the unknown roots of demise afflicting so many helpless and unfortunate little ones.

The image of a doomed infant, before the looking glass, glimpsing itself in wonder—the strange, proverbial aura of mirrors and reflections—draws me back, directs me, to a vision of the Gatlinburg of the present—glass, plastic, neon all flashing and giving back, each to the other, a confusing array of wild, synthetic illusions. If so much of it exists within the realms of images and reflections, where might the true Gatlinburg lie? And what will happen should its various modern effigies reflect each other for too long? What manner of death lies beyond the interval in which this place first glimpsed itself?

   And yet there are the quiet things that exist and return periodically much as they were—the things that speak to me here: once so far away, dimmed by hundreds of miles, now close at hand. On quiet evenings the creek still roars, the late-summer insects holler, and the stars, as the Tennessee poet Charles Wright once described them, "come out to graze, wild-eyed in the new dark." Black bear—agile and evasive despite their great bulk—periodically wander into town, mauling bird feeders and wrecking suburban gardens—vanishing back into the mountains before any action may be taken, often without ever having been seen.

Even a few wolves are rumored to have returned to the hills, loping and sniffing along the dry, steep creek beds, their survival ghostly and tenuous beyond the human boundaries they can neither sense nor abide.

And close by me now, evening in a hollow outside Gatlinburg: a corn-crib and barn built of chestnut sometime during the nineteenth century, full of hay, still in use, the hill falling away from the aged rock foundations—testaments to the ingenuity of the people who built them, the time and care in selecting the appropriate trees, the framing of the building. Here stands a lost work wrought of materials now extinct—the layered boughs a neglected, unknown exhibit on display, humbly carrying on its age-old function. It remains, too, stands in truth still, that from the things we have constructed and the work we have done emerges the people we were and are—living reflections of the wounds and in-clinations of a shared soul. The fortunes of my people have always gone with the land, for they have always farmed, an occupation that spans backward as far as I can trace my ancestors. What imprint does the vocation of centuries on end leave on the person of the present, both within and beyond us? What should it mean that I now exist, man of the twenty-first century, on the small farm where I live, waking at first light though my chores be few: working the ground, mow-ing the fields, child of my ancestors?

Ever do we crave to be told the missing stories of ourselves even as time and the weather wear away the houses that our fathers built. Or are these merely the phenomena that serve to make or seduce us into the beings we believe to be ourselves? Wisdom or illusion, being alone must now be enough for me, for I am tired of traveling, the journey having ended where the man begins, though he never stops becoming: the present ever an embarking point—a dock, a doorway—from which we are forever stepping into the world. Heidegger said, "Through anxiety man encounters nothingness and becomes aware of his finitude and the necessity of death; but through resolution man, who moves in time from past to future through the present, appraises himself, chooses with the whole of his being, and thereby achieves authentic existence."

Don't you reckon?

EPILOGUE

There ain't nothing gonna take this road out of my heart.

—Iggy Pop, "Highway Song"

What I set down here is true until someone else passes that
way and rearranges the world in his own style.

—John Steinbeck, *Travels with Charley*

Time is waning us away to our eternal home.
Life is but a winter day, a journey to the tomb.
Youth and vigor soon will flee, blooming beauty lose its
  charm.
All that's mortal soon shall be enclosed in death's cold arms.

—Old Harp Song

The shifting of spaces, the blurring of places across time, the tale of vanishings and arrivals that is our world, our lives. . . .

In the early twentieth century, before the arrival of large-scale tourism, population growth around Gatlinburg and rising land value made it increasingly difficult for folks to farm and get by. Whereas the first of my ancestors to enter the area had enjoyed the rich bottom soil on Middle Creek, my grandfather and his family generally farmed the comparatively rocky ground, the stony earth, of the hollows, most of which are possessed of a thinner, poorer layer of soil that yields much more reluctantly to hoe and plow. Families and young folks began leaving; some had to, forced off their land by the newly arrived National Park Service during the late 1920s and early 1930s. Life was just as hard in the places most of them journeyed: coal mines, textile mills, or—in the case of my family—a farm in the red clay Virginia Piedmont. The mountains within the park boundaries have been unpopulated now for some time, though they remain haunted places, bearing the signs of the humans who once lived there: the small

sharp-edged stones along the river, the rusted bull-tongue plow among maturing saplings, the gray mossy foundation of stacked river rock glimpsed beneath
the mountain laurel, the old lost roads through the woods undone by nature.
Though monitored by the National Park Service, the area suffers from bad air
quality and acid rain, exacerbated by the heavy annual rainfall, all of which conspire to threaten its diverse bounty of plants and animals. As is the case with
many other places, humans need not live among the Smokies in order to plague
and destroy many of the things that do.

And what of the ancient Indian path? Where did the road become the ground of
my destination, of realized hope? *Athowominee,* or the Path of the Armed Ones or
the Warrior's Path, or whatever it should rightly be called, real or imagined—it
was, after all, a diverging and converging collection of trails—continued south
from Boyd's Creek, which lies north of Sevierville, to the Overhill Cherokee
town called Chota, once known as the "Town of Refuge," now submerged
beneath Tellico Lake, and other towns to the south such as Hiwassee and Tellico,
stretching down into northern Georgia. To the north the trail strays far above
where I took it up in western Maryland, on into Pennsylvania and terminating
in the old Iroquois country of New York. It was never my aim to follow the
entire route or try to master it in the manner that gaunt obsessive hikers breath-
lessly attempt to conquer the Appalachian Trail in a given number of days. More
often than not, that kind of singleness of purpose, of ego-driven drama, induces
travelers to forsake the richest of areas through which they pass without ever
fully coming to note or appreciate them, in the interests of ever moving on. The
Smokies, the hills I could not pass beyond, are home to over nine hundred miles
of Park Service–maintained trails, of which the Appalachian Trail constitutes
only seventy. It holds little relevance for me, the AT, as do the stages of *Athowominee* stretching north and south of my own journey—these are the trails and
stories of others, to be told and remembered in time.

    I, like my ancestors, had happened upon *Athowominee* and commenced to fol-
low it for a certain distance, our section of the route laid out against its entirety
like the linear rise and fall of a single minute civilization on a long timeline
of history, the creator of ruins from which stories are excavated. Among these
arrives a kind of felt message or impression—an impossible transmission sent before my being—murky, old, and barely audible, perhaps altogether fanciful, from
my ancestors, translated through shared experience and borne over great distance,
urging me to be at peace, to be still. Looking back down the road after having
turned aside from it is to glimpse something like yourself spread far and thin be-

yond literal sight. The philosopher Edmund Husserl believed that "spontaneous temporal forms, like all immanent Objects, have their counter-images in reproductive modifications of themselves. The phantasy of judgement is, like every phantasy, itself a temporal form." History—one of time's tenuous measures, a fun-house mirror into which we stare, an oasis in the sands of sorrow, a fanciful gauge at best—is the ongoing human attempt to reflect event and duration, but remains only an imperfect echo of experience, the clumsy weaver of memory. Among its stories of long ago, fantasies of judgment from antiquity, is the tragic tale of the nymph Echo, who was fond of the woods and the hills, but could only repeat what she heard. The love of her life was Narcissus who spurned her but succumbed to his own reflection in a clear, lonely fountain. Ours is a bright land of mirrors without time or space. Echoes and reflections seduce and surround us always, and if they are not all familiar or visible, they are at least masked players in our own collective story, dancing in the wings and whispering in the dark, the semblances of things once lost and far away returning to us, be it ever so brief or imperfect.

To face history, which is to face your own Epicurean mortality, is perhaps the most difficult and crippling human challenge, but it is also the best. And in facing it, we make it as well. As Kierkegaard proclaimed, "Since death is imminent every choice has infinite worth, and every moment is a unique occasion for decisive action; each individual achieves his being through decision." I wonder then at my own questionable choices and their suspect achievement, or the lack thereof—the matter of how I have become in coming to my place of ancestors in the shadow of the mountains: the bitter knowledge of the wanderer—to rove so long and believe what remains the same. The English poet Shelley speculated that writers valiantly attempt to "sound the depths," but usually are astonished, even overwhelmed, at what they find: the difficulties of returning from a voyage, perspectives blunted and memory fading, the world grown small and indistinct in retrospect.

Even in the wake of my wanderings, there is much I do not know and more I never will. Like the character Faust in Goethe's play, I remain, "for all my lore, the wretched fool I was before," and between traveling and writing there are places and events I forgot, falling away from mind and memory though they had once breathed the blood and reality of experience. Likewise, there are hosts of local legends and extraordinary events that never fell upon my ears nor met my eyes from the pages of the many books I pored over. As the Cherokee would say, *"Tsunu'lahun'ski"*: "He tries and fails." To all the places for which I did not possess the proper attention or knowledge, I apologize. The Pyrrhonian skeptics would have told me this was inevitable from the beginning. Yet, for all this, for all the doubt and fear that the perceived pathway to truth may be covered thickly in weeds, we may at least comfort ourselves with the hope that there may be other roads. Like the paths we follow, our lengthy though finite stories, flawed and incomplete as they may be, stretch on in us and reach backward into arcane tongues and cloudy places, beyond oceans, far from this century and continent. . . .

Among them: a sunny May morning in southern Germany, in the foothills of the Alps, the region of my ancestors, in which I, a wanderer in a strange land, once witnessed a memorable farewell: an old man with a heavy worn sack on a dirt road waving goodbye to an elderly woman who stood on the porch of a small roadside cottage, broom in one hand, the other waving to the man. Having turned and taken a few slow, unsteady steps down the road, the old man set down his sack and began hobbling back toward the house, the woman, stiff but moving more easily, coming out to meet him halfway. Stopping awkwardly, he bent forward and kissed her offered cheek before ambling back to his sack, taking up his burden again, effortlessly it seemed to me, a slight spring in his step. Though seen and remembered, passed on here, this farewell remains but one more footnote in the eternal tale of leaving: the tears of departure, the last lingering touch of hands, the giving up of that which we treasure most for the duty of the long, lone journey—the lesson of suffering that teaches us compassion.

And the telling of all these things changes even as the journey continues. For me, and for you too, wherever and whenever you may be: us, who are soon to be parted. Take then now your journey for your own, tell what you find, and believe your words. And may the salt that you taste in departing flow from tears that bear love—the best kind of weeping. For that is a part of it all too: the ordeal of travel, bitter departures, wind at your back on a road brimming with clear, pale light. The long journey ahead.

Appendix I

Brief Timeline of Appalachian Geology and Human Culture

Appalachia spans from Newfoundland to Mississippi, its Blue Ridge flank from North Georgia to Pennsylvania.

900 million–1.2 billion years ago	North America and Africa, along with Siberia and a northern section of Europe were joined as a massive continent called Rodinia.
600–800 million years ago	Rodinia begins breaking up.
550 million years ago	Africa splits off. Southern Appalachia on the equator.
500 million years ago	North America develops a continental shelf.
450 million years ago	Volcanic island string hits North America, resulting in the development of mountains in the Appalachian region.
400 million years ago	The Blue Ridge is a desert.
350 million years ago	Inland sea exists from the Blue Ridge to the Mississippi.
300 million years ago	Large continent collides with North America, producing mountains as high as 25,000 feet. Continents come together to produce the great land mass known as Pangaea.
200 million years ago	Process of extension and erosion, which stretched the mountains and created several basins.
About 60 million years ago	Appalachia begins to take on current shape. First flowering plants have arrived.
No later than 10,000 B.C.	People arrive in Appalachian region.
2500 B.C.	Humans begin forming small villages along rivers, creating primitive pottery, and cultivating plants.
2000 B.C.	Development of the bow and arrow.
0–1000 A.D.	Recognizable Native American tribes begin to form.

Appendix II

Selected Traversed Places

Place	Latitude	Longitude	Elevation in Feet
Maryland			
Frederick (Fredericktown)	39 24 51 N	077 24 39 W	290
West Virginia			
Harpers Ferry (The Hole)	39 19 31 N	077 44 21 W	484
Charles Town	39 17 20 N	077 51 36 W	540
Virginia			
Berryville (Battletown)	39 09 06 N	077 58 57 W	575
Winchester	39 11 08 N	978 09 49 W	720
(Frederick Town)			
Strasburg	39 58 19 N	078 21 32 W	578
Woodstock	38 52 54 N	078 30 22 W	773
Harrisonburg (Rocktown)	38 26 58 N	078 52 09 W	1,352
Staunton	38 08 58 N	079 04 19 W	1,402
Lexington	37 47 02 N	079 26 35 W	1,084
(Gilbert Campbell's Ford)			
Natural Bridge	37 37 48 N	079 32 36 W	1,078
Buchanan	37 31 38 N	079 40 48 W	1,233
Roanoke (Big Lick)	37 16 15 N	079 56 30 W	940
Christiansburg	37 05 30 N	080 25 00 W	2,100
Dublin	37 06 20 N	080 41 08 W	2,080
Pulaski	37 02 52 N	080 46 48 W	1,917
Wytheville	36 56 54 N	081 05 06 W	2,284
Marion (Royal Oak)	36 50 05 N	081 29 48 W	2,178
Abingdon (Wolf Hills)	36 42 35 N	081 58 39 W	2,069
Bristol (Sapling Grove)	36 35 47 N	082 11 19 W	1,700
Tennessee			
Kingsport (Long Island)	36 32 54 N	082 33 43 W	1,208
Bean Station	36 20 37 N	083 17 03 W	1,150
Sevierville	35 52 39 N	083 34 12 W	903
(Forks of Little Pigeon)			
Gatlinburg	35 42 51 N	083 29 48 W	1,289
(White Oak Flats)			

Selected Bibliography

A comprehensive compilation of readings for areas and subjects as rich, diverse, and complex as those I attempt to address probably is impossible. In the interest of preserving a readable style and tone, I made the decision not to burden my pages with scholarly footnotes. However, I have assembled here a small representative collection of titles that provided both technical information and imaginative historical inspiration for this book. These will lead to others, though doubtless there are many worthy and important studies that regrettably escaped my attention. I hope, however, that this brief list will at least embark interested readers on a journey toward relevant narratives and more specialized topics.

Bittinger, Lucy. *The Germans in Colonial Times*. New York: Russell & Russell, 1961.

Branch, Michael P., and Daniel J. Philippon. *The Height of Our Mountains: Nature Writing from Virginia's Blue Ridge Mountains and Shenandoah Valley*. Baltimore: Johns Hopkins University Press, 1998.

Brown, Margaret Lynn. *The Wild East: A Biography of the Great Smoky Mountains*. Gainesville: University Press of Florida, 2000.

Caruso, John Anthony. *The Appalachian Frontier: America's First Surge Westward*. Knoxville: University of Tennessee Press, 1959.

Faust, Albert Bernhardt. *The German Element in the United States*. Baltimore: Clearfield, 1927.

Frome, Michael. *Strangers in High Places: The Story of the Great Smoky Mountains*. Knoxville: University of Tennessee Press, 1980.

Hackett, David, and James C. Kelly. *Bound Away: Virginia and the Westward Movement*. Charlottesville: University Press of Virginia, 2000.

Hofstra, Warren R. *The Planting of New Virginia: Settlement and Landscape in the Shenandoah Valley*. Baltimore: Johns Hopkins University Press, 2004.

Kincaid, Robert L. *The Wilderness Road*. New York: Bobbs-Merrill, 1947.

Mitchell, Robert D. *Appalachian Frontiers: Settlement, Society, and Development in the Preindustrial Era*. Lexington: University Press of Kentucky, 1981.

Moltmann, Günter, ed. *Germans to America: 300 Years of Immigration, 1683 to 1983*. Stuttgart: Institute for Foreign Cultural Relations, 1982.

Nead, Daniel Wunderlich. *The Pennsylvania-German in the Settlement of Maryland*. Lancaster, PA: Pennsylvania-German Society, 1914.

Rouse, Parke, Jr. *The Great Wagon Road: From Philadelphia to the South*. New York: McGraw-Hill, 1973.

Shaw, Russell. *The Gatlinburg Story*. Gatlinburg, TN: Shaw, 1960.

Acknowledgments

This book owes a great deal to a vast number and variety of people, the majority of whom probably will remain forever nameless to me. Perhaps I should thank them first: the good folks who offered a drink from a garden hose or some ground to sleep on and many other kindnesses, great and small. Overwhelmingly, the people I encountered during my wanderings were generous and tolerant of what most often probably took the form of a strange and unexpected, albeit inadvert, intrusion into their lives and places.

Several sections of the book appeared independently in the following venues: *ISLE: Interdisciplinary Studies in Literature and Environment, Lynchburg College Magazine, Magazine Americana, Muscadine Lines, River Walk Journal, Rhizomes, Southern Hum,* and *Tapestries.* During its composition, portions of *The Warrior's Path* were presented at the following events: the Appalachian Studies Association conference (Radford University, 2005, and Maryville College, 2007), the September 2006 Shenandoah Valley Regional Studies Seminar (James Madison University), the South Atlantic Modern Language Association conference (Roanoke, Virginia, 2004, and Charlotte, North Carolina, 2006), and the 2006 Virginia Forum conference (Shenandoah University). I am thankful for having been given the opportunity to share these separate portions of the manuscript with a diverse array of thoughtful, genuinely helpful editors, listeners, and readers.

A number of specific organizations and individuals aided me in thinking about and developing this book. I would like to thank my friends and colleagues from the National Endowment for the Humanities Summer Institute entitled "Regionalism and the Liberal Arts: Appalachia Up Close" (including guest lecturers, Ferrum College organizers, and residents of McDowell County, West Virginia), the fellowship residency at the Virginia Foundation for the Humanities in Charlottesville, the Mednick fellowship program of the Virginia Foundation for Independent Colleges, the Lillian Gary Taylor fellowship residency at the University of Virginia's Harrison Institute, the visiting fellows program at the University of South Carolina's Institute for Southern Studies, and the English Department at Lynchburg College. The following individuals have my enduring gratitude for offering general support as well as diversely significant, yet equally helpful, feedback on the manuscript: Fred Chappell, Thelma Dalmus,

Pablo Davis, R. H. W. Dillard, George Garrett, Maurine Harrison, Jennifer Holland, Laura Long, Robert Morgan, Joyce Pair, Mark Roberts, and David Spears—as well as several Clabough relatives (Armalee, Avery, Erin, Francis, Frank, Gardner, Howard, Jeanne, Seth, Shirley, Whitaker), the anonymous readers for the University of Tennessee Press, and a number of students at Lynchburg College. My literary agent, Sorche Fairbank, and the University of Tennessee Press staff—especially Scot Danforth and Gene Adair—oversaw the complicated transition from manuscript to book with skill and enthusiasm.

My wife, Rochelle, remains central to everything I do in ways that are difficult to articulate but evoke all my praise.